Trout Streams of Northern New England

Trout Streams of Northern New England

David Klausmeyer

An Angler's Guide to the Best
Fly-Fishing in Vermont,
New Hampshire, and Maine

BACK COUNTRY

Backcountry Guides
Woodstock, Vermont

Library of Congress Cataloging-in-Publication Data
Klausmeyer, David, 1958–
   Trout streams of northern New England : an angler's guide to the
   best fly-fishing in Vermont, New Hampshire, and Maine / David
   Klausmeyer
      p. cm.
   ISBN 0-88150-462-9
      1. Trout fishing—Vermont—Guidebooks. 2. Trout fishing—New
Hampshire—Guidebooks. 3. Trout fishing—Maine—Guidebooks. 4. Ver-
mont—Guidebooks. 5. New Hampshire—Guidebooks. 6. Maine—Guide-
books. I. Title.

SH688.U6 K635 2001
799.1'24'0974—dc21

                                                          2001037543

Maps by Paul Woodward, © 2001 The Countryman Press
Design by Bodenweber Design
Cover photograph © Richard V. Procopio
Interior photographs by David Klausmeyer

Published by Backcountry Guides
A division of The Countryman Press
P.O. Box 748, Woodstock, Vermont 05091

Distributed by W. W. Norton & Company, Inc.
500 Fifth Avenue,
New York, NY 10110

Printed in the United States of America

10 9 8 7 6 5 4

DEDICATION

For my wonderful children, Erik and Sandra.

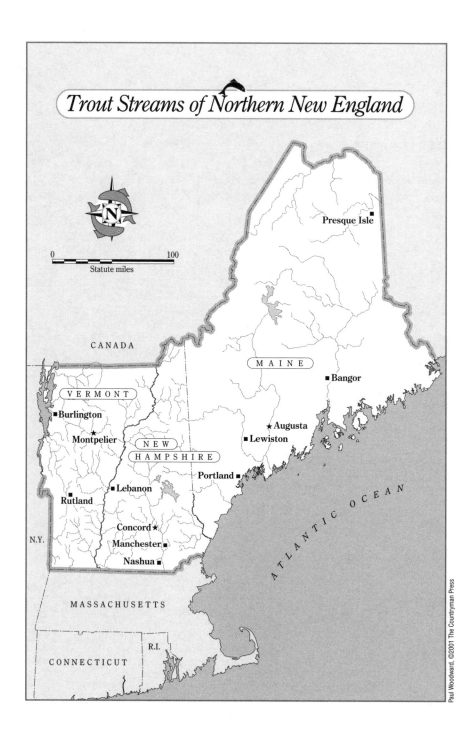

Trout Streams of Northern New England

Statute miles

0 ——— 100

CANADA

VERMONT

■Burlington

★ Montpelier

NEW
HAMPSHIRE

■Lebanon

Rutland ■

Concord ★

Manchester ■

Nashua ■

N.Y.

MASSACHUSETTS

CONNECTICUT

R.I.

MAINE

■ Bangor

Presque Isle ■

★ Augusta

■ Lewiston

Portland ■

ATLANTIC OCEAN

Contents

Part III. Maine

I once told this story in print. I don't remember where, or in what context; I only know that it was in some magazine article. It's a true story, and this is an excellent place to retell it.

I was born in St. Louis, Missouri. Although we lived in the city and its suburbs, the members of my family always enjoyed hunting and fishing. There's even a branch of my family that owned a boat dock and restaurant on the Mississippi. It was called My River Home, which I always thought was a nice name for boat dock.

I remember visiting My River Home a couple of times with my mother and father. We cooked barbecue and fished for Mississippi carp with dough balls; we always threw the carp back or gave them to the other carp fishermen along the bank. We even baited a couple of Eagle Claw hooks—the snelled kind that came in a package with the picture of the guy holding a stringer of trout—with the skins from the chicken thighs and breasts the adults would barbecue that evening. If I caught a catfish with the chicken skins, I could keep it.

That's how I started fishing: dough balls, carp, chicken skins, and catfish. I also dunked my share of worms for sunfish. But I believed there was far more to the sport.

When I visited my grandfather, I sat in his chair and flipped through the outdoors magazines he kept in an old brass kindling rack: *Outdoor Life*, *Field & Stream*, and the like. I didn't read the stories, but I liked the pictures. I was especially captivated by the photos and paintings of backwoods cabins, campfires, flies, trout, salmon, and canoes. This was the type of fishing I wanted to do, and I came to believe that this was the way fishing was really meant to be practiced. Unfortunately, this type of fishing didn't exist anywhere near St. Louis.

Soon my father's company transferred him from our home near the Mississippi to another part of the country also far away from really good fly-fishing. Then there was another move, and yet another—always to places with virtually no opportunities to fly-fish. Or so I thought.

We ended up in Tulsa, Oklahoma (there would eventually be one more move, to Oklahoma City). At the time, about 30 years ago, a local sporting goods store sponsored a weekly outdoors television show. Every Wednesday evening the host featured films of local hunting and fishing. One night, he devoted a show to fly-fishing for bass. The gentleman they featured in that show was an expert at catching largemouth bass with floating deer hair frogs and mice. The fish fell all over his flies. I was glued to the television screen, and I thought what he did made perfect sense.

At the end of the show, the host announced that his guest would be giving a fly-tying demonstration the following Saturday at the sporting goods store. My parents agreed to take me. I listened to that fellow's stories and watched him tie his bass bugs. This was the way fishing was supposed to be practiced, I thought. I was hooked.

Over the years I have learned to tie my own flies and make split-bamboo fly-rods; I've traveled across North America to fish for trout, salmon, steelhead, bass, and many saltwater species. I've moved around a bit, and 10 years ago made my home on the coast of Maine about an hour from the Canadian border. I'm finally living in a place where I can fish the way it is meant to be practiced.

Northern New England—Maine, New Hampshire, and Vermont—offers some of the finest fly-fishing opportunities in the United States. There are countless streams, rivers, lakes, and ponds containing brook, rainbow, and brown trout, landlocked salmon, togue (lake trout), and various trout hybrids. Throw in the largemouth and smallmouth bass, pike, muskie, and other warm-water species, and you have literally hundreds of opportunities for good fishing.

This book describes several dozen of the best places to fish for trout and landlocked salmon in Vermont, New Hampshire, and Maine. Some of the destinations are well known; others see few visitors. All offer excellent fly-fishing.

Each entry in this book contains the maps you will need to get around. In addition, you will find references to maps in the DeLorme *Atlas and Gazetteers* for Vermont, New Hampshire, and Maine. The *Atlas and Gazetteers* have become the bibles for navigating the North Woods; you'll find them in the trucks of every logger, game warden, forester, land manager, and guide.

I also describe each piece of water, convenient access points, the best asset of each piece of water as well as its biggest drawback, the local fishing regulations, and a selection of flies you'll want to carry. All of these descriptions will get you to the destination and help you start fishing, but be prepared to do a bit of exploring on your own; each piece of water is complex, and you'll have to match your wits with those of the fish.

There are many people I need to thank. They've all helped me in different ways related to fishing, writing, and publishing: Barbara, Erik, Sandra, Richard, and Dolores; the patient folks at The Countryman Press; my good friends at Abenaki Publishers; Larry Largay, the finest fly-fishing artist and illustrator in the country; an old English teacher named Mrs. Stewart; a whole bunch of fishing and hunting buddies . . . to name just a few.

At the top of the list, though, is the fellow at that sporting goods store who tied bass bugs. That was 30 years ago, and I just can't remember his name. Wherever he is, I know he's still fishing.

Enjoy northern New England!

I | VERMONT

Vermont offers fly-fishers many excellent opportunities to catch trout and landlocked salmon, as well as several other species of fish. While my main focus is the best places to catch trout and salmon, the lower sections of many trout streams and rivers contain smallmouth bass, largemouth bass, northern pike, and pickerel; these areas will be mentioned when they apply.

I cover Vermont by starting in the southern end of the state and moving north. Along the way I'll investigate some of fly-fishing's most storied waters, as well as little-known, out-of-the-way places; all offer great fishing, sight-seeing, hiking, and other opportunities to enjoy the outdoors.

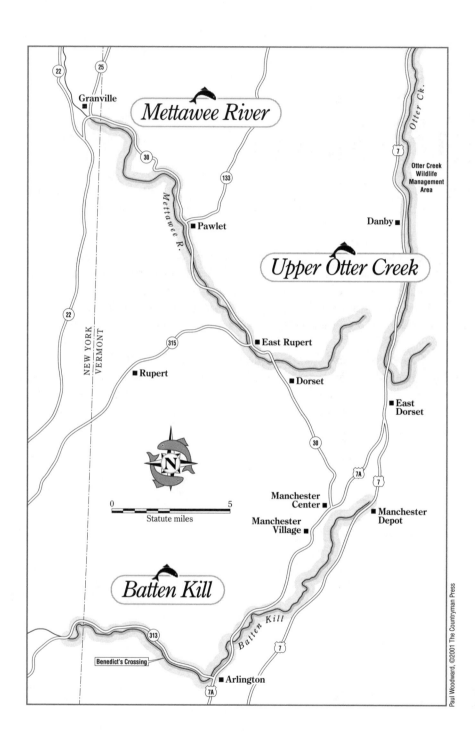

Mettawee River

Granville

22 25

30

133

Mettawee R.

Pawlet

Otter Ck.

7

Otter Creek
Wildlife
Management
Area

Danby

Upper Otter Creek

22

NEW YORK
VERMONT

315

Rupert

East Rupert

Dorset

East
Dorset

N

30

0   5

Statute miles

7A

7

Manchester
Center

Manchester
Village

Manchester
Depot

Batten Kill

313

Benedict's Crossing

Batten Kill

7

Arlington

7A

1 | Southern Vermont

Southern Vermont is readily accessible from several major metropolitan areas: Boston, Hartford, New York City—really, the entire Northeast. Southern Vermont is also blessed with numerous inns, bed & breakfasts, restaurants, and other facilities. Any one of the rivers discussed would make the perfect destination for a weekend getaway. If you have more time, you could spend a couple of weeks, visit several pieces of water, and never fish the same place twice.

I have limited the discussion to several of the more prominent, easy-to-find streams and rivers. These should make the backbone of any fishing trip to southern Vermont. For the more adventuresome, I also discuss fishing the small, remote trout streams of the area. Vermont is the home of the Green Mountain National Forest, which is an unsung angling opportunity; if you want to get away from the crowds and fish for native brook trout in an unspoiled setting, strap on your hiking boots and head up one of the forest's many freestone brook-trout streams.

THE METTAWEE RIVER

Maps *The Vermont Atlas and Gazetteer,* pages 24 and 28.

Description The Mettawee River starts as a small mountain stream in Vermont's Green Mountains, flows northwest, and builds into a medium-sized river before entering New York State. The lower section of the river flows through rolling farmland. The Mettawee is easy to wade, and offers good fishing for rainbow trout.

Access VT 30 follows the Mettawee for much of its course. Look for access wherever the road crosses the river. There is also one state-maintained pull-out next to the river. Much of the Mettawee flows through dairy farms, and many of the farmers grant permission to fish—just ask.

Best Asset Scenery. The Mettawee Valley is dairy country, and the scenery is superb. The river is also highly wadable. The caddis hatches are very dependable.

Biggest Drawbacks Access is rather limited. While VT 30 follows the general course of the Mettawee, many sections of the river are hard to get to. I also find it difficult to believe that having all of the cattle standing in the river, doing what cattle do, doesn't have a negative effect on the fish (but who knows—maybe it actually helps).

Regulations The legal fishing season runs from the second Saturday in April through the last Sunday in October. There are no length restrictions on the fish you may keep. Daily bag limit: The total number of brook trout, brown trout, and rainbow trout is 12 fish; total number of brown and rainbow trout is 6 fish.

Favorite Flies Mickey Finn (#6–8), Olive Woolly Bugger (#6–8), Black Woolly Bugger (#6–8), Brown Woolly Bugger (#6–8), Muddler Minnow (#4–8), Woolly Worm (#6–8), Royal Coachman (#6–10), Hare's Ear Nymph (#8–14), Pheasant Tail Nymph (#8–14), Bead Head Nymph (#8–14), Olive Sparkle Caddis Pupa (#8–14), Brown Sparkle Caddis Pupa (#8–14), Cream Sparkle Caddis Pupa (#8–14), Olive Caddis Larva (#8–14), Brown Caddis Larva (#8–14), Elk Hair Caddis (#10–14), Hendrickson (#14), Sulphur (#12), Adams (#10–14), March Brown (#8–12), Yellow Sally Stonefly (#10), Lime Sally Stonefly (#14), Dave's Hopper (#10), Letort Cricket (#10), Black Ant (#12).

The Mettawee flows through one of the most picturesque corners of New England. It begins as a small freestone mountain stream in the hills southeast of Dorset, Vermont. From its origins in the Green Mountains, the Mettawee flows northwest for 16 miles before crossing the state line into New York. Along the way, the Mettawee passes through beautiful dairy farms that seem right out of a Winslow Homer painting.

The Mettawee starts in the mountains above the town of Dorset. This stretch is most easily reached by taking Lower Hollow Road out of Dorset. The river is narrow here and best fished using a small rod and dry flies: Royal Wulffs, Humpies, and Elk Hair Caddises. I prefer doing this type of fishing in June and July, and I like to fish "wet" (without waders), rock-hopping from pool to pool.

Access to the middle section of the Mettawee, from East Rupert to Pawlet, is along VT 30. While the dairy farms provide a wonderful backdrop for fishing, they also restrict access to much of the Mettawee. You can find access at many of the bridges crossing the river; there is also one state-maintained access site on VT 30. Most landowners will allow you to cross their land to fish if you ask permission, but who has time to track down a

The headwaters of the Mettawee River above Dorset are a very beautiful place to fish. The river runs along the base of this old mill.

farmer? I usually fish up- and downstream from the bridges, but occasionally I'll see an angler on this part of the river, which tips me off to an access point I've overlooked.

Near North Pawlet the dairy farms begin to give way to woodlands, and access to the Mettawee is found on two roads off VT 30. The first, a local road marked TH1, continues to follow the Mettawee. You'll find access to the river where TH1 meets TH16 on the left. TH16 crosses the river, and you can walk down to the water at this bridge. This lower section of the Mettawee contains rainbow and brown trout.

The main stem of the Mettawee flows through fields and dairy farms. This angler is skating imitations of adult caddis across the surface of the water. As I watched, he caught trout.

Another option is to turn onto VT 153 (TH1 also intersects with VT 153). The bridge where VT 153 crosses the Mettawee offers easy access to the river. There is ample parking near the bridge, and you can wade upstream for a fairly long distance; you'll find a mix of riffles and pools (I've never run out of water to fish in this area). I like to fish dry flies and weighted nymphs while wading upstream, and wet flies and small streamers when I wade downstream back to the car. This part of the river is about 25 feet wide and easy to wade. Be sure to try the big pool under the bridge.

VT 149 west, also called Button Falls Road, heads to New York State and offers additional access to the Mettawee. There is a large set of falls in this section, but the area is heavily posted against trespassing. Park near the large concrete Fred N. Mason Jr. Memorial Bridge, cross the river, and look for the heavily used footpath leading upstream. This path will take you to a favorite local swimming hole. When there are no swimmers, the large pool at the bottom of the falls offers an excellent chance to catch very large rainbow trout.

"You can start fishing the Mettawee earlier than some other rivers such as the Batten Kill," said Walter Hoetzer, the co-owner of Batten Kill Outfitters in Manchester, Vermont. "The Mettawee is a totally different valley system, and there are many times when the water in that river will be lower than the water in the Batten Kill. Sometimes you can start fishing the Mettawee around the first of May.

"As for as hatches," he continued, "the big difference between the Mettawee and other rivers is that it does have stoneflies. Not the really big stones like you'll find out West, but they're about a size 10 yellow stonefly. There's also a bright green stonefly that we tie in about size 14."

If you visit the Mettawee, also go prepared with the usual complement of patterns: Hendricksons, Sulphurs, and Elk Hair Caddises. Obviously, the fields lining the river teem with grasshoppers in late summer, and a Dave's or Joe's Hopper is a good imitation of a grasshopper that has made the mistake of flying out over the river and fallen to the surface. Your fly box for the Mettawee should also contain an assortment of small Bead Head Nymphs and caddis larvae and pupae.

The last half of May and all of June is the favorite time to fish the middle and lower sections of the Mettawee. The river's middle section lacks overhanging vegetation, and in late summer the temperature of the water can rise to dangerous levels for trout. If you visit at this time of year, concentrate your efforts on the deep pools where cool feeder streams enter the river.

THE BATTEN KILL

Maps *The Vermont Atlas and Gazetteer,* pages 24 and 25.

Description The Batten Kill starts at the confluence of Mad Tom and Little Mad Tom Brooks in Dorset north of Manchester, Vermont. It flows southwest, turns west at Arlington, and then flows into New York State. It's a medium-sized stream holding brook and brown trout. The river flows through a mixture of hard- and softwood forests and farms. Most of it is quite easy to wade, and in some areas you can fish from the bank.

Access Historic VT 7A follows the Batten Kill from Manchester to Arlington. Side roads, most notably River Road (what else?), come off VT 7A and follow the river, providing access. In Arlington VT 313 parallels the Batten Kill to the New York State line. Look for pulloffs along VT 313, or take one of the bridges across the river to access the other side of the river.

Best Assets Manchester and Arlington contain many bed & breakfasts and lovely inns that will make your stay quite memorable. Manchester is the home of the American Museum of Fly Fishing and the Orvis Company. Visiting the museum and the Orvis store (you can also take a tour of the rod factory) makes a trip to the Batten Kill especially interesting. The museum holds special events throughout the year, and you can plan a trip to coincide with these festivities. There is also ample access to the river.

Biggest Drawbacks When I first visited Manchester about 15 years ago, it was still a fairly small village. I remember seeing notices for a public meeting to discuss the building of an outlet store; apparently some of the residents were concerned that this outlet would alter the nature of their quiet community. Today Manchester has several dozen outlet stores, which has increased the congestion in this small town. If you're interested only in fishing, you won't even know that these stores and the hordes of people they attract are there; the outlets might even be an attraction to the nonfishing members of your family. However, they have taken much of the quaintness out of Manchester.

Locals tell me that the river doesn't fish nearly as well as it did years ago (but I hear that wherever I go). State biologists admit that the numbers of fish have declined. The Batten Kill is managed as a wild trout fishery and is not stocked. However, a serious angler can still catch fish.

Regulations The legal fishing season on the Batten Kill is from the second Saturday in April to the last Sunday in October. There is excellent news for fly-anglers: The entire Batten Kill from Dufresne Pond to the New York State border is now being governed under catch-and-release regulations.

Favorite Flies Hornberg (#6–10), Gray Ghost (#4–8), Black Ghost (#4–8), Mickey Finn (#6–8), Olive Woolly Bugger (#6–8), Black Woolly Bugger (#6–8), Brown Woolly Bugger (#6–8), Muddler Minnow (#4–8), Woolly Worm (#6–8), Royal Coachman (#6–10), Ballou Special (#4–8), Hare's Ear Nymph (#8–14), Pheasant Tail Nymph (#8–14), Bead Head Nymph (#8–14), Olive Sparkle Caddis Pupa (#8–14), Brown Sparkle Caddis Pupa (#8–14), Cream Sparkle Caddis Pupa (#8–14), Olive Caddis Larva (#8–14), Brown Caddis Larva (#8–14), Elk Hair Caddis (#10–14), Hendrickson Dun (#14), Hendrickson Spinner (#14), Sulphur Dun (#12), Adams (#10–14), Gray Fox (#14), March Brown (#8–12), Trico Spinner (#18–22), Black Ant (#14), Dave's Hopper (#10).

The Batten Kill is one of the most famous rivers in the annals of American fly-fishing. Old-timers will tell you that the river of today is mostly a ghost of its former glory, yet it still contains brown trout in the 14- to 18-inch range, and brook trout averaging 8 to 10 inches long.

I've fished the Batten Kill for a number of years, and I only recently learned how to consistently catch the stream's wily brown trout. I first became acquainted with the river about 15 years ago while visiting the American Museum of Fly Fishing in Manchester, Vermont. I was a fledgling split-bamboo rod maker, and I traveled to Vermont to see the museum's wonderful collection of classic rods. In the evenings I fished the Batten Kill.

I started fishing here with fairly standard wet flies and the down-and-across method of presentation, and I caught a couple of fish that week. As I continued visiting the museum over the next decade, I used a variety of flies and fishing techniques—all pretty standard stuff—and caught the occasional fish.

When visiting the Batten Kill, be sure to stop by the American Museum of Fly Fishing. This institution maintains the largest collection of fly-fishing tackle in the world.

I finally learned how to fish the Batten Kill when I spent a summer living in Bennington, Vermont. One evening I was fishing the Benedict's Crossing section of the river along VT 313 between the town of Arlington and the New York State border. As the sun was setting below the horizon, several nice fish started rising; from the large size of the rings, I could tell that they were the river's prized brown trout. I cast a number of flies over those fish, but they showed no interest. Frustrated, I set my rod on the bank, bent over, and began examining the surface of the water. That's when I noticed a number of oddly proportioned mayfly spinners. The insects had size 16 bodies, but size 14—maybe size 12—wings. There was no sign of spinner activity in the area where I was fishing; the insects had obviously mated upstream, fallen to the water, and were just now washing downstream. That's why I'd missed seeing the spinners on the water. This must be what's capturing the trouts' attention, I thought.

I rummaged through my fly boxes and found one small spinner imitation. I quickly tied the fly to my tippet and began casting to the closest rising trout. I'm telling you the truth when I say that I caught a fat 14-inch-long brown trout on my first cast. I continued working upstream, carefully presenting my fly to every rising fish. I landed six trout before I finished, the smallest measuring 12 inches.

For all of the negative views I hear about today's Batten Kill, I consider that a fine evening of serious match-the-hatch fly-fishing.

I've since learned that that unusually proportioned mayfly is of the family Baetiscidae (genus *Baetisca*). Tom Rosenbauer, a local angling authority, wrote of the importance of the *Baetisca* spinner in an article about the Batten Kill for *American Angler* magazine. I've also learned that the *Baetisca* is a very rare mayfly, living in only the Batten Kill, Michigan's Pere Marquette River, and perhaps just a few other rivers. Having a spinner imitation of the correct size certainly spelled the difference between frustration and success on that late-June evening.

Walter Hoetzer of the Batten Kill Outfitters in Manchester can give you the latest information on the river. According to Hoetzer, the Batten Kill always offers good fishing. Ultimately, however, it depends upon the rains and the water level.

In the 2000 season, he said, "The heavy rains in the spring affected the hatches. Even with the higher-than-normal water, some of the hatches have been better than what I've seen in the past.

"The Hendrickson is the hatch everyone associates with the Batten Kill," Hoetzer continued. "You have two shots at the Hendricksons. They come off at around three in the afternoon. You fish the hatch, and then go have an early dinner. After dinner you get back on the river and fish the spinner fall. Mid-May is the best time to fish the Hendricksons. Sometimes they start hatching around the end of April, or they'll peak at the end of May, but mid-May is a good target date.

"After the Hendricksons, we get a few gray foxes, and of course the caddis are on the water. The next really big hatch is when the sulphurs come off. That's in June and sometimes into July. You also have an *Isonychia* hatch in June.

"As far as caddis, we have an early-season caddis that's about a size 12. It's not a heavy hatch, but it's a good one. As the season progresses, all of the flies get smaller. In August we get a few olives and of course the tricos."

Fishing can get tough on the Batten Kill late in the summer. Even though there are numerous feeder streams and springs, the temperature of the river rises and the fish become sluggish. If you fish early in the morning before the sun cracks over the horizon, however, the water will be cooler and the fish will be active.

"The river did decline over the past several years. I spent 10 years living out West and came back to open the fly shop. The quality of the fishing did decline while I was away," lamented Hoetzer. "The one thing that has had an immediate impact on improving the river is the introduction of catch-and-release regulations. The entire Vermont stretch of the Batten Kill is now catch-and-release. Now we don't have those old-time wormers down there taking their 12 fish.

"The state of Vermont is showing a renewed interest in the Batten Kill," he continued. "The state also received $200,000 to conduct studies on the river. We're seeing more small fish than ever before, and we're also seeing a lot of big fish. The Batten Kill is definitely coming back."

Hoetzer warned that the Batten Kill isn't an easy river to fish: "This is a technical type of fishing. These are wild trout, and they're not easy to catch. Many guys haven't developed the skill to catch these type of fish, but it's not impossible. I've seen beginners have good luck on the river. When you catch a 15- or 16-inch trout on the Batten Kill, you know you've done something."

Even though the Manchester area is becoming increasingly developed, you can still enjoy a lot of access to the Batten Kill. Its main stem is formed in Manchester where the West and East Branches, as well as several small feeder streams, come together. Access is rather limited, but there are several spots where you can reach the river and wet a line. River Road in Manchester periodically crosses the Batten Kill, and you can gain access next to the bridges. There is also a Vermont Fish and Wildlife public access area on VT 7A in the town of Sunderland.

VT 313 west out of Arlington parallels the north side of the river. Three roads head south from VT 313 and cross the river; you can gain access near these bridges. The vicinity of the river near the middle bridge is known as

Benedict's Crossing. This is a favorite area among fly-fishers and is managed under artificial-lures-only regulations. This is where I discovered the importance of fishing spinners on the Batten Kill.

Manchester is a special place for fly-fishers. It's the home of the Orvis Company, and you can visit the showroom, take a tour of the rod factory, attend a fly-fishing class, and even test a rod on the company's casting pool. And you can't visit the Batten Kill without stopping by the American Museum of Fly Fishing. This nonprofit institution contains the largest collection of historic fly-fishing artifacts in the world, including the tackle of such famous anglers as Ernest Hemingway, Andrew Carnegie, Daniel Webster, and Presidents Carter, Bush, Hoover, and Eisenhower. The museum occasionally holds dinners in Manchester and at other locations around the country. These are fun affairs, and you'll get the opportunity to meet a lot of interesting fellow anglers.

UPPER OTTER CREEK

Map *The Vermont Atlas and Gazetteer,* page 25.

Description Upper Otter Creek is a small freestone stream flowing through the Green Mountains. The casting is tight for feisty native brook trout.

Access US 7 follows upper Otter Creek. There are places to park and access the river. U.S. Forest Service Road No. 10 follows Big Branch, an important, easily accessed tributary of Otter Creek. Be sure to try any of the small tributaries flowing into this section of the creek.

Best Assets The lovely mountain scenery. Odds are also very good you'll have the stream to yourself, especially if you visit during the week.

Biggest Drawback As on all mountain streams, the upper reaches of Otter Creek are subject to extreme water fluctuations; a couple of days of heavy rain can bring the stream up out of its banks.

Regulations The legal fishing season runs from the second Saturday in April through the last Sunday in October. There are no length restrictions on the fish you may keep. Daily bag limit: The total number brook trout, brown trout, and rainbow trout is 12 fish.

Favorite flies Olive Woolly Bugger (#8–12), Black Woolly Bugger (#8–12), Brown Woolly Bugger (#8–12), Woolly Worm (#8–10), Royal Coachman (#6–10), Hare's Ear Nymph (#8–14), Pheasant Tail Nymph (#8–14), Bead Head Nymph (#8–14), Olive Sparkle Caddis Pupa (#8–14), Brown Sparkle Caddis Pupa (#8–14), Cream Sparkle Caddis Pupa (#8–14), Olive Caddis Larva (#8–14), Brown Caddis Larva (#8–14), Elk Hair Caddis (#10–14), Royal Wulff (#8–12), Adams Wulff (#10–12), March Brown (#8–12).

The headwaters of Otter Creek flow out of the Green Mountain National Forest. This is a beautiful place to fish for native brook trout.

Otter Creek is an unusual piece of flowing water. In a state where so many of the rivers and streams are rather short, this creek stretches for more than 100 miles—from its source in Emerald Lake near East Dorset to Lake Champlain in the northern end of the state. The river flows from south to north and offers a variety of fishing opportunities, from brook trout to smallmouth bass and northern pike. Since I'm examining Vermont from south to north, I'll limit my discussion to upper Otter Creek.

Otter Creek starts at Emerald Lake in Emerald Lake State Park north of East Dorset. This is a picturesque setting at the base of the Green Mountain National Forest. There are numerous access points along US 7, which parallels Otter Creek; be sure to check near every bridge that crosses the creek. One of the chief access points is the Otter Creek Wildlife Management Area on US 7. This section provides good fishing in spring and summer, and is best fished by canoe. The area is rich in insects, but favorite patterns are Hendricksons and March Browns in spring and early summer. Weighted nymphs and Bead Head Nymphs are good bets when there are no rising fish, as well as Green and Tan Caddis Larvae and Pupae. Be sure to try terrestrial patterns in late summer, when grasshoppers, beetles, and ants thrive in the nearby fields. This section of Otter Creek contains a good supply of brook trout measuring 8 to 10 inches.

Big Branch, in Mount Tabor, is the first major tributary of Otter Creek. Big Branch is a mountain stream worth fishing for brook trout. Here I use a short rod and bushy dry flies: Royal Wulffs, Humpies, and the like. Work upstream and make a couple of casts into every small pool. Work quickly and cover a lot of water. I think you'll be surprised by just how many fish a small stream like Big Branch contains. Fishing mountain streams is contagious; it's easy to get hooked on the beautiful brook trout and the solitude.

A U.S. Forest Service road parallels Big Branch for much of its course. The lower section of Big Branch, especially where the tributary meets Otter Creek, contains a mixture of brook, brown, and rainbow trout.

Although I've discussed only 10 or so miles of upper Otter Creek, this is the most productive section for trout fishing. As the stream heads north, it slows and warms. There are several cool tributaries that enter the creek and provide suitable trout habitat, but these stretches are short and difficult to find. Later, when I examine central Vermont, I'll return to Otter Creek and discuss the trout fishing opportunities in that part of the state.

THE WEST RIVER

Maps *The Vermont Atlas and Gazetteer*, pages 22 and 26.

Description The West River begins as a freestone mountain stream in the Green Mountain National Forest in Weston. It flows southeast to its conflu-

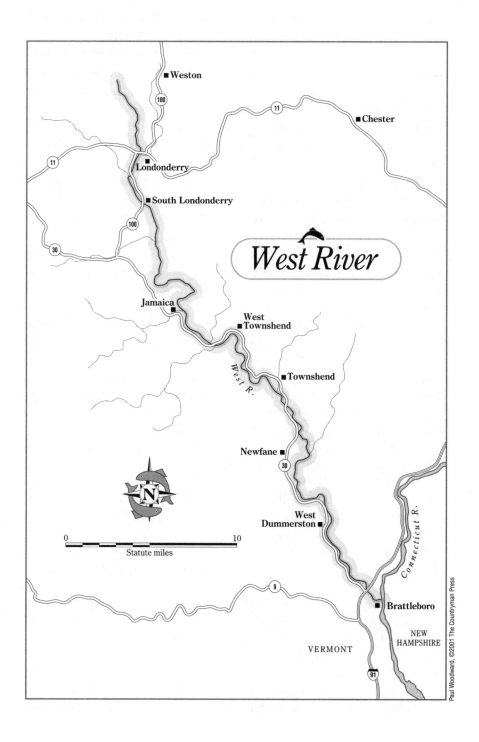

Weston

Chester

Londonderry

South Londonderry

West River

Jamaica

West
Townshend

West R.

Townshend

Newfane

West
Dummerston

Connecticut R.

N

0   10
Statute miles

Brattleboro

NEW
HAMPSHIRE

VERMONT

ence with the Connecticut River in Brattleboro. Much of the river is wadable. The West River Valley is forested and quite beautiful. A little-known waterway, it's well worth visiting on your next fishing trip to southern Vermont.

Access VT 100 follows along the headwaters of the West River through Weston and Londonderry, Vermont, providing ample parking and places to fish. From Jamaica on, VT 30 follows the river to Brattleboro.

Best Assets You can easily access much of the West River, and you'll see very few other anglers. The river valley is quite beautiful and spotted with covered bridges.

Biggest Drawback Parts of the West River can get quite low and warm in summer, making fishing difficult.

Regulations The legal fishing season for the West River runs from the second Saturday in April through the last Sunday in October.

From the VT 100 bridge in Jamaica to the headwaters, the following regulations apply. Daily bag limit: The total number of brook, rainbow, and brown trout is 12 fish; the total number of brown and rainbow trout is six fish.

From Townshend Dam in Townshend to the VT 100 bridge in Jamaica: Total number of brook, brown, and rainbow trout is six fish daily, weighing not more than a total of 5 pounds.

Favorite Flies Hornberg (#6–10), Gray Ghost (#4–8), Black Ghost (#4–8), Mickey Finn (#6–8), Olive Woolly Bugger (#6–8), Black Woolly Bugger (#6–8), Brown Woolly Bugger (#6–8), Muddler Minnow (#4–8), Woolly Worm (#6–8), Royal Coachman (#6–10), Ballou Special (#4–8), Hare's Ear Nymph (#8–14), Pheasant Tail Nymph (#8–14), Bead Head Nymph (#8–14), Olive Sparkle Caddis Pupa (#8–14), Brown Sparkle Caddis Pupa (#8–14), Cream Sparkle Caddis Pupa (#8–14), Olive Caddis Larva (#8–14), Brown Caddis Larva (#8–14), Elk Hair Caddis (#10–14), Adams (#10–14), Light Cahill (#12–16), Green Drake (#4–6), March Brown (#8–12).

The West is another of Vermont's relatively unsung rivers. By Vermont standards, it's fairly long. I recommend concentrating your efforts in two sections.

First, try the headwaters of the West River along VT 100 in Weston. Once again you're at the edge of the Green Mountain National Forest, so you know the scenery will be good. This section of the river and its tributaries are home to brook trout. Look for access to the water at pullouts from the road and wherever VT 100 crosses the river. Use a short rod and high-floating dry flies. Cast upstream and be ready for the splashy rises of these delightful little fish. Fishing the upper West River is a great way to spend the afternoon.

VT 30 eventually follows the West River into Brattleboro. Along the way the river widens and enters two reservoirs designed to control flooding. Townshend Dam, which forms the Townshend Lake Flood Control Reservoir, is a huge and impressive project. There is a nice picnic area here, and you can fish for brown trout in the flowing water below the dam. Walk onto the dam, look down through the steel-grate section of the road, and you'll see just how high you really are; my stomach spun a bit as I looked through the grate. It may remind you of some of the larger dams in the western United States.

My second firm recommendation is to fish for smallmouth bass in the section of the West River in Brattleboro. In reality, the entire lower section of the West River is better known as a smallmouth-bass fishery, and there are some really large "smallies" in the slow-moving water in Brattleboro where the West meets the Connecticut River. On one July evening I encountered several smallmouth bass rising along the inaccessible edge of the river along the far shore. I waded out almost to the top of my chest waders, and did the best I could to cast a small, panfish-sized Woolly Bugger to the cliff face on the other side of the river. After several casts my line became taut, and I was tethered to a big smallmouth bass. I let him peel line off the reel while I carefully waded back to shore to fight him. After about 10 minutes I landed one of the largest smallmouth bass I've ever caught. I also suggest bringing a canoe to explore this entire section of the river.

THE BLACK RIVER

Maps *The Vermont Atlas and Gazetteer,* pages 27, 30, and 31.

Description The Black River is a medium-sized river in south-central Vermont. It begins as a mountain freestone stream but is quickly tamed by several dams, which form Amherst Lake, Echo Lake, and Lake Rescue. The surrounding valley is mountainous and forested.

The headwaters of the Black River, which are in the Calvin Coolidge State Forest, contain primarily brook trout. The section of the river flowing through Cavendish, which is accessed along VT 131, is stocked with brook, rainbow, and brown trout. The lakes contain bass and a variety of panfish.

Access VT 100, which runs north to south through much of Vermont, parallels the Black River from the Calvin Coolidge State Forest to Ludlow. There are numerous pulloffs and picnic areas. The lakes along this section of the river are also worth a try.

Your next best chances at fishing for trout are along VT 103 from Ludlow to Proctorsville, and along VT 131 from Proctorsville to Downers. Both of these roads parallel the river and have pulloffs offering access.

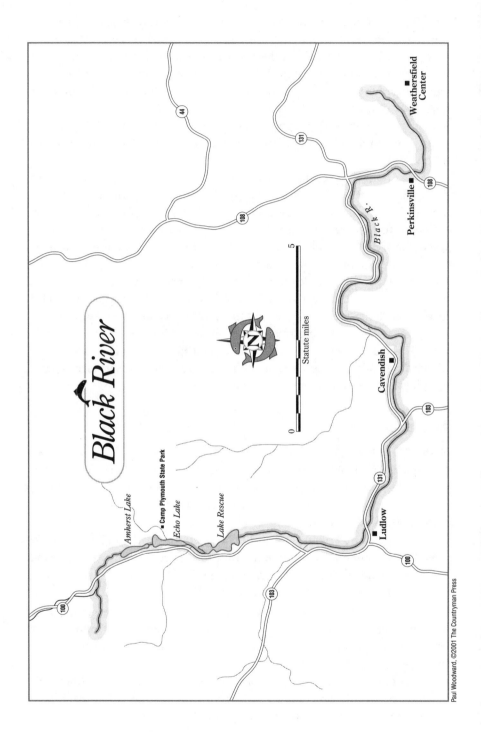

Black River

Amherst Lake
■ Camp Plymouth State Park
Echo Lake
Lake Rescue

Statute miles

Weathersfield
Center

Perkinsville

Black R.

Cavendish

Ludlow

Paul Woodward, ©2001 The Countryman Press

Best Assets There is ample access to the Black River along major routes. Although the fishing is quite good, you will see few other anglers. Fish attractor dry flies—Wulff patterns and Humpies on size 12 hooks—in the headwaters, and look for hatches of caddis- and mayflies in the main stem of the river below Ludlow.

Biggest Drawback The flow of the river is regulated by the dams on the river. Generally, though, the water remains at fishable levels.

Regulations The legal fishing season runs from the second Saturday in April through the last Sunday in October.

From the Downers covered bridge in Weathersfield to the Howard Hill bridge in Cavendish: The total daily creel limit for brook, brown, and rainbow trout is two fish. No minimum length.

From the Howard Hill bridge to the headwaters: the total daily creel limit for brook, brown, and rainbow trout is 12 fish.

Favorite Flies Gray Ghost (#6–10), Black Ghost (#6–10), Mickey Finn (#6–8), Olive Woolly Bugger (#6–10), Black Woolly Bugger (#6–10), Brown Woolly Bugger (#6–10), Muddler Minnow (#4–8), Woolly Worm (#6–10), Royal Coachman (#8–10), Ballou Special (#6–10), Hare's Ear Nymph (#8–14), Pheasant Tail Nymph (#8–14), Bead Head Nymph (#8–14), Olive Sparkle Caddis Pupa (#8–14), Brown Sparkle Caddis Pupa (#8–14), Cream Sparkle Caddis Pupa (#8–14), Olive Caddis Larva (#8–14), Brown Caddis Larva (#8–14), Elk Hair Caddis (#10–14), Hendrickson Dun (#14), Adams (#10–14), Light Cahill (#12–16), Green Drake (#4–6), March Brown (#8–12).

The Black River starts in the Calvin Coolidge State Forest above the town of Plymouth Union. This section of the river, from the state forest to Amherst Lake, is a mountain freestone stream: cool water, easy to wade, and full of native brook trout. The Black then enters a series of small lakes—Amherst Lake, Echo Lake, and Lake Rescue—that contain brown trout, rainbow trout, and lake trout. There are pulloffs along VT 100, which parallels this section, and boat ramps at the lakes.

In Ludlow the Black River bears east and contains primarily rainbow trout. VT 103/131, which closely follows this part of the river, offers pulloffs; there is additional access at the bridges crossing the river.

The Black River figures into Vermont's and the federal government's efforts to restore Atlantic salmon to the Connecticut River. The Black receives stockings of salmon fry in the hope that these fish will grow, head down the Black and the Connecticut Rivers to the Atlantic Ocean, and return one day as adult spawning salmon. In addition to the salmon fry, the state also stocks the river with rainbow and brown trout. Occasionally stocked brown trout measure more than 16 inches.

Favorite flies for fishing the main stem of the Black River from Ludlow to the Downers covered bridge include weighted nymphs—Gold Ribbed Hare's Ears, Bead Head Nymphs, and other small nymphs—as well as Elk Hair Caddises, Hendricksons, Quill Gordons, and March Browns. The best time to fish the Black is from mid-May to the first of July.

THE GREEN MOUNTAINS

Maps *The Vermont Atlas and Gazetteer,* pages 21, 22, 25, 26, 29, 30, 33, and 34.

Description The Green Mountain National Forest has many miles of streams containing native brook trout. These fish are plentiful but receive scant attention compared with the trout living in more publicized rivers and streams.

The name *Green Mountains* can be taken quite literally: These peaks, averaging around 2,800 feet, are heavily forested and lush. Freestone mountain streams rush in the valleys between the peaks. These streams, flowing in the shade of the trees, stay cool throughout the summer, and the fishing remains good. The streams are also quite easy to wade.

Access Study maps of the Green Mountain National Forest and you'll see dozens of small streams. Look for streams paralleling U.S. Forest Service roads and hiking trails. Some also flow near state highways, such as the streams along VT 9 east of Bennington. VT 100, which travels north and south through the middle of the state, is a main artery opening many miles of streams to your exploration. The maps in *The Vermont Atlas and Gazetteer* offer a wealth of information for finding out-of-the-way, seldom-fished freestone mountain streams.

Best Asset Very few anglers work these small mountain streams. Indeed, you may be able to fish a stream all summer and not see another angler. It's not that it doesn't contain trout—they're there—but too many anglers think you have to visit brand-name water to catch fish. Enjoy the solitude and the native fish—and keep your little stream a secret.

Give yourself a treat: take a small rod, a single box of dry flies, and wade "wet" (without waders).

Biggest Drawbacks I love to fish mountain streams for native trout, so I'm pushing to find something negative to say. I look at a;; tjese negatives as positives, frankly, but here goes:

1. You'll have to do a little research to find the best places to fish.
2. Most fly shops will try to steer you to the big-name pieces of water, so they're usually of little help.
3. You'll have to do a little hiking to get into some of these streams.

Regulations The legal fishing season runs from the second Saturday in April through the last Sunday in October. There are no minimum length restrictions on the fish you may keep. Daily bag limit: The total number of brook trout, brown trout, and rainbow trout is 12 fish; the total number of brown and rainbow trout is 6 fish.

Special Note The Green Mountain National Forest covers a wide piece of southern and central Vermont, and some streams are governed under special regulations. Many times these regulations are applied because a stream is a tributary of an important piece of water. Consult the latest edition of the *Vermont Guide to Hunting, Fishing, and Trapping Laws* for any special regulations governing the streams and ponds you fish.

Favorite Flies Olive Woolly Bugger (#10), Black Woolly Bugger (#10), Brown Woolly Bugger (#10), Woolly Worm (#10–12), Royal Coachman (#10–12), Hare's Ear Nymph (#8–14), Pheasant Tail Nymph (#8–14), Bead Head Nymph (#8–14), Olive Sparkle Caddis Pupa (#8–14), Brown Sparkle Caddis Pupa (#8–14), Cream Sparkle Caddis Pupa (#8–14), Olive Caddis Larva (#8–14), Brown Caddis Larva (#8–14), Elk Hair Caddis (#10–14), March Brown (#8–12), Royal Wulff (#8–12).

Fishing mountain streams is one of the most overlooked angling opportunities I know of. The entire Appalachian Mountain range from Georgia to Vermont offers great fishing for brook trout, and sometimes brown and rainbow trout. Vermont, in particular, offers hundreds of miles of mountain streams teeming with brookies. In their mad rush to get to the Batten Kill and other famous rivers, many anglers pass up more rewarding, and often more productive, fishing opportunities. I guess it all comes down to how you measure a successful day of fishing. If it's strictly by the size of the fish you catch, then head for the larger water. Of course, you'll have to work harder to gain access to those rivers, and you'll probably have to share the water with other anglers once you get there.

On the other hand, if you're interested in catching brightly colored fish in a remote, quiet setting, try the small freestone streams of the Green Mountains. The chances are that you'll catch far more fish than at one of the better-known destinations.

Vermont's Green Mountains are blessed with dozens of small, cold-water streams chock-full of brook trout. And because many of these streams are located in the Green Mountain National Forest, access isn't a problem; you're limited only by your willingness to take a hike.

Actually, as you begin to explore the Green Mountain National Forest, you'll discover many small streams that travel next to the gravel roads maintained by the U.S. Forest Service. Even though these little jewels are easily accessible, they're visited by few anglers; hike a mile or two upstream and you'll be casting to trout that see no more than four or five artificial flies during the entire year—if that many. And while common courtesy on a more popular and crowded river dictates that you give a fellow angler a wide berth, you'll probably want to stop and chat with any other fly-rodder you see on the high mountain streams—but don't count on seeing any.

There are two ways to fish mountain streams. The first is to use a long rod—9 to 9½ feet—and weighted nymphs. The idea is to flip and dangle nymphs into the small pools as you wade upstream. I don't much like this method, because I find it too difficult to hike or wade small streams while carrying a long rod. It also eliminates the joy of seeing a bright brook trout dash and pluck your dry fly from the surface of the water. And most long rods are too heavy to let you enjoy the tussle you'll get from these small fish.

When I fish mountain streams, I prefer using a rather short, lightweight rod—my favorite is a 6½-foot-long split-bamboo wand that carries a 3-weight double-tapered line. I also prefer using medium-sized, bushy dry flies, usually Royal Wulffs and Elk Hair Caddises tied on size 12 and 14 hooks. I wade "wet"—without waders—and work upstream. I cast my fly onto every small pool; even a pool the size of a bathtub can contain two or three brook trout. I work quickly and silently, and rarely cast more than four or five times onto each pool. These trout are not selective, and they usually strike on the first presentation. Often you'll see an orange streak start sev-

A native Green Mountain trout. Though small, these little gems are a delight to catch. Use lightweight tackle, bushy dry flies, and enjoy!

eral feet from your fly and end in a splashy rise. These trout average 8 to 9 inches in length; a 10-inch fish is an outstanding example. That's another reason for the light rod; these fish are more enjoyable on the banty tackle.

There are far too many worthy mountain streams to attempt to name all of them. Topographical maps are indispensable aids in discovering small mountain streams teeming with brook trout that other anglers overlook. And Vermont isn't the only state offering this type of unique fishing; New Hampshire and Maine, too, are full of small, out-of-the-way mountain streams offering solitude and excellent fishing. In southern Vermont try these fairly easy-to-find mountain streams:

Roaring Branch—East of Bennington along VT 9. Miles of access from VT 9.

Bolles Brook—A tributary of Roaring Branch in the town of Woodard east of Bennington. Parallels a U.S. Forest Service gravel road.

Cold Brook—North of Wilmington. Cold Brook is a tributary of the Deerfield River and parallels a U.S. Forest Service road.

Mad Tom Brook—A tributary of the Batten Kill east of East Dorset.

Big Branch—I discussed this mountain stream in the section on Otter Creek. It contains a mixture of rainbow and brook trout. Well worth the effort.

Mill River—This is another tributary of Otter Creek. Try the upper reaches of the Mill River along VT 103 for some good brook trout fishing.

This list just scratches the surface of the opportunities for fishing mountain streams in southern Vermont. The best places are usually out of the way and are closely guarded secrets of knowledgeable local anglers. With a topographical map and a pair of hiking boots, you'll be able to unlock your own secrets to some wonderful fishing.

Other Stocked Trout Waters Worth Exploring

Adams Reservoir (Woodford), Amherst Lake (Plymouth), Beebe Pond (Sunderland), Big Cold Spring Brook (Shaftsbury), Big Mud Pond (Mount Tabor), Black Pond (Hubbardton), Black River (Cavendish), Bourn Pond (Sunderland), Branch Pond (Sunderland), Broad Brook (Guilford), Castleton River (Fair Haven), Colby Pond (Plymouth), Lower Cold River (Clarendon), Cooks Pond (Ludlow), Daily Pond (Shaftsbury), Dewey Brook (Bennington), Dufresne Pond (Manchester), Furnace Brook (Shaftsbury), Gayle Pond (Shaftsbury), Glen Lake (Castleton), Griffith Pond (Mount Tabor), Hapgood Pond (Peru), Hoosic River (Pownal), Jewett Brook (Bennington), Lake Bomoseen (Castleton), Lefferts Pond (Chittenden), Little Cold Spring Brook (Shaftsbury), Little Rock Pond (Wallingford), McIntosh Pond (Royalton), Mill River (Shrewsbury), Mill Pond (Windsor), East Branch of the North River (Whitingham), Patch Brook (Ludlow), Prentice Pond (Dorset), Red Mill Pond (Woodford), Rescue Lake (Ludlow), Roaring Banch (Sunderland), Sacketts Brook (Putney), Lower Saxtons River (Rockingham), Shaftsbury Hollow

Brook (Shaftsbury), Smith Pond (Pittsford), South Pond (Marlboro), Stamford Stream (Woodford), Thompsonburg Brook (Londonderry), Turkey Mountain Brook (Jamaica), Walloomsac River (Bennington), Wardsboro Branch (Wardsboro), Wheelerville Brook (Mendon), Whetstone Brook (Brattleboro), Whipple Hollow Brook (West Rutland), Lower Williams River (Chester).

Where to Stay in Southern Vermont

Greenwood Lodge & Campsites Box 246, Bennington, VT 05201 802-442-2547.
Camping on the Batten Kill Historic VT 7A, Arlington, VT 05250 802-375-6663.
Manchester Highlands Inn Highland Ave., Manchester, VT 05255 1-800-743-4565.
Equinox Hotel Historic VT 7A, Manchester, VT 05254 802-362-4700.

Local Guide Services

Batten Kill Outfitters Route 7A, Manchester, VT 05254
Bill's Guide Service P.O. Box 653, Manchester, VT 05254 802-325-3966.
Blue Ridge Outfitters 20 Chittenden Road, South Chittenden, VT 05701 802-747-4878.
Kevin Ladden Guide & Outfitter 64 Tucker Road, Ludlow, VT 05149 802-228-5195.
Peter Basta Guide Service & Outfitter P.O. Box 540, Dorset, VT 05251 802-867-4103.

Of Special Interest

American Museum of Fly Fishing Historic VT 7A, Manchester, VT 05254 802-447-3600.
Orvis Historic VT 7A, Manchester, VT 05254 802-362-3750.

2 | Central Vermont

Central Vermont is a mixture of forests and farms, with its own share of development. There are many inns, bed & breakfasts, and other facilities to help make your stay a pleasant experience. Many of the streams and rivers of central Vermont don't get the same amount of fishing pressure as the waters in the southern part of the state, especially the Batten Kill. The streams of central Vermont do, however, offer excellent opportunities to enjoy some great fishing.

LOWER OTTER CREEK

Maps *The Vermont Atlas and Gazetteer,* pages 32, 33, and 38.

Description The area surrounding lower Otter creek features farms interspersed with some swampy areas. There is little shade to protect the river from the heat of the summer sun. Several dams slow the flow, providing good habitat for bass. However, brown and rainbow trout are stocked in Rutland and Middlebury.

Access Explore the roads off US 7 to gain access to lower Otter Creek, especially Beldens Dam Road and the Rivers Bend Campground.

Best Assets In addition to stocked trout, lower Otter Creek offers excellent smallmouth bass fishing. The water is fertile and hosts a variety of good mayfly and caddisfly hatches.

Biggest Drawback Due to the slow flow of the water, which can lose oxygen in summer, lower Otter Creek offers limited trout fishing.

Regulations The legal fishing season runs from the second Saturday in April through the last Sunday in October.

From the falls at Vergennes to Rutland Falls: The total daily creel limit for brook, brown, and rainbow trout is six fish, not to exceed a total weight

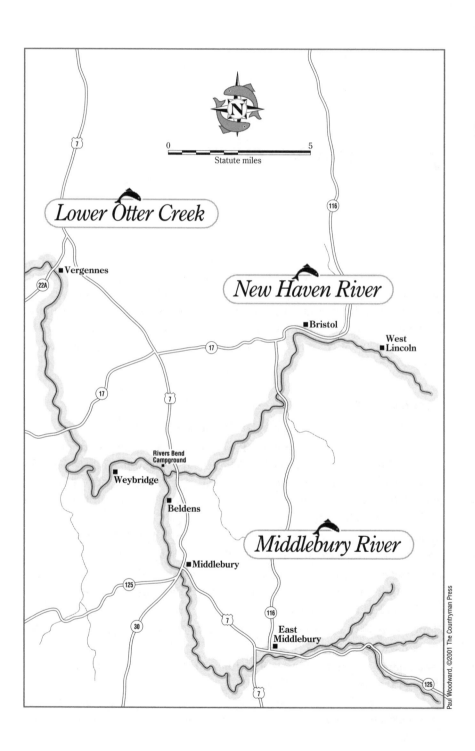

Lower Otter Creek

New Haven River

Middlebury River

■Vergennes

■Bristol

West
■Lincoln

Rivers Bend
Campground
■

■
Weybridge

■
Beldens

■Middlebury

East
Middlebury
■

Statute miles

0   5

Paul Woodward, ©2001 The Countryman Press

of 5 pounds; the total number of lake trout and landlocked salmon is two fish. There is no minimum length on brook, rainbow, and brown trout. There is an 18-inch minimum limit on lake trout, and a 15-inch minimum limit on landlocked salmon.

From Lake Champlain to the falls at Vergennes, there is no closed season. The daily creel limit for brook, brown, and rainbow trout is three fish. The minimum length for these trout is 12 inches. There is a three-fish limit for lake trout (minimum length 15 inches), and a two-fish limit for landlocked salmon (minimum length 15 inches).

Favorite Flies Hornberg (#6–10), Gray Ghost (#4–8), Black Ghost (#4–8), Mickey Finn (#6–8), Olive Woolly Bugger (#6–8), Black Woolly Bugger (#6–8), Brown Woolly Bugger (#6–8), Muddler Minnow (#4–8), Woolly Worm (#6–8), Royal Coachman (#6–10), Ballou Special (#4–8), Hare's Ear Nymph (#8–14), Pheasant Tail Nymph (#8–14), Bead Head Nymph (#8–14), Olive Sparkle Caddis Pupa (#8–14), Brown Sparkle Caddis Pupa (#8–14), Cream Sparkle Caddis Pupa (#8–14), Olive Caddis Larva (#8–14), Brown Caddis Larva (#8–14), Elk Hair Caddis (#10–14), Adams (#10–14), Light Cahill (#12–16), Green Drake (#4–6), March Brown (#8–12).

There isn't a tremendous amount of good trout fishing in the lower sections of Otter Creek. The river widens, and a series of dams slows the flow and allows the water to warm. The best trout water is below Beldens Dam near the town of Middlebury. This section of the river is accessed by following Beldens Dam Road off US 7. It holds a population of stocked rainbow and brown trout, many more than 10 inches in length. Favorite flies are Woolly Buggers, Mickey Finns, and other streamers. Weighted nymphs also work in lower Otter Creek.

To be perfectly honest, the best trout fishing in the lower section of Otter Creek is in the tributaries. These offer a mixture of brook, rainbow, and brown trout, and access is generally pretty good. I suggest exploring the Middlebury River, the New Haven River, the Neshobe River, and Furnace Brook.

THE MIDDLEBURY RIVER

Map *The Vermont Atlas and Gazetteer,* page 33.

Description The Middlebury River is a tributary of lower Otter Creek. The Middlebury begins as a series of freestone mountain streams. As the tributaries join—Goshen Brook, Crystal Brook, Alder Brook, and the South, Middle, and North Branches of the Middlebury—the river gains strength before joining Otter Creek south of the town of Middlebury. The South, Middle, and North Branches are stocked with brook, brown, and rainbow trout. Some of the fish stocked into the lower section of the river, near the town of Middlebury, measure better than 10 inches long; that's not a bad size for a stocked fish.

Access VT 125 follows the South Branch of the Middlebury and a section of the main stem of the river. There are pulloffs and picnic areas where you can park and gain access to the river.

A section of the Middlebury River flows through Middlebury Gorge, whose bottom lies 150 feet below VT 125. There are paths leading down into the gorge, but they are steep and treacherous. If you're more mountain goat than human and make it to the bottom, you'll find that wading and access up- and downstream are very difficult. I suggest passing up the stretch of the river flowing through Middlebury Gorge to concentrate on other areas.

Best Assets The Middlebury and its tributaries see few anglers. You might be able to fish all day and not see another fisherman. The branches are well stocked.

Biggest Drawback Middlebury Gorge. The water below is productive, but it's not worth getting hurt to reach.

Regulations The legal fishing season runs from the second Saturday in April through the last Sunday in October. There are no length restrictions on the fish you may keep. Daily creel limit: The total number of brook trout, brown trout, and rainbow trout is 12 fish daily; the total number of brown and rainbow trout is 6 fish.

Favorite Flies Hornberg (#6–10), Mickey Finn (#6–8), Olive Woolly Bugger (#6–8), Black Woolly Bugger (#6–8), Brown Woolly Bugger (#6–8), Muddler Minnow (#4–8), Woolly Worm (#6–8), Royal Coachman (#6–10), Ballou Special (#4–8), Hare's Ear Nymph (#8–14), Pheasant Tail Nymph (#8–14), Bead Head Nymph (#8–14), Olive Sparkle Caddis Pupa (#8–14), Brown Sparkle Caddis Pupa (#8–14), Cream Sparkle Caddis Pupa (#8–14), Olive Caddis Larva (#8–14), Brown Caddis Larva (#8–14), Elk Hair Caddis (#10–14), Hendrickson (#14), Royal Wulff (#12), Adams (#10–14), Light Cahill (#12–16), Green Drake (#4–6), March Brown (#8–12).

The Middlebury River is one of the major tributaries of Otter Creek. It begins at Pleiad Lake near Middlebury Gap on VT 125. This section of the river is the South Branch of the Middlebury. The South Branch is joined by the Middle Branch in the town of Ripton; the North Branch joins the growing flow near Middlebury Gorge. This is a lovely area, there is ample access to the water along VT 125, and there are several picnic areas where you can stop to enjoy lunch before fishing. The Middlebury remains cool throughout the summer, making it ideal brook trout habitat. It fishes very well in June and July.

Middlebury Gorge is a particularly beautiful area, and its deep pools hold large brook and rainbow trout. However, the gorge is nearly 150 feet deep, and safe access is almost impossible. The lower section of the Middlebury, near its confluence with Otter Creek, is a good spot to fish for brown trout.

THE NEW HAVEN RIVER

Map *The Vermont Atlas and Gazetteer,* page 39.

Description The New Haven River is visited by very few anglers and features some of the best scenery in Vermont. It also offers good trout fishing.

The river is a heavily wooded, freestone mountain stream originating in the Green Mountains and flowing into Otter Creek. The area features the Bristol Cliffs Wilderness Area and the New Haven River Gorge.

Best Assets The scenery will keep any angler coming back—the good fishing for native brook trout and stocked rainbow and brown trout is just a bonus. And there's a good chance that you'll fish most of the day and not see another angler.

Biggest Drawback As on so many lesser-known rivers, it's tough to find a guide here if you want one. Other than that, this river has much to recommend it.

Regulations The legal fishing season runs from the second Saturday in April through the last Sunday in October. There are no length restrictions on the fish you may keep. Daily creel limit: The total number brook trout, brown trout, and rainbow trout is 12 fish; total number of brown and rainbow trout is 6 fish.

Favorite Flies Hornberg (#6–10), Gray Ghost (#4–8), Black Ghost (#4–8), Mickey Finn (#6–8), Olive Woolly Bugger (#6–8), Black Woolly Bugger (#6–8), Brown Woolly Bugger (#6–8), Muddler Minnow (#4–8), Woolly Worm (#6–8), Royal Coachman (#6–10), Ballou Special (#4–8), Hare's Ear Nymph (#8–14), Pheasant Tail Nymph (#8–14), Bead Head Nymph (#8–14), Olive Sparkle Caddis Pupa (#8–14), Brown Sparkle Caddis Pupa (#8–14), Cream Sparkle Caddis Pupa (#8–14), Olive Caddis Larva (#8–14), Brown Caddis Larva (#8–14), Elk Hair Caddis (#10–14), Adams (#10–14), Hendrickson (#14), Royal Wulff (#8–12), Light Cahill (#12–16), Green Drake (#4–6), March Brown (#8–12).

The New Haven is a major tributary of Otter Creek. Starting on the side of Bread Loaf Mountain in Ripton, it flows north toward Lincoln and Rocky Dale. This section of the river, which is classic mountain freestone water, is accessed by taking Lincoln Gap Road from VT 116 in Bristol. This road follows the twisting course of the river as it flows through the New Haven River Gorge. Continue following Lincoln Gap Road until it becomes a dirt road and then a footpath on the side of Bread Loaf Mountain, and you'll find pools that see very few other anglers. Fish the upper stretch of the New Haven using a short, light rod and dry flies. The choice of flies doesn't seem to matter, as long as they float well and are visible.

From below the town of Bristol to its confluence with Otter Creek, the New Haven supports brook, rainbow, and brown trout. This is standard trout water, requiring a medium-sized rod and the usual collection of flies: weighted nymphs, caddis larvae, and a smattering of dry flies. Small streamers and Woolly Buggers are also good flies for fishing the lower New Haven.

The section of the river near the town of New Haven is stocked with brown and rainbow trout; brook trout are stocked near Lincoln.

FURNACE BROOK

Maps *The Vermont Atlas and Gazetteer,* pages 29 and 33.

Description Furnace Brook, a tributary of Otter Creek, starts as a forested mountain freestone stream in the Green Mountain National Forest. Easy to wade, it offers good fishing for brook, rainbow, and brown trout.

Access Look for access where VT 3 and US 7 cross Furnace Brook. Also, a well-maintained road north of Grangerville follows the stream and leads to the Pittsford National Fish Hatchery. The road continues north of the hatchery and follows along the stream to the Proctor Village Forest.

Best Assets As on all of Vermont's mountain freestone streams, the scenery is one of Furnace Brook's biggest assets. And like many of the tributaries of Otter Creek, you might be able to fish the entire day and see few other anglers. Also drop by the Pittsford National Fish Hatchery for a tour.

Biggest Drawback The water level is subject to extreme fluctuations; a couple of days of rain might ruin the fishing for the next week.

Regulations The legal fishing season runs from the second Saturday in April through the last Sunday in October. There are no length restrictions on the fish you may keep. Daily creel limit: The total number of brook trout, brown trout, and rainbow trout is 12 fish; the total number of brown and rainbow trout is 6 fish.

Favorite Flies Mickey Finn (#8–10), Olive Woolly Bugger (#8–10), Black Woolly Bugger (#8–10), Brown Woolly Bugger (#8–10), Woolly Worm (#10), Royal Coachman (#6–10), Ballou Special (#4–8), Hare's Ear Nymph (#8–14), Pheasant Tail Nymph (#8–14), Bead Head Nymph (#8–14), Olive Sparkle Caddis Pupa (#8–14), Brown Sparkle Caddis Pupa (#8–14), Cream Sparkle Caddis Pupa (#8–14), Olive Caddis Larva (#8–14), Brown Caddis Larva

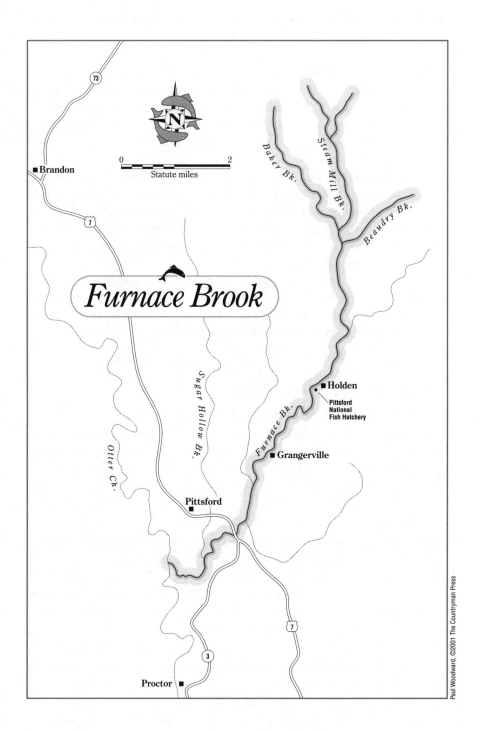

(#8–14), Elk Hair Caddis (#10–14), Adams (#10–14), Hendrickson (#14), Light Cahill (#12–16), Royal Wulff (#10).

Furnace Brook is a fascinating little stream worth trying if you want to get away from the usual crowds that gather at Vermont's more famous waterways. It's formed where North Brook and Bee Brook join above the town of Holden in the Green Mountain National Forest. Furnace Brook tumbles down the mountainside and then quickly flattens out near Pittsford, where it empties into Otter Creek.

Although the Pittsford National Fish Hatchery is operated on Furnace Brook, the stream is managed as a wild trout fishery and is not stocked. It is, however, the home of a population of brook, rainbow, and brown trout. As with the other tributaries of Otter Creek, you'll find more brook and rainbow trout near the headwaters of the stream, and more brown trout in the slower section downstream.

Furnace Brook enjoys good hatches throughout the spring and summer. Bead Head and other small, weighted nymphs work well here. Attractor dry flies seem to work about as well as imitative patterns; Wulffs and Humpies are particularly effective. Plan on fishing Furnace Brook from mid-May to the first half of July.

THE OTTAUQUECHEE RIVER

Maps *The Vermont Atlas and Gazetteer,* pages 30 and 31.

Description The Ottauquechee River starts as a mountain freestone stream in Killington, Vermont. It flows southeast through Bridgewater and Woodstock, gaining strength from several small tributaries. Below the town of Woodstock, the Ottauquechee flows through 165-foot-deep Quechee Gorge. The river continues east until it empties into the Connecticut River. The best trout fishing is from Quechee Gorge to the headwaters.

Access US 4 parallels the Ottauquechee. There are several unmarked pullovers where you can park and gain access to the river. Rainbow trout are the fish of choice in the water above the Quechee Gorge. Two trails lead down into the gorge, but be careful: This section of the river lies below three dams and is subject to fluctuating water levels. Quechee Gorge contains several large pools holding big brown trout.

Best Assets The wooded areas of the headwaters are particularly beautiful. And if you don't mind the hike, the Quechee Gorge is a spectacular place to fish; it's probably the only place like it in the eastern United States.

Biggest Drawback The dams regulating the water in Quechee Gorge make fishing a dicey proposition. Be alert for rising water and you'll be safe.

Regulations The legal fishing season for the Ottauquechee River runs from the second Saturday in April through the last Sunday in October. There are no length restrictions on the fish you may keep. Daily bag limit: The total number of brook trout, brown trout, and rainbow trout is 12 fish; total number of brown and rainbow trout is 6 fish.

New Hampshire fishing regulations apply to that section of the Ottauquechee from the Connecticut River upstream to the first highway bridge: The legal trout fishing season is from January 1 to October 15. The daily bag limit (brook, brown, and rainbow trout) is five fish, not to exceed a total weight of 5 pounds.

Favorite Flies Hornberg (#6–10), Gray Ghost (#4–8), Black Ghost (#4–8), Mickey Finn (#6–8), Olive Woolly Bugger (#6–8), Black Woolly Bugger (#6–8), Brown Woolly Bugger (#6–8), Muddler Minnow (#4–8), Woolly Worm (#6–8), Royal Coachman (#6–10), Ballou Special (#4–8), Hare's Ear Nymph (#8–14), Pheasant Tail Nymph (#8–14), Bead Head Nymph (#8–14), Olive Sparkle Caddis Pupa (#8–14), Brown Sparkle Caddis Pupa (#8–14), Cream Sparkle Caddis Pupa (#8–14), Olive Caddis Larva (#8–14), Brown Caddis Larva (#8–14), Elk Hair Caddis (#10–14), Adams (#10–14), Light Cahill (#12–16), Green Drake (#4–6), March Brown (#8–12).

The Ottauquechee is another river nestled in the beautiful Vermont countryside. It starts as a classic mountain stream near the town of Killington, and flows southeast before entering the Connecticut River. The short upper stretch contains brook trout; lower portions contain brown and rainbow trout. Because the river eventually widens and the temperature rises, it's best to confine your trout fishing to the first 10 to 15 miles. The favorite time to fish the Ottauquechee is May through the first week of July.

There is a lot of access to the Ottauquechee along US 4, which parallels the river; look for pullouts along the road and try your luck. There are also several tributaries that contain brook trout. Pinney Hollow Brook, near Coolidge State Park, and North Brook, which runs through Bridgewater Center, are easy to access.

You won't need a large assortment of flies to score on the Ottauquechee, but it's best to go prepared with a variety of patterns. In the early season Hendricksons are the most important: Hendrickson Dun dry flies to match the adults and Gold Ribbed Hare's Ears to match the nymphs, all tied on size 14 hooks, are good to have in your fly box. As the season progresses, try the Gray Fox, Gray Quill, and Blue Winged Olive. If you fish the small tributaries of the Ottauquechee, you'll want to cast Royal Wulffs and other bushy dry flies.

One place on the Ottauquechee River you'll want to see, if not fish, is

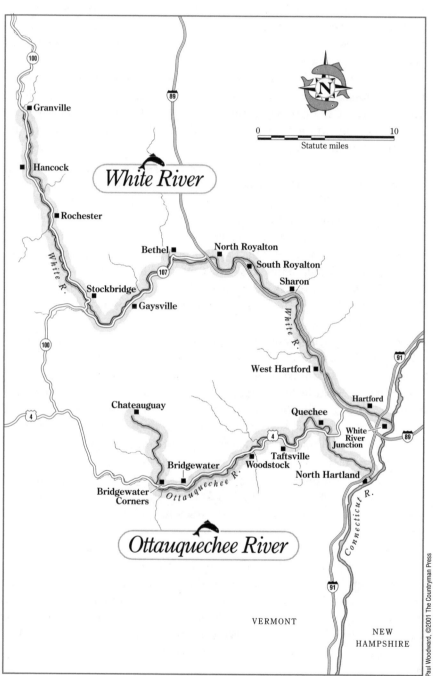

Granville

Hancock

Rochester

White River

Bethel

North Royalton

South Royalton

Sharon

Stockbridge

Gaysville

West Hartford

Hartford

Chateauguay

Quechee

White River Junction

Bridgewater

Taftsville

Woodstock

North Hartland

Bridgewater Corners

Ottauquechee R.

Ottauquechee River

White R.

White R.

Connecticut R.

0   10
Statute miles

VERMONT

NEW HAMPSHIRE

Paul Woodward, ©2001 The Countryman Press

the Quechee Gorge. This gorge near the town of Woodstock is a 165-foot-deep canyon. US 4 crosses it, and there are places to park and take pictures. If you're a hardy soul and wish to try your luck here, two trails lead to different parts of the river. Where US 4 crosses the gorge, look for a trail on the west side of the river. This trail leads upstream to the beginning of the gorge; a trail on the east side of the river heads downstream to the end of the gorge. Although the Quechee Gorge is known to contain some very large brown trout, remember that the water flow is regulated by a dam and fluctuates dramatically. Use extreme caution when fishing here.

THE WHITE RIVER

Maps *The Vermont Atlas and Gazetteer,* pages 31, 34, and 35.

Description The White River is one of the largest and most important rivers in Vermont. There are several branches and many tributaries, all offering opportunities to fish for trout.

The West Branch, Robbins Branch, Clark Brook, Patterson Brook, Deer Hollow Brook, Third Branch, and other tributaries of the White River start in the heart of the Green Mountains. These headwaters are mountain freestone streams, tumbling cool and clear through the mountain valleys.

As the headwater streams join together, the river gathers strength as it flows toward the Connecticut River at White River Junction. The headwater streams are very easy to wade, but the pools deepen in the middle stretch of the river around Rochester and Pittsfield, and wading becomes more difficult. From Stockbridge to White River Junction, the river deepens and widens, and fishing is best done from a canoe. The lower sections of the river are a mixture of woodlands and farms.

Access Several roads lead along the tributaries and main stem of the White River. VT 100 follows the main stem from Granville to Stockbridge. There are many places to park and access the river. VT 107 continues following the main stem of the White River from Stockbridge to Royalton. Although it's best to float this section, there are pulloffs where you can park and fish. VT 14 follows the river from Royalton to White River Junction.

Best Asset The White River offers a variety of fishing opportunities. Whether you like wading small mountain streams, prefer a medium-sized river with larger pools, or enjoy the adventure of taking a float trip, this river has it all.

Biggest Drawback I-89 follows and crosses the White River from Royalton to White River Junction. The noise of the interstate in this section of the river detracts from the experience.

Regulations The legal fishing season runs from the second Saturday in April through the last Sunday in October.

From Lillieville Brook in Stockbridge to the headwaters, there are no length restrictions on the fish you may keep. Daily bag limit: The total number brook trout, brown trout, and rainbow trout is 12 fish; the total number of brown and rainbow trout is 6 fish.

From Cleveland Brook in Bethel to Lillieville Brook in Bethel, artificial-lures-only and fly-fishing-only rules apply. You may keep one trout (the minimum length is 18 inches).

From the US 5 bridge in Hartford to the VT 107 bridge in Royalton: The daily creel limit (brook, brown, and rainbow trout) is a total of six fish, not to exceed a total of 5 pounds.

From the Connecticut River to the Route 5 bridge in Hartford: The fishing season is from January 1 to October 15, and the daily creel limit for trout is five fish, not to exceed a total of 5 pounds.

Favorite Flies Hornberg (#6–10), Gray Ghost (#4–8), Black Ghost (#4–8), Mickey Finn (#6–8), Olive Woolly Bugger (#6–8), Black Woolly Bugger (#6–8), Brown Woolly Bugger (#6–8), Muddler Minnow (#4–8), Woolly Worm (#6–8), Royal Coachman (#6–10), Ballou Special (#4–8), Hare's Ear Nymph (#8–14), Pheasant Tail Nymph (#8–14), Bead Head Nymph (#8–14), Olive Sparkle Caddis Pupa (#8–14), Brown Sparkle Caddis Pupa (#8–14), Cream Sparkle Caddis Pupa (#8–14), Olive Caddis Larva (#8–14), Brown Caddis Larva (#8–14), Elk Hair Caddis (#10–14), Adams (#10–14), Light Cahill (#12–16), Green Drake (#4–6), March Brown (#8–12).

The White is one of Vermont's most famous rivers for a couple of reasons. First, it once provided key spawning habitat for Atlantic salmon returning to the Connecticut River each year. Dams built on the Connecticut River in the 19th century blocked the returning salmon and destroyed the runs, but state and federal fisheries biologists are working hard to return this important species to the Connecticut and the White Rivers. The White River National Fish Hatchery, which is located at the junctions of VT 107 and VT 12, is playing a key role in this restoration effort. Plan on visiting the hatchery to learn more about this important recovery effort.

Second, the White River is noteworthy for the quality of its fishing. While the Connecticut was being destroyed by dams and development, the White was largely spared. Even today there are many miles of access, all providing excellent fly-fishing opportunities.

The White River is classified as a freestone river, with wild brook trout populating the upper stretches and many of the tributaries. The river starts as a small mountain stream in Granville near the base of Braintree Mountain. VT 100 parallels the headwaters of the White River, providing easy access to anglers interested in fishing for wild brook trout. The small White River quickly gains size as tributaries—Robbins Branch, Thatcher Brook,

Howe Brook, and others—join the flow. All of these freestone tributaries of the upper White River hold brook trout and are worth investigating with a light rod and high-floating dry flies.

The White River jumps in size in Rochester near the intersection of VT 100 and VT 73. VT 100 continues to follow the river for approximately 12 miles, offering access at pullouts along the way.

The Tweed River adds its flow to the growing White River where VT 100 and VT 107 meet in Pittsfield. The Tweed is a relatively short river—it's only about 15 miles long—offering a mixture of brook and rainbow trout. Access to the Tweed is at pullouts along VT 100.

VT 107 follows the White River from the town of Stockbridge to Bethel. This section of the river is a combination of freestone bottom and deep pools, and holds a mixture of stocked trout and salmon. Locust Creek joins the White near the White River National Fish Hatchery where VT 107 and VT 12 meet; this freestone tributary contains a supply of stocked rainbow trout.

In Bethel the Third Branch of the White River meets the main stem. This long freestone tributary is followed by VT 12A for much of its course, and there is a lot of access at pullouts along the road. The best fishing is in the upper sections around Roxbury for native brook trout, although the lower stretch contains a nice population of brown trout.

The First and Second Branches of the White River join the main stem in Royalton. The First Branch, which begins in the western corner of Washington, Vermont, is followed by VT 110. There is quite a bit of access at pullouts and especially the bridges where VT 110 crosses the stream. The First Branch is better known for its healthy population of rainbow and brown trout, although there are brookies in its upper reaches.

The Second Branch of the White River is paralleled by VT 14. Sadly, access is limited in the upper sections, but you can reach the stream from VT 14 near the spot where the Second Branch dumps into the White River. This is a good area to catch large brown trout and smallmouth bass.

From Bethel to White River Junction, where the White meets the Connecticut, the White is followed by VT 14 and I-89. This section is wider, slower, and deeper, and is a favorite among canoeists. It does contain some very large brown and rainbow trout, as well as a good supply of smallmouth bass.

The best time to fish the White River and its tributaries is from the middle of May through the middle of July. During the early part of summer, begin by using Hendricksons and March Browns, and switch to Blue Winged Olives as the season wears on. By the middle of July Tricos and terrestrial patterns grow in importance. Of course, as the main stem of the river warms in midsummer, the tributaries remain cool and the fishing continues to be good; here you'll want to use light tackle and dry flies.

A favorite tactic in the lower section of the river where the large rainbow and brown trout live is to use heavily weighted nymphs and Woolly Buggers, as well as streamers such as Muddler Minnows, with a sinking-tip line. In midsummer it's best to fish the lower White River in the early morning and early evening, when the water is cooler.

THE WINOOSKI RIVER

Maps *The Vermont Atlas and Gazetteer,* pages 40, 41, 44, 45, 46, and 47.

Description The Winooski River starts as a small stream in Marshfield, Vermont, then flows northwest to enter Lake Champlain near Burlington. On its way, major tributaries—the Mad River, Dog River, Stevens Branch, Little River, and others—enter, and the Winooski gains considerable size.

The surrounding Winooski River Valley is a combination of wooded mountains and farmland. Parts of the Winooski are rather easy to wade, yet the river is so large that a canoe will open up many more miles of river. This gently flowing river is a safe canoe trip for even a novice paddler.

Access Primary access is along US 2 in Middlesex and Moretown; the road follows the river, providing opportunities to park and walk to the river. River Road, which follows the south side of the river in Duxbury and Bolton, is one of my favorite sections of the Winooski; there is ample parking and plenty of places to access the water. This is a popular area to fish.

Best Assets The Winooski River is easily accessed, and there is enough water to accommodate a large number of anglers. It's a good river for beginning fly-fishers because it's wide and open, giving plenty of room for backcasts. There are also prolific hatches of caddis- and mayflies.

Biggest Drawbacks The Winooski is subject to water releases from dams, which will affect your ability to safely wade. If you like solitude when you fish, the Winooski might not be for you, especially on weekends. It's a popular river and gets a considerable amount of traffic in late spring and early summer.

Regulations The legal fishing season runs from the second Saturday in April through the last Sunday in October. From the US 2 bridge in Waterbury to the headwaters, there are no length restrictions on the fish you may keep. Daily creel limit: The total number of brook trout, brown trout, and rainbow trout is 12 fish; the total number of brown and rainbow trout is 6 fish.

From the railroad bridge in Waterbury to the US 2 bridge in Waterbury, the daily creel limit is two trout.

From the railroad bridge in Waterbury to Bolton Dam, the daily creel limit for brook trout, brown trout, and rainbow trout is 12 fish; the total number of brown and rainbow trout is 6 fish.

From the ledges west of US 7 in Winooski to Bolton Dam, the daily creel

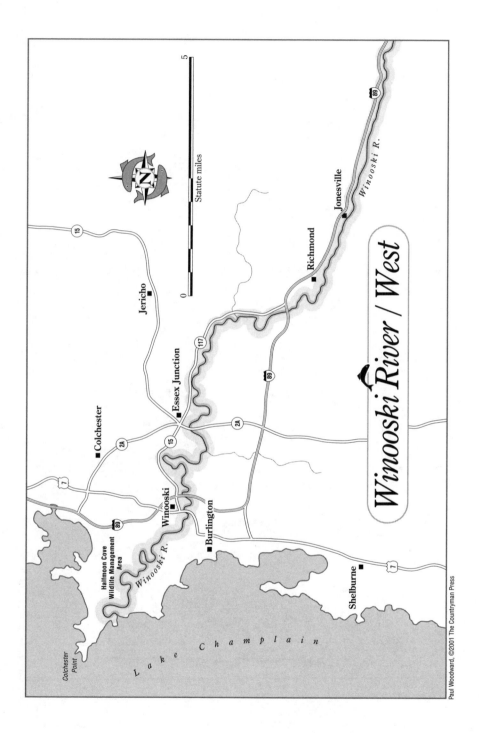

Winooski River / West

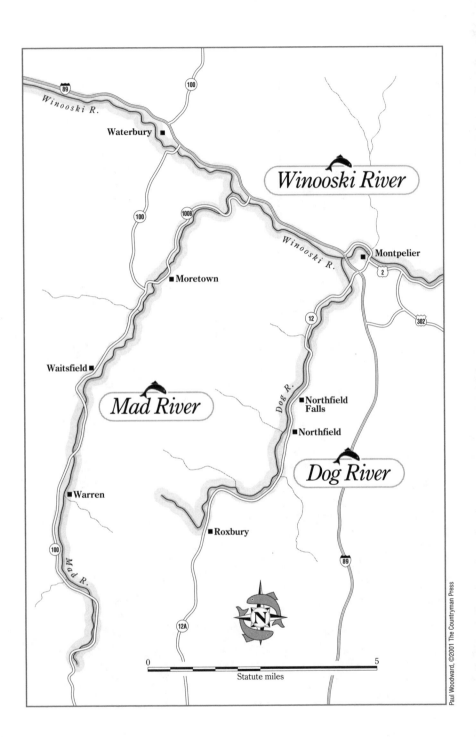

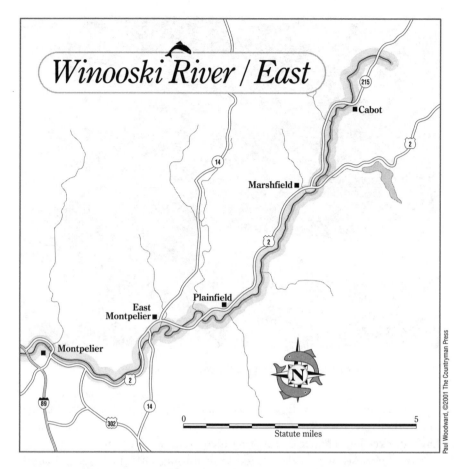

Winooski River / East

Cabot

Marshfield

Plainfield

East
Montpelier

Montpelier

N

0 — — — — — 5
Statute miles

limit for brook, rainbow, and brown trout is six fish, not weighing more
than a total of 5 pounds.

Favorite Flies Hornberg (#6–10), Gray Ghost (#4–8), Black Ghost (#4–8), Mick-
ey Finn (#6–8), Olive Woolly Bugger (#6–8), Black Woolly Bugger (#6–8),
Brown Woolly Bugger (#6–8), Muddler Minnow (#4–8), Woolly Worm (#6–8),
Royal Coachman (#6–10), Ballou Special (#4–8), Hare's Ear Nymph (#8–14),
Pheasant Tail Nymph (#8–14), Bead Head Nymph (#8–14), Olive Sparkle Cad-
dis Pupa (#8–14), Brown Sparkle Caddis Pupa (#8–14), Cream Sparkle Cad-
dis Pupa (#8–14), Olive Caddis Larva (#8–14), Brown Caddis Larva (#8–14),
Elk Hair Caddis (#10–14), Adams (#10–14), Light Cahill (#12–16), Green
Drake (#4–6), March Brown (#8–12), Black Ant (#14), Dave's Hopper (#10).

The Winooski is a major waterway in north-central Vermont. After traveling across much of the middle of the state, the river empties into Lake
Champlain in Burlington.

The Winooski is a wide river. It contains a healthy population of stocked trout.

The Winooski is a wide, almost intimidating, river; it's certainly unlike most other rivers in Vermont. However, if you know where to start, you'll have an excellent chance at catching nice rainbow and brown trout.

The lower section of the Winooski in Burlington contains smallmouth bass, salmon, steelhead, and even walleyes from Lake Champlain. The most popular area in the lower part of the river is the Salmon Hole below the power dam in the town of Winooski. Access to the Salmon Hole is from Riverside Avenue on the Burlington side of the river, or at the fish trap and canoe access points in Winooski. The Salmon Hole is closed to fishing from the middle of March to the first of June to protect spawning walleyes, but the rest of the year you can catch perch, pike, pickerel, and lake trout. Among local anglers the favorite time to fish the Salmon Hole is fall, when the steelhead and landlocked salmon run up the Winooski to the base of the dam. In 1993 a trap-and-truck program was instituted to trap the migrating fish at the dam and drive them upriver to complete their spawning runs. While the Salmon Hole might not be the prettiest place on the river—you are fishing in the center of small city—it does offer a good opportunity to catch a variety of nice fish.

The section of the Winooski from Burlington to Montpelier, the capital of Vermont, sees the most fly-anglers. River Road follows the Winooski for several miles on the south side of the river in Duxbury, providing good access to the water. Look for River Road where the bridge crosses the Winooski in the town of Jonesville. You can also pick up River Road in Waterbury off VT 100.

Wading this section is fairly easy, because the river bottom is made of fine gravel; there are several obvious pullouts where you can park. While you can use hip waders, chest waders will give you more mobility and open up this entire section to you. Many stretches of this wide river become warm in summer, but this area remains cool. The water flowing in from the Mad River and discharges from the dam in Duxbury keep the water at a temperature the trout prefer. This section of the Winooski hosts a wide variety of insects, especially caddisflies and stoneflies; try fishing imitations of caddis pupae down and across stream, and stonefly nymphs upstream. With respect to mayflies, the river contains Hendricksons early in the season, and sulphurs and light cahills in June. As the season wears on, the golden drake emerges. By mid- to late summer tricos and blue-winged olives take control. In late summer and early fall large numbers of grasshoppers live along the river's grassy banks. These insects frequently fly over and flop on the water; a grasshopper imitation, fished with a slight twitching action, can sometimes fool a fish that is wise to the presence of the naturals. This popular section of the Winooski is populated with brown and rainbow trout. The entire river is liberally stocked with rainbow and brown trout as well as landlocked salmon.

THE DOG RIVER

Map *The Vermont Atlas and Gazetteer,* page 40.

Description The Dog is a medium-sized river flowing through a mixture of forested hills and farmlands. It starts in the wooded hills of northern Roxbury and flows north to the Winooski. The Dog River is easy to wade, and some anglers say it has some of the best brown trout fishing in the state of Vermont.

Access VT 12, which follows the Dog from Montpelier to Roxbury, is your key to the river. There are several prominent parking areas and access points along the river; other stretches are within fenced farmlands, making access very difficult.

Best Assets I think the scenery is one of the best features of the Dog River. The rolling farmlands add a nice touch to the surrounding valley. This is also a comfortable river to fish: It's easy to wade, and there's ample room to cast.

Biggest Drawbacks There is good access to the water as the river flows through Berlin, Vermont, as well as the section of the river flowing through northern Roxbury and southern Northfield. However, the sections of the river flowing near Norwich University and the town of Northfield are much more difficult to access. The lower sections are also a bit silty, making the rocks very slippery. Even though the water is slow, be sure to wade with care.

Regulations The legal fishing season runs from the second Saturday in April through the last Sunday in October. There are no length restrictions on the fish you may keep. Daily creel limit: The total number of brook trout, brown trout, and rainbow trout is 12 fish; the total number of brown and rainbow trout is 6 fish.

Favorite Flies Hornberg (#6-10), Gray Ghost (#4-8), Black Ghost (#4-8), Mickey Finn (#6-8), Olive Woolly Bugger (#6-8), Black Woolly Bugger (#6-8), Brown Woolly Bugger (#6-8), Muddler Minnow (#4-8), Woolly Worm (#6-8), Royal Coachman (#6-10), Ballou Special (#4-8), Hare's Ear Nymph (#8-14), Pheasant Tail Nymph (#8-14), Bead Head Nymph (#8-14), Olive Sparkle Caddis Pupa (#8-14), Brown Sparkle Caddis Pupa (#8-14), Cream Sparkle Caddis Pupa (#8-14), Olive Caddis Larva (#8-14), Brown Caddis Larva (#8-14), Elk Hair Caddis (#10-14), Adams (#10-14), Hendrickson (#12-14), Light Cahill (#12-16), Green Drake (#4-6), March Brown (#8-12), Dave's Hopper (#10), Letort Cricket (#10), Black Ant (#14).

The Dog River is an important tributary of the Winooski River (see map on page 52). The lower section of the Dog flows through a mix of dairy farms and wooded areas before emptying into the Winooski in Montpelier. The Dog River Valley is extremely beautiful and well worth your time to visit.

There are several access points to the Dog River along VT 12 south out of Montpelier. The first is located about 1 mile after VT 12 passes under I-89; look for a dirt road on the right with a small parking area. This is a popular area, and there are often a couple of anglers in this section in the early evening from the last half of May through June. Continue driving upstream, and to the left you'll find a dirt road that crosses the tracks for the Central Vermont Railway. You can walk up the tracks to gain access to this section of the river. Continue driving south on VT 12 and look for pullouts providing access.

The next major access point is the Dog River Natural Area in the town of West Berlin. This small nature preserve features wooden benches and a footpath on the north side of the river. This area is very easy to wade, and there are several nice pools. If you're a fan of covered bridges, then you'll want to spend some time exploring Northfield Falls, Vermont—a little town

The lower section of the Dog River flows through a mixture of forests and dairy farms. It holds some very large brown trout.

with four covered bridges. You'll also be able to access the river at the bridges spanning the Dog River.

From Northfield Falls to Northfield Center, access is very limited. Posted land, businesses, and homes prevent access to much of this part of the river.

VT 12A follows the Dog beginning in Northfield Center. The next best access point is along VT 12A above the Northfield Country Club. These headwaters of the Dog, which cascade over the rocky streambed, are overgrown with vegetation. Casting is tight, but the water remains cool throughout the summer.

The entire Dog River contains brown trout interspersed with rainbows. In spring and early summer, the river boasts the usual complement of mayflies and caddisflies, so be prepared with an assortment of nymphs, larvae, and dry flies. Imitations of Hendricksons are important if you fish the Dog at the end of May, but you'll want to have a few March Browns and Gray Quills for June. The trico hatch takes over by mid-August, and you'll also want to have an assortment of terrestrials: grasshoppers, crickets, and ants. Favorite streamers include medium-sized Woolly Buggers and Muddler

Minnows; these are especially effective in the lower sections of the river in the early evening, when the big brown trout go on the prowl.

THE MAD RIVER

Maps *The Vermont Atlas and Gazetteer,* pages 34 and 40.

Description The Mad River is very similar to its cousin to the east, the Dog River. The Mad starts as a small freestone mountain stream in the Green Mountains. It tumbles northeast, gaining strength as it flows toward the Winooski River. The upper reaches of the Mad are easy to wade; the lower sections contain riffles interspersed with very deep pools. The section flowing through Waitsfield and Moretown passes through farms and between forested hills.

Access VT 100B from Middlesex to southwestern Moretown closely follows the river. Several parking areas offer good access to the river.

VT 100 follows the Mad River from southwestern Moretown to its headwaters in the Green Mountain National Forest in Granville. There are a few pulloffs where you can park and fish near the town of Warren, but your best bet is to fish the lower sections of the river and then head to the headwaters in Granville. The road closely follows the river in Granville, where there are pulloffs and plenty of access to the water.

Best Assets I like the fact that you can fish the Mad River for a few hours, and then hop over to the Winooski or Dog River. The Mad also offers two distinct types of fishing: the upper freestone mountain headwaters requiring small tackle and accurate casting, and the deeper, slower-moving lower river where you will use standard-sized tackle and weighted flies to fish the big pools.

Biggest Drawback The Mad River area is a bit of a tourist destination, and a lot of folks use the river. Around Waitsfield you'll have to yield some of the better pools to the swimmers and canoeists.

Regulations The legal fishing season runs from the second Saturday in April through the last Sunday in October. There are no length restrictions on the fish you may keep. Daily creel limit: The total number of brook trout, brown trout, and rainbow trout is 12 fish; the total number of brown and rainbow trout is 6 fish.

Favorite Flies Hornberg (#6–10), Gray Ghost (#4–8), Black Ghost (#4–8), Mickey Finn (#6–8), Olive Woolly Bugger (#6–8), Black Woolly Bugger (#6–8), Brown Woolly Bugger (#6–8), Muddler Minnow (#4–8), Woolly Worm (#6–8), Royal Coachman (#6–10), Ballou Special (#4–8), Hare's Ear Nymph (#8–14), Pheasant Tail Nymph (#8–14), Bead Head Nymph (#8–14), Olive Sparkle Caddis Pupa (#8–14), Brown Sparkle Caddis Pupa (#8–14),

The lower Mad River is a good spot to hook a good-sized brown or rainbow trout.

Cream Sparkle Caddis Pupa (#8–14), Olive Caddis Larva (#8–14), Brown Caddis Larva (#8–14), Elk Hair Caddis (#10–14), Adams (#10–14), Light Cahill (#12–16), Green Drake (#4–6), March Brown (#8–12), Dave's Hopper (#10), Letort Cricket (#12).

The Mad River is another major tributary of the Winooski (see map on page 52). The Mad starts in Warren in the Green Mountain National Forest where Austin Brook, Stetson Brook, and Mills Brook come together. The upper part of the river is a narrow mountain freestone stream. It travels through the forest and is quite beautiful, especially in summer and fall. As on all mountain streams, the water is subject to rapid fluctuations, and high water is more of a problem than low. This section of the Mad River remains cool throughout much of summer, especially where small tributaries join the main flow. In the heat of summer, it's always best to look for trout below these tributaries. VT 100 follows the Mad River from Moretown to its source in Warren. There are numerous pullouts along VT 100 where you can park and fish, and there is also a state-maintained streamside picnic site.

The Mad River begins to broaden from Waitsfield to Moretown. This area is more developed, and access becomes a problem. Still, there are spots where you can park; a short walk through the woods will lead you to the river. In the heat of summer, the most obvious places become the haunts of local swimmers and sunbathers, but you will be able to fish these areas early in the morning and many evenings.

Below Moretown, where the Mad makes its final approach to the Winooski, the river begins to broaden and access improves. This stretch of the river is followed by VT 100B, along which are several pullouts where you can park and fish. The upper section of the river is populated with brook trout, but this broad, slower lower stretch contains brown trout.

Most of the tributaries of the Mad River contain brook trout, but Mill Brook in Fayston is a particularly nice and easily accessed stream (this is a different stream from the Mills Brook in Warren). VT 17 (also called McCullough Highway) parallels Mill Brook out of Irasville. This small stream is best fished with a short rod and dry flies. It's a classic mountain freestone stream in the heart of the Green Mountains.

The area around the Mad River is a popular ski destination in winter, and there are numerous hotels, restaurants, and other facilities. Waitsfield is also the home of Mad River Canoes.

Mid-May to the first week in July is the best time to fish the Mad River. The same flies you use to fish the Winooski and Dog Rivers will work on the Mad: Hendricksons, March Browns, Light Cahills, and Blue Winged Olives are popular mayfly imitations. Elk Hair Caddises, as well as caddis larvae and pupae, work on all of these rivers. As the season wears on, the fields of the dairy farms along the Mad are filled with grasshoppers, crickets, and ants, and floating terrestrial imitations can encourage a trout to come up from the bottom of almost any pool in the river. When the water is high, or when you're fishing the wider section of the lower river, try streamers such as Woolly Buggers and various bucktail patterns.

Other Stocked Trout Water Worth Exploring

Baker Pond (Brookfield), Browns River (Jericho), Colton Pond (Killington), Currier Brook (Wolcott), Elmore Brook (Woodbury), First Banch (Chelsea), Greenwood Lake (Woodbury), Harvey's Lake (Barnet), Hollow Brook (Hinesburg), Joiner Brook (Bolton), Judd Brook (Woodbury), Kato Brook (Woodbury), Kettle Pond (Groton), Lewis Creek (Starksboro), Mirror Lake (Calais), Nelson Pond (Calais), Nichols Pond (Woodbury), Notch Brook (Bristol), Noyes Pond (Groton), Tabor Branch (Topsham), Thatcher Brook (Waterbury), Waits River (Topsham).

Where to Stay in Central Vermont

All Seasons Inn 112 Main Street, Ludlow, VT 05149 1-888-228-8100.
The Quechee Inn Clubhouse Road, Quechee, VT 05059 1-800-253-3133.

Woodstock Motel Taftsville Road, Woodstock, VT 05091 802-457-2500.

Local Guide Services

Fly-fish Vermont 954 South Main Street, Stowe, VT 05672 802-253-3964.
Fly Rod Shop Box 960, Stowe, VT 05672 1-800-535-9763.
Green Mountain Outdoor Adventures HCR 32, Middlesex, VT 05602
802-229-4246.

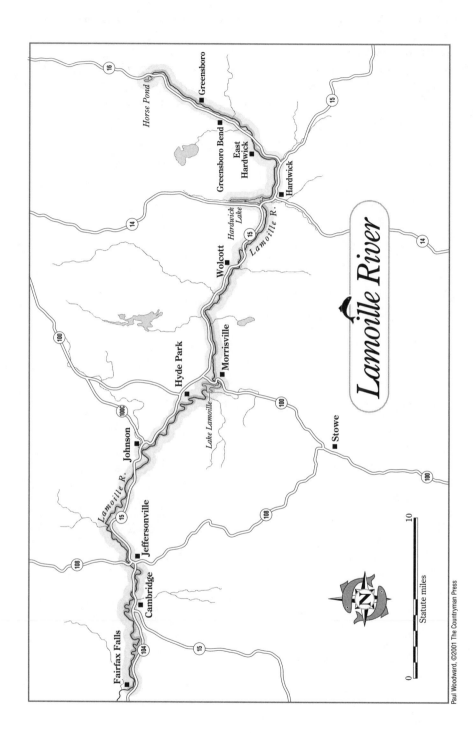

Lamoille River

Paul Woodward, ©2001 The Countryman Press

Statute miles

0   10

3 | Northern Vermont

Northern Vermont—also known as the Northeast Kingdom—is a favorite destination for anglers and other outdoors enthusiasts wanting to get away from the crowds that gather at more popular rivers such as the Batten Kill, Mettawee, and Winooski. Spring comes late to this part of Vermont, and snowpack can keep rivers running high until the first of June. These rivers make wonderful destinations for the last week of May through July.

THE LAMOILLE RIVER

Maps *The Vermont Atlas and Gazetteer,* pages 46, 47, and 48.

Description The Lamoille is one of the major rivers of northern Vermont, traveling across the state from the eastern corner of Greensboro to Lake Champlain.

The Lamoille beings at the outflow of Horse Pond and flows southwest through the forests of Greensboro and Hardwick. This section of the river is freestone and rather easy to wade. The upper Lamoille quickly gains strength as several tributaries enter.

In south-central Hardwick the Lamoille bends to the west. The river also gains in size as a productive tributary called Haynesville Brook adds its flows. At this point the Lamoille becomes a respectably sized stream, but it's still rather easy to wade. This larger section of the river is lovely and holds bigger fish.

It's a curious fact that in July and August, the water temperatures in the upper section of the Lamoille can be higher than in the lower stretches. It's not uncommon to find the water in the upper river to be 80 degrees F or higher, certainly not what you'd associate with good trout fishing. In the heat of summer, the trout migrate to the mouths of the tributaries and even into the tributaries themselves to seek cooler water.

The lower Lamoille, below Lake Lamoille in Cadys Falls, is larger and can be fished by either foot or canoe. This section of the river contains larger trout. It remains relatively cool throughout the summer thanks to several major tributaries, including the Gihon River, the North Branch of the Lamoille, and the Green River. All of these tributaries are stocked and worth exploring for good trout fishing.

Access VT 16 follows the upper Lamoille River from its origins in Horse Pond to south-central Hardwick. VT 15 (the Grand Army of the Republic Highway) parallels the Lamoille from Hardwick to Cambridge. Both roads have pulloffs and picnic areas offering easy access to the river. Wade the upper sections of the Lamoille, and wade the shallows or fish from canoe from Cady Falls to Cambridge.

Best Assets The Lamoille offers a variety of opportunities to catch brown, rainbow, and brook trout. There is ample access to the river at pulloffs and picnic grounds. Several tributaries also offer excellent fishing. The river is liberally stocked with brown, brook, and rainbow trout as well as landlocked salmon. In one stocking alone the state placed 80,000 fingerling salmon into the Lamoille.

Biggest Drawback In recent years development in the area has allowed silt to enter the river. Local anglers say this material is beginning to effect the once prolific hatches of may- and caddisflies. Fortunately the Lamoille River Anglers Association is working hard to protect the river and increase the quality of the fishery.

Regulations The legal fishing season runs from the second Saturday in April through the last Sunday in October. The *Vermont Guide to Hunting, Fishing, and Trapping Laws* guidebook recognizes several sections of the Lamoille, each governed by its own set of regulations. The following regulations pertain to the best trout-fishing sections of the river.

From Fairfax Falls Dam to the headwaters: There are no length restrictions on the fish you may keep. Daily creel limit: The total number of brook trout, brown trout, and rainbow trout is 12 fish; the total number of brown and rainbow trout is 6 fish.

From the VT 104 bridge in Fairfax to the Georgia High Bridge in Georgia: The daily creel limit for trout is a total of two fish.

Favorite Flies Gray Ghost (#4–8), Black Ghost (#4–8), Mickey Finn (#6–8), Olive Woolly Bugger (#6–8), Black Woolly Bugger (#6–8), Brown Woolly Bugger (#6–8), Muddler Minnow (#4–8), Woolly Worm (#6–8), Royal Coachman (#6–10), Ballou Special (#4–8), Hare's Ear Nymph (#8–14), Pheasant Tail Nymph (#8–14), Bead Head Nymph (#8–14), Olive Sparkle Caddis Pupa (#8–14), Brown Sparkle Caddis Pupa (#8–14), Cream Sparkle Caddis Pupa (#8–14), Olive Caddis Larva (#8–14), Brown Caddis Larva (#8–14), Elk Hair

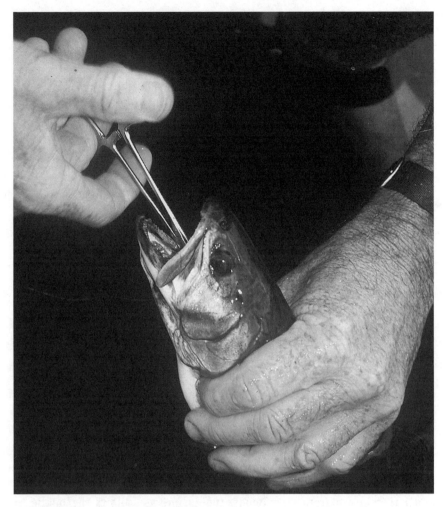

Say "aaaahhhh. . . ." It's been said that a nice trout is too valuable to be caught only once. Please practice catch-and-release.

Caddis (#10–14), Adams (#10–14), Light Cahill (#12–16), Green Drake (#4–6), March Brown (#8–12), Royal Wulff (#12).

The Lamoille is a river with many faces. Cutting across the top quarter of the state, it starts in eastern Greensboro as a classic trout stream, gaining strength and becoming populated with largemouth and smallmouth bass before emptying into Lake Champlain.

The Lamoille originates at Horse Pond in Greensboro, and begins its journey by flowing south beside VT 16. It flows into Wheelock, is joined by Page and Morrison Brooks, and then reenters Greensboro. This is good brook trout water and easy to wade. Look for pullouts along the highway, and don't be afraid to take a hike through the woods; your efforts will be rewarded with good fishing in a secluded setting. The upper stretch of the Lamoille is narrow and best fished with a short, light rod and dry flies: Wulffs, small parachute mayflies, Humpies, and Elk Hair Caddises. As the Lamoille journeys toward East Hardwick, numerous cool tributaries—Mud Pond Brook, Greensboro Brook, Stevens Brook, and others—join the flow. Any of these small feeder streams can provide good fishing for brook trout and is worth exploring. All should be fished using your lightest tackle and bushy dry flies.

Below East Hardwick the Lamoille takes a sharp turn to the west. Access to the river is now provided by VT 15, also called the Grand Army of the Republic Highway. The best access is at the bridges where the road crosses the river and at several unmarked pullouts. While you can wade the upper river and its tributaries "wet," you will be more comfortable exploring the middle and lower sections of the Lamoille wearing waders. You can also step up the size of your tackle—perhaps an 8½-foot-long rod and a 5-weight line—and use weighted nymphs, Woolly Buggers, and small streamers. The river now gets fairly wide, but there are several deep sections containing good trout. In this stretch the brook trout give way to rainbows, and there are also some brown trout averaging 14 inches.

A dam near the town of Wolcott gives anglers the opportunity to fish a tailwater; there is another dam in Morrisville. This second dam forms Lake Lamoille, and its discharge forms what is considered the lower section of the Lamoille River. Cadys Falls, below Lake Lamoille, is a particularly good place to fish.

Ten Bends, a private fishing reserve between Hyde Park and Johnson, offers an excellent opportunity to catch rainbow trout averaging 12 inches and larger brown trout. Ten Bends, though private, allows the public to enjoy its waters provided they register upon arriving, practice catch-and-release, and report their catch when leaving. This is good dry-fly water, especially in the early morning and early evening. Hendricksons, March Browns, and Blue Winged Olives are among the favorite flies, as well as attractor patterns. The Lamoille also hosts a variety of caddisflies, and the Elk Hair Caddis as well as caddis pupae and larvae all catch fish.

Below Johnson the Lamoille continues to widen; its temperature rises during the summer, making life rather uncomfortable for the trout. If you're interested in fishing the Lamoille, you'll probably have better luck in the upper half of the river, above Johnson.

The Lamoille, like many of Vermont's major rivers, is blessed with a system of cold-water tributaries that also provide excellent trout fishing. I've already mentioned a couple of tributaries worthy of exploration, but there are several others. The Browns River, south of Fairfax Falls, is a good spot to catch rainbow and brook trout. Access is a little tough, but you'll be able to get to the water next to the bridges where VT 128 crosses the river.

The Brewster River is another important tributary of the Lamoille. It flows out of Jeffersonville along VT 108. There are several pullouts along the road, providing good opportunities to catch brook trout. The Brewster starts in Mount Mansfield State Forest. This is a narrow stream requiring small, lightweight tackle.

The North Branch of the Lamoille is yet another place to wet a line. It begins in the eastern corner of Belvidere near the Avery Gore Wildlife Management Area, and ends where it flows into the main stem of the Lamoille in Cambridge. VT 109 follows the North Branch for much of its length, providing access at pullouts and bridges. The lower section of the North Branch, below the dam in Waterville, holds brown trout; above the Waterville impoundment you will encounter brown trout, and then brook trout in the headwaters of the stream.

The Gihon River is another small stream with excellent potential for catching brook trout. It starts at Lake Eden in Eden Mills and flows southeast until it meets the Lamoille in Johnson. VT 100 follows the Gihon throughout much of its course.

The Green River is the last tributary of the Lamoille I will mention. This short stream flows only about 3 miles from its origins below Green Lake to its intersection with the Lamoille. In this short distance, however, you can catch brook, rainbow, and brown trout. The only drawback is access: You're limited to a footpath heading upstream from the mouth of the river. Look for this path where VT 15 crosses the Green. If you don't mind a bit of walking, you'll be well rewarded.

THE MISSISQUOI RIVER

Maps *The Vermont Atlas and Gazetteer,* pages 52 and 53.

Description The Missisquoi River can be conveniently discussed in several sections.

First, the lower section—from Lake Champlain to Enosburg Falls—contains more bass and other warm-water species than trout. However, this stretch does occasionally yield a large brown trout. If you're in northern Vermont and want to fish the Missisquoi for trout, head to upper sections of the river.

The river begins by draining the mountains of Lowell, Vermont. This section of the Missisquoi is in the Northeast Kingdom, known for its forested mountains. The headwaters of the Missisquoi—Burgess Branch, Notch Brook, LeClair Brook, and Snider Brook—are small freestone mountain

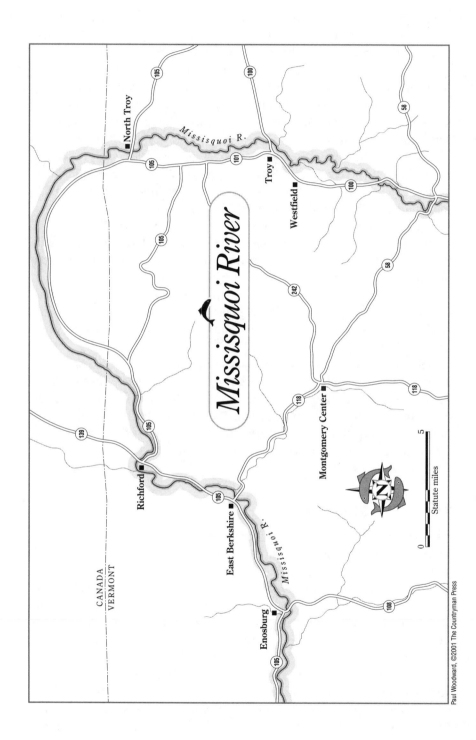

Missisquoi River

CANADA
VERMONT

North Troy

Missisquoi R.

Troy

Westfield

Richford

East Berkshire

Missisquoi R.

Enosburg

Montgomery Center

Statute miles

0   5

Paul Woodward, ©2001 The Countryman Press

streams. From Lowell to Westfield, the Missisquoi flows through a mixture of woodlands, farms, and fields. It enters Quebec at North Troy.

The river then reenters Vermont from Quebec in Richford. This section continues through a mixture of wooded hills and farmland. Here the best trout fishing is from the Canadian border to Enosburg Falls. From Enosburg Falls to Lake Champlain, you'll probably catch more bass than trout.

Best Assets The Missisquoi River flows through the heart of the Northeast Kingdom. The countryside is quite beautiful. Be sure to fish the headwater streams for native brook trout.

Biggest Drawback The Missisquoi is far north; cold spring temperatures can delay spring runoff and the hatches.

Regulations The legal fishing season runs from the second Saturday in April through the last Sunday in October. There are different sets of regulations governing the various sections of the Missisquoi River. These are the laws pertaining to the most popular trout-fishing areas.

From Rixford Dam to the headwaters, there are no length restrictions on the fish you may keep. Daily creel limit: The total number of brook, brown, and rainbow trout is 12 fish; the total number of brown and rainbow trout is 6 fish.

From Highgate Falls Dam to Swanton Dam, the daily creel limit is a total of six trout, not weighing more than a total of 5 pounds.

From 850 feet below Swanton Dam to Swanton Dam, the daily creel limit is three trout each measuring not less than 12 inches in length. This section of the river is closed to all fishing from March 16 to June 1.

Favorite Flies Hornberg (#6–10), Gray Ghost (#4–8), Black Ghost (#4–8), Mickey Finn (#6–8), Olive Woolly Bugger (#6–8), Black Woolly Bugger (#6–8), Brown Woolly Bugger (#6–8), Muddler Minnow (#4–8), Woolly Worm (#6–8), Royal Coachman (#6–10), Ballou Special (#4–8), Hare's Ear Nymph (#8–14), Pheasant Tail Nymph (#8–14), Bead Head Nymph (#8–14), Olive Sparkle Caddis Pupa (#8–14), Brown Sparkle Caddis Pupa (#8–14), Cream Sparkle Caddis Pupa (#8–14), Olive Caddis Larva (#8–14), Brown Caddis Larva (#8–14), Elk Hair Caddis (#10–14), Adams (#10–14), Light Cahill (#12–16), Green Drake (#4–6), March Brown (#8–12).

Now I'm getting well into northern Vermont. It's hard to pick the very best time to visit this part of the state, because the area remains so beautiful throughout the season. Spring, however, can bring high runoff, depending on the size of the snowpack. But this is Vermont, and it always snows in the winter.

One of the best times to visit the Missisquoi is fall. This is when the brown trout begin their spawning run, and their colors are in their full glory; this is also when the surrounding maples and other trees reach their splendor.

The Missisquoi is formed where a number of small feeder streamers come together in Lowell. These tributaries—LeClair Brook, Notch Brook, Burgess Branch, East Branch, and Ace Brook—offer good brook trout fishing and should be part of any fishing trip to the Missisquoi. VT 100 follows the Missisquoi from its headwaters in Lowell to the town of Troy. Access to the Missisquoi is gained at various unmarked pullouts and wherever VT 100 crosses the river. The Missisquoi flows north into Quebec before turning west and crossing back into Vermont to flow to Lake Champlain.

The upper Missisquoi fishes best in late spring and early summer, before the waters recede entirely. This is a small but respectable stretch of river, and hosts a good population of brook trout. These average 8 to 10 inches, but don't be surprised if you hook a 12-inch-long brook trout; that's a very nice-sized mountain brookie. Autumn is also a good time to fish the upper Missisquoi, because the brown and brook trout are spawning.

The Missisquoi twists through the countryside in northern Lowell. This section contains some very good pools that hold some of the river's best brook trout. A wide variety of patterns works in this area, so whether you are a devotee of dry flies, nymphs, or streamers, you stand an excellent chance of catching some fish. VT 100 departs from the river in southern Westfield, making access a little tough. The upper Missisquoi is the fastest part of the river and demands some nimble wading.

The next best place to reach the Missisquoi is along River Road east of Westfield. Look for access to the water wherever River Road crosses it. This is also in the vicinity of the spot where Mill Brook, Taft Brook, and Lilly Brook enter, giving the river a cool drink and keeping conditions favorable for trout. A section of River Road turns into Loop Road. Look near Loop Road for a nice, wadable stretch.

The section around Westfield offers the largest trout in the Missisquoi. The river in this area is slower and contains some very deep pools. Weighted flies—Woolly Buggers, nymphs, and streamers—are used to search these deep holes for trophy brown trout.

VT 100 leaves the river at Troy. As you can see, VT 100 follows some of the best trout fishing in Vermont. The possibilities start in the southern end of the state, and the road travels through the heart of the Green Mountains. It would be worth a week to travel and fish along the entire length of VT 100 (of course, it can be driven in one day). This trip will lead you to some of the best fly-fishing Vermont has to offer.

In Troy, VT 100 heads east, and VT 101 goes north. Almost a mile east of the intersection with VT 101 you'll find River Road heading north. This part of River Road leads to some additional fine fishing on the Missisquoi.

A dam, located on the left, offers good angling for brown trout in the deep pools above and below this structure. This is also a popular swimming hole during summer, so plan on visiting in the early morning and early evening. There is ample parking near the dam.

The dam near Troy is also the beginning of a very good canoe trip. This short trip—a little over 5 miles—ends where the river flows under the covered bridge on Bayou Road, but it will get you into some remote, seldom-fished areas. There are many deep pools here that hold brown trout.

If you're not a canoeist, you can still reach many of these fine pools by traveling River Road. Several pullouts provide parking, and the wading in this section is rather easy. The locals like to fish here in the early evening, when they stand the best chance of catching large brown trout.

Below the covered bridge on Bayou Road you'll find Big Falls, a 50-foot-high waterfall pouring into a large gorge. If you wade downstream from the bridge, you'll fish a stretch of the river that sees few anglers. However, be warned that once you head downstream, you'll have to go almost a mile before you find a good place to climb the streambank to return to your car. The pool below Big Falls contains the largest brown trout in the river. It's also a popular swimming and picnic site. This area can get rather crowded during summer, but it's an excellent place to try for a trophy brown trout in fall.

THE CLYDE RIVER

Maps *The Vermont Atlas and Gazetteer,* pages 54 and 55.

Description The Clyde River begins at Island Pond in Brighton, Vermont. To be specific, the name of the Pherrins River changes to the Clyde River. The Clyde flows through some of the flattest topography in Vermont. During its first several miles, from Island Pond to Charleston, the river drops less than 4 feet per mile.

On its 34-mile course to Lake Memphremagog, the Clyde flows through a series of lakes and ponds: Pensioner Pond, Lubber Lake, Lake Salem, and Clyde Pond. The river slows as it enters each of these bodies of water, and then speeds up at the outflows. The Clyde is fed by a number of cold-water tributaries and lakes, which keep the river cool throughout much of the summer.

Best Assets Besides finding good fishing in the main stem of the river, all of the Clyde's tributaries offer excellent brook trout fishing. Be sure to explore the tributaries leading to Echo Lake and Seymour Lake, as well as Stumpf Brook. All of these tributaries are in Charleston.

The Clyde is stocked with brown, brook, and rainbow trout, as well as landlocked salmon. There is also a growing run of landlocked salmon in the river's lower stretch. The best time to fish for salmon is fall.

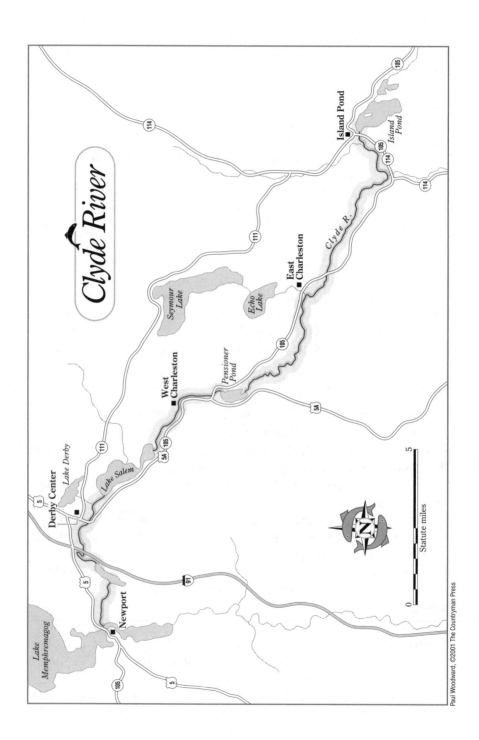

Clyde River

Paul Woodward, ©2001 The Countryman Press

Biggest Drawbacks Some of the tributaries, especially Mad Brook, have seen a considerable amount of siltation in recent years due to increased logging. Also, be aware that certain areas of the river are posted against fishing during key spawning times. Don't worry, however, because there is ample opportunity to fish other sections of the river and its tributaries.

Regulations The legal fishing season runs from the second Saturday in April through the last Sunday in October. There are no length restrictions on the fish you may keep. Daily creel limit: The total number of brook trout, brown trout, and rainbow trout is 12 fish; the total number of brown and rainbow trout is 6 fish.

Favorite Flies Hornberg (#6–10), Gray Ghost (#4–8), Black Ghost (#4–8), Mickey Finn (#6–8), Olive Woolly Bugger (#6–8), Black Woolly Bugger (#6–8), Brown Woolly Bugger (#6–8), Muddler Minnow (#4–8), Woolly Worm (#6–8), Royal Coachman (#6–10), Ballou Special (#4–8), Hare's Ear Nymph (#8–14), Pheasant Tail Nymph (#8–14), Bead Head Nymph (#8–14), Olive Sparkle Caddis Pupa (#8–14), Brown Sparkle Caddis Pupa (#8–14), Cream Sparkle Caddis Pupa (#8–14), Olive Caddis Larva (#8–14), Brown Caddis Larva (#8–14), Elk Hair Caddis (#10–14), Adams (#10–14), Light Cahill (#12–16), Green Drake (#4–6), March Brown (#8–12).

Lake Memphremagog is one of the most legendary lakes in New England. Straddling the border between Vermont and the Canadian province of Quebec, Lake Memphremagog is home to a wide variety of game fish. Anglers travel from throughout the country to fish for the landlocked salmon here.

The Clyde River runs into the southeastern corner of Lake Memphremagog. The lower section of the Clyde is popular among local anglers and can get a bit crowded. The best times to fish the lower Clyde are in spring when the landlocked salmon are feeding on smelt, and in fall when the fish enter the river on their spawning run. In spring, streamers—the Nine-Three, Gray Ghost, Mickey Finn, and Ballou Special—are good choices. In fall, when the salmon seem to be thinking more about spawning than feeding, my choice is a heavily weighted nymph fished along the bottom. In 1994 a portion of Citizen Utilities Number 11 Dam collapsed; the entire dam was eventually removed. The fish now have more access to swim upstream, and local anglers are working to restore the lower Clyde River to its former glory days.

VT 105 follows the upper Clyde, but access is difficult and it would take much effort to find the best access points. Still, if you take the time or opt for a canoe trip down the upper Clyde, you will catch brook and brown trout.

THE CONNECTICUT RIVER

Map *The Vermont Atlas and Gazetteer,* page 37.

Description The Connecticut River, which forms the border between the states of Vermont and New Hampshire, flows through a mixture of forests and farmland. The Connecticut has several dams and impoundments. Much of the river is far too deep and wide to wade. Indeed, much of the Connecticut isn't considered good trout habitat. For purposes of serious trout fishing, head to the upper Connecticut from Beecher Falls to about Maidstone. This stretch of the river is very wadable and relatively easy to fish.

Access VT 102 parallels the best water from the Beecher Falls to Bloomfield. There are many pulloffs offering access to the river.

Best Asset The upper Connecticut sees few out-of-state anglers; they're either visiting the Batten Kill in southern Vermont or fishing the upper Connecticut around Pittsburg, New Hampshire (the Pittsburg area has long been a popular destination among sportsmen). This is good for the locals, but traveling fishermen are missing a great opportunity at some excellent trout. If you're looking for good trout fishing but want to avoid the crowds, head to the upper Connecticut on the Vermont border.

Biggest Drawbacks The Connecticut River quickly broadens, deepens, and slows, becoming a good warm-water fishery with limited trout fishing. The Connecticut, and several of its major tributaries, is blocked by dams. For the best fishing, stick to its upper section.

Regulations The Connecticut River is governed by New Hampshire regulations. It's open to fishing from January 1 to October 15. The daily bag limit is five trout.

Favorite Flies Hornberg (#6–10), Gray Ghost (#4–8), Black Ghost (#4–8), Mickey Finn (#6–8), Olive Woolly Bugger (#6–8), Black Woolly Bugger (#6–8), Brown Woolly Bugger (#6–8), Muddler Minnow (#4–8), Woolly Worm (#6–8), Royal Coachman (#6–10), Ballou Special (#4–8), Hare's Ear Nymph (#8–14), Pheasant Tail Nymph (#8–14), Bead Head Nymph (#8–14), Olive Sparkle Caddis Pupa (#8–14), Brown Sparkle Caddis Pupa (#8–14), Cream Sparkle Caddis Pupa (#8–14), Olive Caddis Larva (#8–14), Brown Caddis Larva (#8–14), Elk Hair Caddis (#10–14), Hendrickson (#14), Gray Fox (#14), Adams (#10–14), Light Cahill (#12–16), Green Drake (#4–6), March Brown (#8–12) Royal Wulff, (#10–12).

Although I've occasionally discussed fly-fishing for smallmouth bass, largemouth bass, and pike, this book is mostly about trout fishing. The Connecticut River is a long, complicated river, and if you fish it from its headwaters in New Hampshire all the way down the eastern boundary of

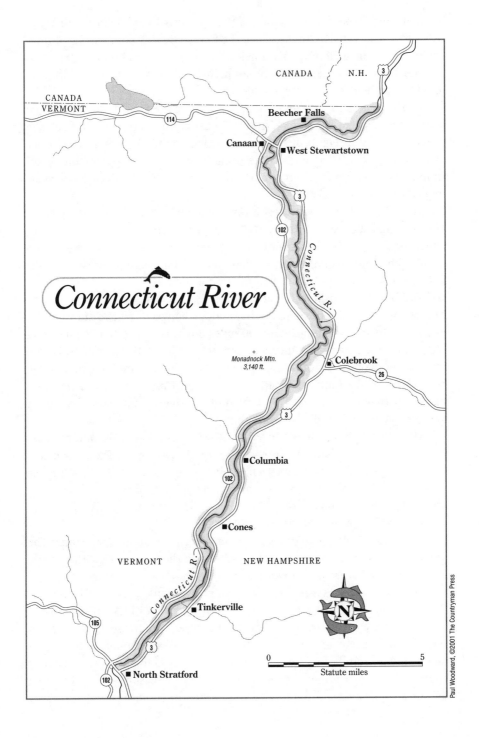

CANADA
N.H.

CANADA
VERMONT

114

Beecher Falls

Canaan ■

■West Stewartstown

3

102

Connecticut R.

Connecticut River

+
Monadnock Mtn.
3,140 ft.

■Colebrook

26

3

■Columbia

102

■Cones

VERMONT

NEW HAMPSHIRE

Connecticut R.

■Tinkerville

105

3

102

■North Stratford

N

0   5

Statute miles

Vermont, you'll be able to catch several species of cold- and warm-water fish. For most of its length, however, the Connecticut is not considered trout habitat. Still, the area of the river below White River Junction is superb bass and northern pike water; if you're not prejudiced against these fish, they do provide excellent sport for fly-rodders.

In all fairness to the Connecticut River, there are areas in its middle and lower sections that do support trout. Trout require cool, well-oxygenated water, and they thrive in the limited areas where they find these conditions in the Connecticut. These spots are usually below places where cold-water tributaries enter, and in the outflow of dams below deep man-made impoundments.

Technically, the state of New Hampshire controls the Connecticut River. This question was settled by the U.S. Supreme Court in 1933. A resident of either state may fish the Connecticut River using his or her own state's license; however, visitors must purchase a New Hampshire nonresident fishing license in order to legally fish the Connecticut.

The best trout fishing in the Connecticut River between Vermont and New Hampshire is from where the river enters between the two states above Beecher Falls to Maidstone, about 30 miles downriver. The first 2-mile-long section, from where the Connecticut enters Vermont to Beecher Falls, is cold water from the outflow of Murphy Dam in New Hampshire (I'll examine the headwaters of the Connecticut River when I turn my attention to the trout fishing of New Hampshire). This stretch of the river contains rainbow trout and the occasional landlocked salmon.

There is a dam on the Connecticut River in Beecher Falls, and the outflow of this dam is home to some very large brown trout. The river below Beecher Falls is a mixture of deep pools and long, slow glides. With the countryside dominated by forests and farms, this is also a very beautiful area to fish. VT 102 parallels the Connecticut from Beecher Falls past Maidstone, providing access at numerous pullouts.

The trout fishing remains good from Beecher Falls to Maidstone. The predominant species is rainbow trout, although the state of New Hampshire also stocks the river with brown and brook trout.

The Connecticut is a fertile river supporting a wide variety of insect life. Hendricksons, blue quills, and early blue-winged olives kick off the season, as well as the early black stoneflies. As the season progresses, gray fox and sulphur duns take over. The Connecticut also hosts a trico hatch; caddisflies and a limited number of stoneflies emerge throughout the season. And of course midsummer brings the onset of grasshopper season; a Dave's Hopper will bring splashy rise from any fish interested in eating terrestrials.

Other Stocked Trout Waters Worth Exploring

Adam White Brook (Craftsbury), Adam's Pond (Enosburg), Annis Brook (Sutton), Bailey Brook (Ferdinand), Baker Pond (Barton), Barton River (Barton), Bean Pond (Sutton), Beaver Meadow Brook (Enosburg), Beck Pond (Newark), Belding Pond (Johnson), Belvidere Bog (Belvidere), Bert Martin Brook (Craftsbury), Blodgett Brook (Lemington), Bog Pond (Morgan), Bolten Brook (Lemington), Branch Brook (Bakersfield), Branch River (Craftsbury), Brewster River (Jeffersonville), Brown Pond (Westmore), Brunswick Springs (Brunswick), Burgess Pond (Lowell), Calender Brook (Sutton), Caspian Lake (Greensboro), Catsbow Brook (Lunenburg), Center Pond (Newark), Church Brook (Bloomfield), Clay Brook (Canaan), Clayhill Brook (Brighton), Clough Brook (Morgan), Coaticook River (Norton), Cobb Brook (Coventry), Cole Hill Brook (Canaan), Cooks Brook (Irasburg), Courser Brook (East Charleston), Crystal Lake (Barton), Dennis Pond (Brunswick), Dennis Pond Stream (Brunswick), Dobis Brook (Canaan), Dolloff Pond (Sutton), Duck Pond (Sutton), Fish Brook (Morgan), Forest Lake (Averill), Fox Stream (Craftsbury), Gihon River (Eden), Granby Stream (Granby), Great Brook (Bloomfield), Greens Brook (Derby), Half Moon Pond (Belvidere), Hartwell Pond (Albany), Hayward Brook (Derby), Hazen Notch Brook (Lowell), Heart Pond (Craftsbury), Holland Pond (Holland), Hudson Brook (Lemington), Hurricane Brook (Warren Gore), Island Pond (Brighton), Jack Brook (East Haven), Jacobs Chopping Brook (Canaan), Jay Branch (Jay), John Judd Brook (Holland), Jones Brook (Craftsbury), Kelsey Brook (Canaan), Keyer Brook (Canaan), Kidder Pond (Coventry), King Brook (East Haven), Kirby Brook (Ferdinand), Lamphear Brook (Lowell), LeClair Pond (Lowell), Leach Creek (Canaan), Lewis Pond (Lewis), Lightning Brook (Brighton), Little Leach Stream (Canaan), Long Pond (Westmore), Lords Creek (Albany), Lost Pond (Belvidere), Madison Brook (Ferdinand), May Pond (Barton), McAllister Pond (Lowell), Mill Brook (Lemington), Mud Pond (Hyde Brook), Murphy Brook (Ferdinand), Newark Pond (Newark), Norton Pond (Warren Gore), Notch Pond (Ferdinand), Nulhegan Pond (Brighton), Nulhegan River (Bloomfield), East Branch of the Nulhegan River (Lewis), Orcut Brook (Derby), Oswegotchie Brook (Brighton), Paul Stream (Ferdinand), Payne Brook (Brighton), Pherrins River (Morgan), Pine Brook (Averys Gore), South Wheelock Brook (Wheelock), Salem Lake (Morgan), Sargent Pond (Coventry), Seymour Lake (Morgan), Shadow Lake (Glover), South American Pond (Ferdinand), Stevens Brook (Ferdinand), Trout River (Berkshire), Tuffield Willey Brook (Brighton), Tyler Branch (Enosburg), Upper Lightning Brook (Brighton), Vail Pond (Sutton), West Mountain Pond (Ferdinand), Willard Stream (Lemington).

Where to Stay in Northern Vermont

Golden Maple Inn Route 15, Main Street, Wolcott Village, VT 05680
1-800-639-5234.

Vermont Sportsman Lodge 6111 Route 111, Morgan, VT 05853 802-895-4209.

Belview Campground P.O. Box 222, Barton, VT 05822 802-525-3242.

Lynburke Motel Junction of Route 5 and Route 114, Lyndonville, VT 05851
802-626-3346.

Local Guide Services

Northeast Kingdom Casting Golden Maple Inn, Wolcott Village, VT 05680
1-800-639-5234.

Northeast Kingdom Guide Service RFD 2, Box 117, Lyndonville, VT 05851
802-748-8100.

II | NEW HAMPSHIRE

New Hampshire is a sleeper in the fly-fishing world. It's unfortunate, but I don't hear a lot of folks talking about planning a fishing trip to New Hampshire. Don't get me wrong: There are anglers who religiously fish this state. The upper Connecticut River Valley—above the town of Pittsburg, for instance—has a thriving industry of fine fishing lodges and guide services. But there are also other fine areas to visit and fish.

One of my favorite fishing destinations in New Hampshire, the White Mountain National Forest, offers some of the finest trout fishing in New England. Yet despite the great opportunities to catch trout, the streams and ponds of the White Mountains are visited by mostly local anglers. If you're looking for a nice fishing trip, great scenery, and the opportunity to see moose and other wildlife, the White Mountain National Park, and most of New Hampshire, should be on your list of places to visit.

Just as I did with Vermont, I'll start with southern New Hampshire and work my way north.

The Sugar River, a narrow freestone stream, offers good fishing for brook trout. Use light-weight tackle and dry flies.

4 | Southern New Hampshire

Southern New Hampshire is developing a reputation for its fine saltwater fishing. Today a growing number of fly-fishers are casting for bluefish and sea-run striped bass; indeed, the entire Northeast coast is in the middle of a saltwater fly-fishing boom. Southern New Hampshire also offers several good opportunities to fly-fish for trout.

THE ASHUELOT RIVER

Maps *The New Hampshire Atlas and Gazetteer,* pages 19 and 25.

Description The Ashuelot River starts at Ashuelot Pond in southwestern Washington, New Hampshire. The river flows through a mixture of wooded areas, farmland, and a number of towns, the largest being Keene. It flows into the Connecticut River at Hinsdale. The upper Ashuelot is a medium-sized stream and wadable.

Access Washington Road parallels the east side of the upper Ashuelot from Phelps Square to Ashuelot Pond. Several pulloffs offer access.

NH 10 parallels the Ashuelot from Phelps Square to Gilsum. Look for marked and unmarked pulloffs offering access to the river.

From Gilsum to Surry, NH 12A parallels the river. The section of the Ashuelot flowing through Surry is boggy and difficult to access, but the section that flows through western Gilsum and northern Surry is close to the road; look for pulloffs along the river.

Best Assets The Ashuelot receives regular stockings of rainbow, brook, and brown trout, giving you an excellent opportunity to catch fish. This is also a lightly fished river compared with New Hampshire's more popular trout streams.

Biggest Drawbacks: The Ashuelot has much to recommend it, but this isn't a

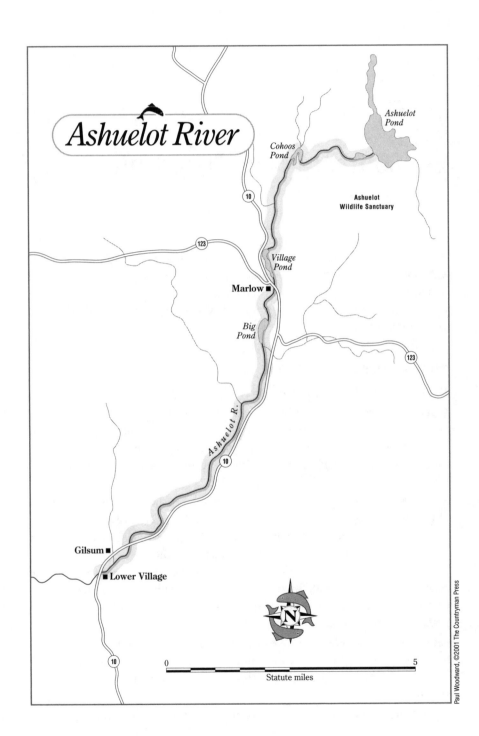

Ashuelot River

Cohoos Pond

Ashuelot Pond

Ashuelot Wildlife Sanctuary

10

123

Village Pond

Marlow ■

Big Pond

123

Ashuelot R.

10

Gilsum ■

■ Lower Village

10

N

0   5
Statute miles

"wild" river. State roads parallel much of the river, making privacy difficult to find. Still, if you're in the area, the Ashuelot is a great choice for an early evening fishing trip.

Regulations The fishing season runs from January 1 to October 15. The daily creel limit is a total of five trout, not to exceed 5 pounds. There is no length limit.

Favorite Flies Hornberg (#6–10), Gray Ghost (#4–8), Black Ghost (#4–8), Mickey Finn (#6–8), Olive Woolly Bugger (#6–8), Black Woolly Bugger (#6–8), Brown Woolly Bugger (#6–8), Muddler Minnow (#4–8), Woolly Worm (#6–8), Royal Coachman (#6–10), Ballou Special (#4–8), Hare's Ear Nymph (#8–14), Pheasant Tail Nymph (#8–14), Bead Head Nymph (#8–14), Olive Sparkle Caddis Pupa (#8–14), Brown Sparkle Caddis Pupa (#8–14), Cream Sparkle Caddis Pupa (#8–14), Olive Caddis Larva (#8–14), Brown Caddis Larva (#8–14), Elk Hair Caddis (#10–14), Adams (#10–14), Light Cahill (#12–16), Green Drake (#4–6), March Brown (#8–12).

The Ashuelot River is one of southern New Hampshire's better opportunities to fly-fish for trout. It begins in Ashuelot Pond above Marlow.

The best fishing on the Ashuelot is above the town of Gilsum. This entire stretch of water is only about 10 miles long, but it offers a lot of good fly-fishing opportunities. NH 10 parallels the river from Gilsum to Marlow, and there is access at numerous picnic sites along the road. Above Marlow, Washington Road follows the river all the way to Ashuelot Pond.

The river is heavily stocked with brook, brown, and rainbow trout, and a wide variety of flies will work. Try small streamers—Woolly Buggers, Mickey Finns, and Edson Tigers—and weighted nymphs.

Unfortunately, the river has been polluted below Keene, and so the best fishing is limited to that section of the Ashuelot above Gilsum.

The South Branch of the Ashuelot is a small stream that also offers good opportunities to catch rainbow, brown, and brook trout. It begins near Troy where several feeder streams come together. There is a fly-fishing-only section between East Swanzey and Troy. This is smaller water requiring light-weight tackle.

THE LAMPREY RIVER

Maps *The New Hampshire Atlas and Gazetteer,* pages 28 and 29.

Description The Lamprey River begins in northern Deerfield, flows south to Raymond, and then heads east to Great Bay. It flows through a combination of farmland and developed areas. The upper sections of the Lamprey, between Freeses Pond in Deerfield and Raymond, are easy to wade, while the

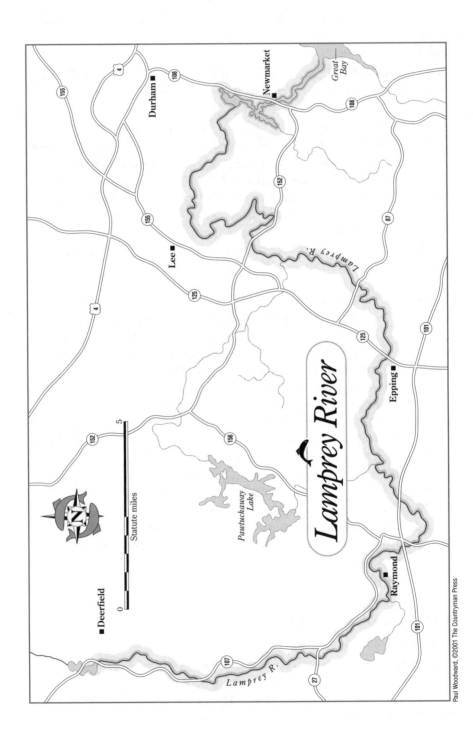

Lamprey River

Paul Woodward, ©2001 The Countryman Press

lower section between Newmarket and Lee can be waded or floated by canoe.

Access Several roads offer access to the Lamprey River. From Freeses Pond to Raymond, NH 107 and NH 27 parallel and cross the river. These roads contain pulloffs offering access to the water. This section is narrower and easier to wade. A popular and heavily fished section flows through Raymond.

Best Assets The Lamprey receives generous stockings of rainbow, brook, and brown trout. The river is also easy to reach for anglers living in southern New Hampshire and the Boston area.

Biggest Drawback Unfortunately, the Lamprey flows through a very populated area, and it sees a lot of fishing pressure. If you want to get away from the crowds, you might not enjoy the Lamprey. On the other hand, if you want to get away for an hour of fishing in the evening during the week, the well-stocked Lamprey might be a good alternative.

Regulations The fishing season is from January 1 to October 15. The daily creel limit is a total of five trout not to exceed 5 pounds. There is no length limit.

Favorite Flies Hornberg (#6–10), Gray Ghost (#4–8), Black Ghost (#4–8), Mickey Finn (#6–8), Olive Woolly Bugger (#6–8), Black Woolly Bugger (#6–8), Brown Woolly Bugger (#6–8), Muddler Minnow (#4–8), Woolly Worm (#6–8), Royal Coachman (#6–10), Ballou Special (#4–8), Hare's Ear Nymph (#8–14), Pheasant Tail Nymph (#8–14), Bead Head Nymph (#8–14), Olive Sparkle Caddis Pupa (#8–14), Brown Sparkle Caddis Pupa (#8–14), Cream Sparkle Caddis Pupa (#8–14), Olive Caddis Larva (#8–14), Brown Caddis Larva (#8–14), Elk Hair Caddis (#10–14), Adams (#10–14), Light Cahill (#12–16), Green Drake (#4–6), March Brown (#8–12).

The Lamprey River benefits from a regular stocking program of rainbow, brook, and brown trout. Because of this intense stocking, the river also attracts a lot of anglers. Still, it's a great place to wet a line and enjoy an evening of fishing.

The best trout fishing is in the upper reaches. This section is in Deerfield and the northeastern corner of Raymond. Here you can expect to catch brook and rainbow trout. The lower section of the Lamprey, in Epping and Lee, offers excellent fishing for largemouth bass and yellow perch.

NH 107 parallels much of the upper stretch of the Lamprey. Look for unmarked pullouts and near all bridges to gain access to the water. The Lamprey isn't a large piece of water, and it's rather easy to wade. It sees a lot of anglers; fly-fishers work side by side with bait-fishermen and hardware chuckers. Despite the pressure, there is plenty of fish for everyone.

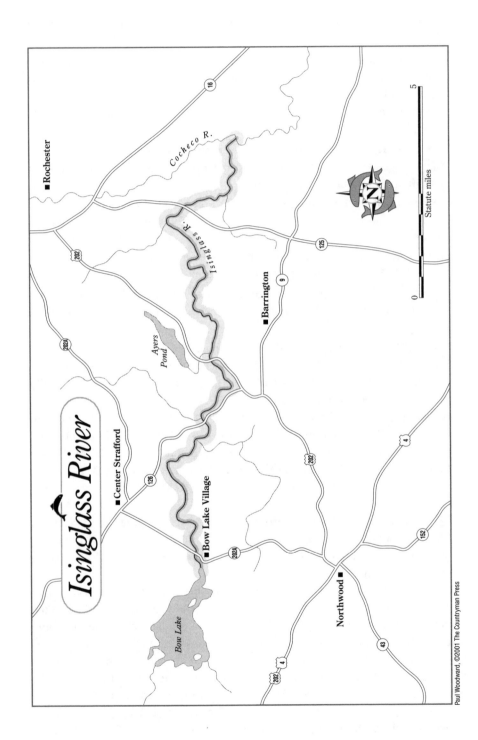

Isinglass River

Paul Woodward, ©2001 The Countryman Press

Since the majority of the fish in the Lamprey are stocked, they don't seem to be in rhythm with the hatches of insects occurring in the river, and a wide variety of flies work. Black and Olive Woolly Buggers are always favorites, as are weighted nymphs.

The Lamprey has also received stockings of Atlantic salmon, but the reintroduction of this great game fish has met with mixed results.

THE ISINGLASS RIVER

Map *The New Hampshire Atlas and Gazetteer,* page 29.

Description The Isinglass is a short, 14-mile-long river flowing out of Bow Lake in Strafford to its confluence with the Cocheco River in the southern corner of Rochester. It's a medium-sized stream and easy to wade. It flows through a mixture of woodlands and development.

Access There is parking and access to the Isinglass near the intersection of NH 126 and US 202 in Barrington. There is additional parking along the Green Hill Road in western Barrington.

Best Assets The Isinglass River is heavily stocked with brown, brook, and rainbow trout. There is ample access, and the river is relatively easy to wade.

Biggest Drawbacks The Isinglass gets a lot of fishing pressure. The water warms considerably in summer.

Regulations The fishing season is from January 1 to October 15. The daily bag limit is a total of five trout, not to exceed 5 pounds. There is no length limit.

Favorite Flies Hornberg (#6–10), Gray Ghost (#4–8), Black Ghost (#4–8), Mickey Finn (#6–8), Olive Woolly Bugger (#6–8), Black Woolly Bugger (#6–8), Brown Woolly Bugger (#6–8), Muddler Minnow (#4–8), Woolly Worm (#6–8), Royal Coachman (#6–10), Ballou Special (#4–8), Hare's Ear Nymph (#8–14), Pheasant Tail Nymph (#8–14), Bead Head Nymph (#8–14), Olive Sparkle Caddis Pupa (#8–14), Brown Sparkle Caddis Pupa (#8–14), Cream Sparkle Caddis Pupa (#8–14), Olive Caddis Larva (#8–14), Brown Caddis Larva (#8–14), Elk Hair Caddis (#10–14), Adams (#10–14), Light Cahill (#12–16), Green Drake (#4–6), March Brown (#8–12).

The Isinglass is a rather short river maintained by the state of New Hampshire as a put-and-take fishery. It's stocked with brook, rainbow, and brown trout, so you can almost always find good fishing until the water warms in midsummer.

The Isinglass River begins at Bow Lake in Strafford. It travels east for 14 miles before emptying into the Cocheco River south of Rochester. The riverbed is a mix of sand and slick rocks, so you'll want to be careful while wading.

The best access to the Isinglass is at one of the many pulloffs near the intersection of US 202 and NH 126 in Barrington, and along Tolend Road east of this intersection.

The good fishing begins during the last week of April and continues until the water warms. Because the fishing begins so early, an imitation of a small black stonefly—a common early-season insect—can sometimes take a fish from the frigid springtime waters. As the season progresses, try small Woolly Buggers and Woolly Worms. You'll be casting to hatchery-raised trout that don't require the same variety of flies needed for careful match-the-hatch fishing.

THE SUGAR RIVER

Maps *The New Hampshire Atlas and Gazetteer,* pages 33 and 34.

Description The Sugar River flows through the hilly, wooded section of southwest New Hampshire. It emerges from the western side of Lake Sunapee and enters the Connecticut River in Claremont.

Access NH 11 and NH 103 parallel much of the Sugar River. Look for pulloffs offering access to the water. There is also a fly-fishing-only section between the Kellyville and Oak Street bridges in Kellyville. The Sugar River may either be waded or floated by canoe.

Best Asset A fly-fishing-only section is always of interest to fly-anglers.

Biggest Drawback The Sugar is a rather short river, but maybe that's really not such a drawback.

Regulations The fishing season is from January 1 to October 15. The daily bag limit is a total of five trout, not to exceed 5 pounds. There is no length limit.

The stretch of the Sugar River from the Kellyville bridge to the Oak Street bridge is fly-fishing only. The daily limit for brook trout in this section is two fish.

Favorite Flies Hornberg (#6–10), Gray Ghost (#4–8), Black Ghost (#4–8), Mickey Finn (#6–8), Olive Woolly Bugger (#6–8), Black Woolly Bugger (#6–8), Brown Woolly Bugger (#6–8), Muddler Minnow (#4–8), Woolly Worm (#6–8), Royal Coachman (#6–10), Ballou Special (#4–8), Hare's Ear Nymph (#8–14), Pheasant Tail Nymph (#8–14), Bead Head Nymph (#8–14), Olive Sparkle Caddis Pupa (#8–14), Brown Sparkle Caddis Pupa (#8–14), Cream Sparkle Caddis Pupa (#8–14), Olive Caddis Larva (#8–14), Brown Caddis Larva (#8–14), Elk Hair Caddis (#10–14), Adams (#10–14), Royal Wulff (#12), Light Cahill (#12–16), March Brown (#8–12).

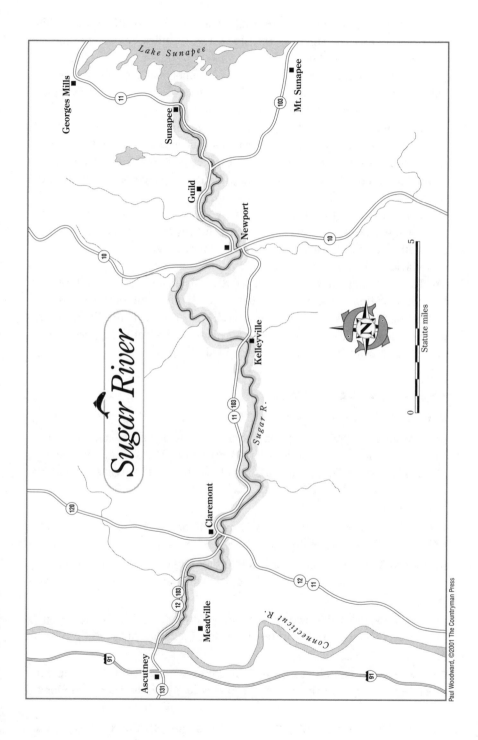

Sugar River

Paul Woodward, ©2001 The Countryman Press

The Sugar River is another nice trout stream in southwest New Hampshire. It begins at Lake Sunapee and flows for 35 miles before entering the Connecticut River in Claremont.

The best fishing in the Sugar is in its upper reaches, above Newport. This is a good area to catch native brook trout. The river receives regular stockings of brown, brook, and rainbow trout.

The upper section of the main stem of the Sugar is accessed along NH 11. In this area the river is fairly narrow and you can use lighter tackle. Access becomes more of a problem below Newport, but NH 11 continues to parallel the Sugar; look for unmarked pullouts and side roads leading to the river.

The Sugar is fed by several small freestone mountain streams. Its two major tributaries are the South Branch and Croydon Branch. Both of these small streams are stocked with brown, rainbow, and brook trout. Both are easily accessed from pullouts and picnic areas along NH 10.

The best time to visit the Sugar River is from the last half of May through the first week of July. Come with lightweight tackle to fish the upper Sugar and its tributaries; for the lower section of the river, be prepared with a slightly larger rod and a selection of Woolly Buggers, Woolly Worms, and Bead Head and other weighted nymphs.

THE SOUHEGAN RIVER

Map *The New Hampshire Atlas and Gazetteer,* page 21.

Description The Souhegan flows from the Massachusetts border in New Ipswich to the Merrimack River in Merrimack. The surrounding area is developed, but the Souhegan is a good choice for anglers living in southeast New Hampshire who are looking for an evening's fishing. The river is generously stocked with trout.

Access NH 31 from Greenville to Wilton provides access to the best stretch of the river. There are pulloffs and access to the water.

Best Assets The Souhegan River offers urban anglers an opportunity to fish without traveling too far. It's well stocked with rainbow, brown, and brook trout.

Biggest Drawback I live way out in the country and am not interested in crowds and congestion. If you feel the same, the Souhegan might not be for you.

Regulations The fishing season is from January 1 to October 15. The daily creel limit is a total of five trout, not to exceed 5 pounds. There is no length limit.

Favorite Flies Hornberg (#6–10), Gray Ghost (#4–8), Black Ghost (#4–8),

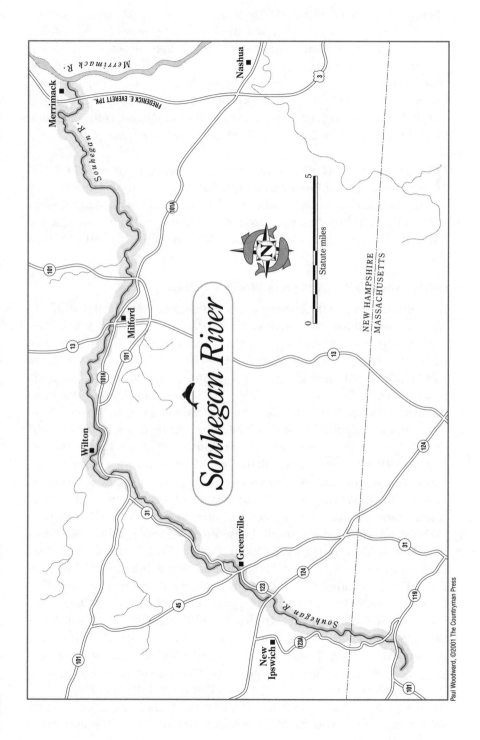

Souhegan River

Statute miles

NEW HAMPSHIRE
MASSACHUSETTS

Nashua

Merrimack

Milford

Wilton

Greenville

New
Ipswich

Mickey Finn (#6–8), Olive Woolly Bugger (#6–8), Black Woolly Bugger (#6–8), Brown Woolly Bugger (#6–8), Muddler Minnow (#4–8), Woolly Worm (#6–8), Royal Coachman (#6–10), Ballou Special (#4–8), Hare's Ear Nymph (#8–14), Pheasant Tail Nymph (#8–14), Bead Head Nymph (#8–14), Olive Sparkle Caddis Pupa (#8–14), Brown Sparkle Caddis Pupa (#8–14), Cream Sparkle Caddis Pupa (#8–14), Olive Caddis Larva (#8–14), Brown Caddis Larva (#8–14), Elk Hair Caddis (#10–14), Adams (#10–14), Light Cahill (#12–16), Green Drake (#4–6), March Brown (#8–12).

The Souhegan is one of New Hampshire's southernmost rivers. It begins in Massachusetts and flows northeast before meeting the Merrimack River.

The best fishing in the Souhegan is from the border with Massachusetts to the town of Wilton. You can access this section from NH 31, NH 123, and NH 123A. The best time to fish the Souhegan is from the last half of May to the end of June.

Other Stocked Trout Waters Worth Exploring

Amy Brook (Henniker), Archery Pond (Allenstown), Area Pond (Gilford), Ayers Brook (Gilmanton), Baboosic Brook (Merrimack), Bailey Brook (Nelson), Barbadoes Pond (Madbury), Bartlett Pond (Atkinson), Batchelders Pond (Hampton), Bear Brook (Allenstown), Beards Brook (Hillsboro), Lower Beech Pond (Tuftonboro), Beehole Brook (Loudon), Bellamy River (Dover), Berry Brook (Rye), Bicknell Brook (Enfield), Big Island Pond (Derry), Big River (Barnstead), Black Brook (Sanbornton), Blackwater River (Andover), Blanchard Brook (Walpole), Blood Brook (Meriden), Bogle Brook (Peterborough), Branch River (Milton), Brickyard Brook (Litchfield), Brush Brook (Dublin), Burnham Brook (Canterbury), Butterfield Pond (Wilmot), Caldwell Pond (Alstead), California Brook (Swanzey), Canning Factory Brook (Greenland), Cascade Brook (Wilmot), Cascade Pond (Loudon), Catamount Pond (Allenstown), Catesbane Brook (Chesterfield), Cemetery Pond (Deering), Center Pond (Nelson), Chapin Pond (Newport), Chase Brook (Litchfield), Churchill Brook (Brookfield), Clark Brook (Alexandria), Clough Pond (Loudon), Club Pond (New Durham), Cocheco River (Farmington), Coffin Brook (Alton), Cold River (Acworth), Cold Spring Pond (Stoddard), Cold Rain Pond (New Durham), Cole Pond (Enfield), Conservation Pond (Epping), Crooked Run Brook (Barnstead), Curtis Brook (Lyndeborough), Dames Brook (Farmington), Danforth Brook (Bristol), Deer Pond (New Boston), Demag Pond (Hillsboro), Derby Pond (Canaan), Dions Pond (Franklin), Dolf Pond (Hopkinton), East Kingston Pond (Kingston), Ela River (Farmington), Evas Marsh (Hancock), Exeter River (Brentwood), Ferguson Brook (Hancock), Ferrin Pond (Weare), Flints Brook (Hollis), Argue Pond (Pittsfield), Gilmore Pond (Jaffrey), Golden Brook (Windham), Gould Mill Brook (Brookline), Granite Brook (Nelson), Great

Brook (Antrim), Gridley River (Sharon), Gulk Brook (Chesterfield), Gustin Pond (Alstead), Hackett Brook (Canterbury), Hartford Brook (Deerfield), Hayes Brook (Farmington), Hedgehog Pond (Salem), Hogback Pond (Greenfield), Hopkins Pond (Andover), Horn Pond (Wakefield), Hot Hole Pond (Loudon), Hoyte Brook (Bradford), Hunkins Pond (Sanbornton), Hurd Brook (Alton), Joe English Brook (Amherst), Kidder Pond (Alstead), Knights Pond (Dublin), Knox Mountain Brook (Sanbornton), Lamberts Pond (Kensington), Lily Pond (Alstead), Lougee Pond (Barnstead), Lovejoy Brook (Enfield), Mace Brook (Campton), Magoon Brook (New Hampton), Manning Lake (Gilmanton), Martin Brook (Swanzey), Melvin River (Tuftonboro), Mill Brook (Grafton), Mt. Williams Pond (Weare), Needleshop Brook (Hill), Nineteen Mile Brook (Tuftonboro), North Branch River (Antrim), Nubanusit River (Harrisville), Number Seven Brook (Orange), Osgood Brook (Milford), Otter Brook (Peterborough), Perry Brook (Swanzey), Picataquog River (Goffstown), Poorfarm Brook (Gilford), Purgatory Brook (Milford), Rand Brook (Francestown), Roaring Brook (Winchester), Rum Brook (Canterbury), Smith Brook (Grafton), Spaulding Brook (Brookline), Spickett River (Salem), Spring Brook (Bennington), Tates Brook (Somersworth), Taylor River (Hampton), Tulley Brook (Richmond), Watson Brook (Alton).

Where to Stay in Southern New Hampshire

The Country Porch Bed & Breakfast 281 Moran Road, Hopkinton, NH 03229 603-746-6391.

Rocky Brook Motel & Cabins 850 Marlboro Road, Keene, NH 03431 603-352-4236.

The Old Mill House Box 224, VT 9, Munsonville, NH 03457 603-847-3224.

Cathedral House B&B 63 Cathedral Entrance, Rindge, NH 03461 603-899-6790.

The Inn at East Hill Farm Monadnock Street, Troy, NH 03465 603-242-6495.

Local Guide Services

Richard A. Bernard 11 King Edward Drive, Londonderry, NH 03053 603-434-2193.

Stuart May 453 Center Road, Lyndeborough, NH 03082 603-672-1315.

Kevin Cote 11 Cheryl Drive, Concord, NH 03303 603-229-1669.

James St. Laurent East Hill Farm, Troy, NH 03456 603-242-3242.

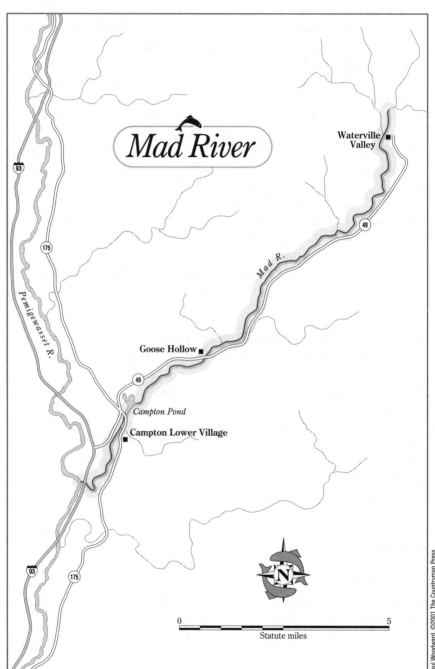

Mad River

Waterville
Valley

93

175

Pemigewasset R.

Mad R.

49

Goose Hollow

49

Campton Pond

Campton Lower Village

93

175

N

0   5
Statute miles

5 | Central New Hampshire

Central New Hampshire is one of the most beautiful areas in New England. While the coastal southern section of the state is heavily developed and populated, the central (and northern) parts of the state are more rural and forested.

There are many good places to visit and vacation in central New Hampshire. The heart of the region is in the White Mountain National Forest. You can spend a week fishing here and never visit the same piece of water twice. In this section, I'll discuss several of the best places to fish for trout in central New Hampshire.

THE MAD RIVER

Maps *The New Hampshire Atlas and Gazetteer,* pages 39 and 40.

Description The Mad River (this is a different Mad River from the one discussed in the section on Vermont) is a true mountain freestone stream. It drains the southwest corner of mountainous Waterville Valley. The surrounding scenery is green and lush. The small river is easy to wade.

Access: NH 49 parallels the Mad from Waterville Valley to Campton. Look for pullouts offering easy access to the river.

Best Assets You'll be fishing for mostly brook trout, and you'll see few other anglers. Visit during the week and you'll probably have the river to yourself.

Biggest Drawbacks Like all mountain streams, the Mad is subject to rapidly changing water levels. A few days of heavy rain can turn this lovely stream into a rushing torrent. The trees and foliage along the Mad will test your casting skills.

Regulations The fishing season is from January 1 to October 15. The daily bag limit is a total of five trout, not to exceed 5 pounds. There is no length limit.

Favorite Flies Olive Woolly Bugger (#10), Black Woolly Bugger (#10), Brown Woolly Bugger (#10), Woolly Worm (#10–12), Royal Coachman (#6–10), Hare's Ear Nymph (#8–14), Pheasant Tail Nymph (#8–14), Bead Head Nymph (#8–14), Olive Sparkle Caddis Pupa (#8–14), Brown Sparkle Caddis Pupa (#8–14), Cream Sparkle Caddis Pupa (#8–14), Olive Caddis Larva (#8–14), Brown Caddis Larva (#8–14), Elk Hair Caddis (#10–14), Adams (#10–14), Light Cahill (#12–16), March Brown (#8–12), Royal Wulff (#12), Adams Wulff (#12).

New Hampshire's Mad River is the main artery flowing out of Waterville Valley in the White Mountain National Forest. The White Mountain National Forest is a great place to fish; the scenery alone is worth the trip. But the streams and rivers of the forest, such as the Mad River, offer some terrific fishing for brook and rainbow trout.

Why, you might ask, include a small river such as the Mad in a guide to trout fishing? Why not stick to the brand-name water? Because by discussing a stream like the Mad River, I'm showing my prejudice for small streams and solitude. Yes, I fish and enjoy the better-known rivers, but my fondest memories are of fishing the small, out-of-the-way places that see few anglers. If you like to be uninterrupted while enjoying good fishing, the White Mountain National Forest's Mad River and its surrounding streams and ponds might be for you.

NH 49 follows the Mad River for much of its course into the White Mountains. There is ample access at the many pulloffs along the way. You'll also find picnicking and campsites along the river. After traveling only about 5 miles, the Mad empties into the Pemigewasset River. And don't forget to explore some of the many small tributaries feeding into the Mad.

The Mad River is a narrow stream that can be fished with light tackle and high-floating dry flies; Wulffs and Humpies are my favorites.

THE GALE RIVER

Map *The New Hampshire Atlas and Gazetteer,* page 43.

Description The Gale River is a fast mountain stream flowing from southwestern Bethlehem to enter the Ammonoosuc River in Lisbon. It's stocked with brook trout.

Access NH 18 follows the center section of the Gale. There are pulloffs and access to the water. The upper section is accessed from Gale River Road, which is located off NH 142 near the border between Franconia and Bethlehem.

Best Assets The Gale River is a typical freestone stream and easy to wade.

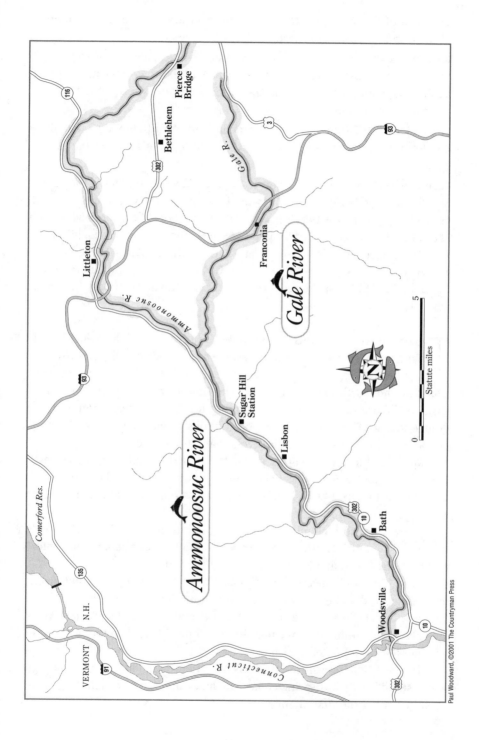

Gale River

Ammonoosuc River

Littleton

Bethlehem

Pierce
Bridge

Gale R.

Franconia

Sugar Hill
Station

Lisbon

Ammonoosuc R.

Comerford Res.

VERMONT

N.H.

Bath

Woodsville

Connecticut R.

Statute miles

0   5

116

302

3

93

93

135

97

302

10

302

10

The town of Franconia, which lies near the central section of the river, offers all the services you might need.

Biggest Drawbacks: Like all mountain streams, the Gale is subject to rapid water fluctuations; a few days of rain can send the river over its banks. To avoid disappointment, make the Gale a part of your fishing itinerary—not the main destination.

Regulations The fishing season is from January 1 to October 15. The daily bag limit is a total of five trout, not to exceed 5 pounds. There is no length limit.

Favorite Flies Olive Woolly Bugger (#10), Black Woolly Bugger (#10), Brown Woolly Bugger (#10), Woolly Worm (#10–12), Royal Coachman (#6–10), Hare's Ear Nymph (#8–14), Pheasant Tail Nymph (#8–14), Bead Head Nymph (#8–14), Olive Sparkle Caddis Pupa (#8–14), Brown Sparkle Caddis Pupa (#8–14), Cream Sparkle Caddis Pupa (#8–14), Olive Caddis Larva (#8–14), Brown Caddis Larva (#8–14), Elk Hair Caddis (#10–14), Adams (#10–14), Light Cahill (#12–16), March Brown (#8–12), Royal Wulff (#12), Adams Wulff (#12).

The Gale River is another stream found in the heart of the White Mountain National Forest. A small freestone stream, it's a delight to fish.

The headwaters of the river are deep in the White Mountains, between Flat Top and North Twin Mountains. The Gale flows northwest for a short distance before turning west and heading toward its intersection with the Ammonoosuc. The Gale River, which contains primarily brook and a scattering of rainbow trout, is slightly less than 20 miles long.

Much of the lower Gale is paralleled by NH 18 through the town of Franconia. However, I prefer fishing the upper stretches of the river, which is followed by NH 142 and Gale River Road. Look for unmarked pullouts providing access to the river.

There are also a couple of important Gale tributaries that can provide some high-quality fishing for brook trout. Plan to spend some time exploring both the North and South Branches of the Gale.

Bead Head and Pheasant Tail Nymphs work well on the Gale, but bushy, high-floating dry flies provide the best action. This is a fast-flowing river, and you'll want to cast your fly onto every small pool and slick spot. Work quickly and continually move upriver; you'll be able to cover a lot of water and possibly catch a lot of fish.

The best time to visit the Gale River is from the middle of May through the first half of July. If spring comes late and water levels remain high, plan to start fishing the first of June.

The Ammonoosuc River in central New Hampshire contains brook and rainbow trout.

THE AMMONOOSUC RIVER

Maps *The New Hampshire Atlas and Gazetteer,* pages 43, 44, and 47.

Description The headwaters of the Ammonoosuc River are in the White Mountain National Forest. At this point the river and its tributaries are free-stone mountain streams: heavily forested, easy to wade (wade "wet" without waders and rock-hop), and home to brook trout.

The area contains numerous campgrounds and picnic sites, many right along the river. There are many tributaries of the Ammonoosuc worth fishing, most of which contain brook trout.

This is a favorite river among canoeists and should be better known among trout anglers.

Access US 302 follows the Ammonoosuc from its confluence with the Connecticut River to Fabyon, which is almost the entire course of the river. Many pulloffs, picnic sites, and side roads provide access to the water.

Best Assets There is a lot of access to the Ammonoosuc. There are also ample campgrounds where you can pitch a tent or park an RV. I prefer the upper

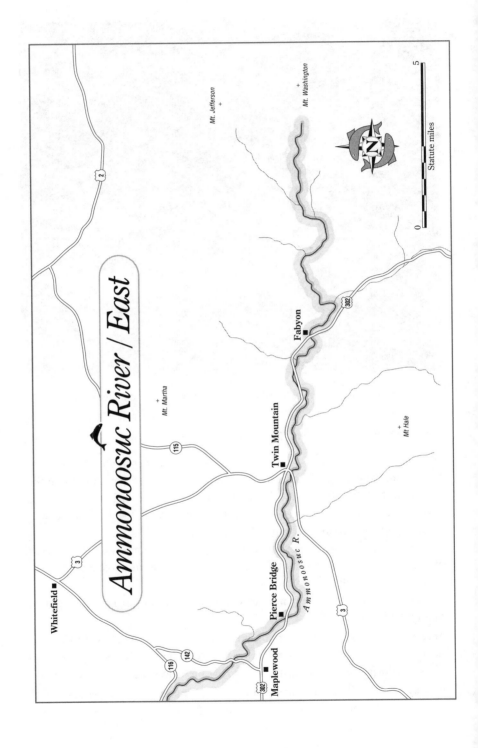

Ammonoosuc River / East

Whitefield

Mt. Martha

Mt. Jefferson

Mt. Washington

Maplewood

Pierce Bridge

Twin Mountain

Fabyon

Mt Hale

Ammonoosuc R.

Statute miles

0   5

stretches of the river, but if you like to canoe and fish, the main stem is an excellent choice. As a side trip, you can visit the Mount Washington Observatory on Mount Washington.

Biggest Drawbacks: The White Mountain National Forest is a popular destination for all nature lovers, and the main river can get busy during summer. You'll have the river pretty much to yourself in May and the first part of June, but canoe traffic increases as summer wears on. Of course, if you like to fish from a canoe, you'll be able to gain access to many more miles of river.

Regulations The fishing season is from January 1 to October 15. The daily creel limit is a total of five trout, not to exceed 5 pounds. There is no length limit.

From Apthorp Dam in Littleton to the confluence with the Connecticut River in Woodsville, it's illegal to take rainbow and brook trout between two hours after sunset and one hour before sunrise. You may catch and keep brown trout anytime of the day or night during the open season.

Favorite Flies Olive Woolly Bugger (#10), Black Woolly Bugger (#10), Brown Woolly Bugger (#10), Woolly Worm (#10–12), Royal Coachman (#6–10), Hare's Ear Nymph (#8–14), Pheasant Tail Nymph (#8–14), Bead Head Nymph (#8–14), Olive Sparkle Caddis Pupa (#8–14), Brown Sparkle Caddis Pupa (#8–14), Cream Sparkle Caddis Pupa (#8–14), Olive Caddis Larva (#8–14), Brown Caddis Larva (#8–14), Elk Hair Caddis (#10–14), Adams (#10–14), Light Cahill (#12–16), March Brown (#8–12), Royal Wulff (#12), Adams Wulff (#12).

The Ammonoosuc River begins on the side of Mount Washington, the highest point in New England (elevation 6,288 feet), and the neighboring peaks. Several streams—Jefferson Brook, Clay Brook, Monroe Brook, Franklin Brook, and Sokokis Brook—come together to form the Ammonoosuc. Monroe Brook starts at one of two scenic ponds called Lakes of the Clouds. All of these tributaries of the Ammonoosuc River are freestone brook trout streams and a lot of fun to fish. The trout may not be large, but they are hearty and plentiful.

The upper Ammonoosuc is the portion above Bethlehem. This section is stocked with brook trout. The headwaters of the Ammonoosuc, east of Fabyon, are paralleled by Base Road. Look for pullouts along Base Road to find access to the river.

US 302 and NH 116 follow the river west of Fabyon until the Ammonoosuc empties into the Connecticut River at Woodsville. While the upper section of the river contains brook trout, the lower Ammonoosuc is stocked with rainbows.

In addition to the Gale River, which I have already discussed, there are several other tributaries worth mentioning. These contain both rainbow and brook trout. Pettyboro Brook, which begins in Bath, is easily accessed along Black Valley Road. Mill Brook, in Landaff, is accessed from pulloffs along Mill Brook. And NH 117 parallels Salmon Hole Brook in Lisbon and Sugar Hill.

One of the most important tributaries of the Ammonoosuc is the Wild Ammonoosuc River. This is a fast-moving freestone stream beginning in the northern corner of Woodstock in the White Mountain National Forest. NH 112 follows the Wild Ammonoosuc through Swiftwater, providing access at numerous pullouts and picnic sites.

The entire Ammonoosuc drainage fishes best from the second half of May through the first week of July. For small mountain streams such as the headwaters of the Ammonoosuc and the various tributaries, I prefer a light-weight rod and dry flies like Wulffs, Humpies, and large terrestrials. Cast these flies onto the surface of every small pool and into the pocket water behind the small boulders in the river. In these fast-flowing streams the fish react quickly to every well-presented morsel.

For the main stem of the lower Ammonoosuc, step up the size of your tackle and start using Woolly Buggers, streamers, and weighted nymphs.

THE SWIFT RIVER

Maps *The New Hampshire Atlas and Gazetteer,* pages 44 and 45.

Description The Swift River is a classic mountain freestone stream: rugged scenery, cool temperatures, and rushing water. It starts in the depths of the White Mountain National Forest in Livermore, and flows for 23 miles to the Saco River in Conway. There are numerous campgrounds along the river, and ample access at picnic areas and pulloffs.

Access NH 112, also known as Kancamagus Highway, follows the Swift from its headwaters to Conway, New Hampshire. There are campgrounds, pulloffs, and picnic areas along the entire river. Any of these spots offers an excellent opportunity to fish.

Heading upstream from Conway on the north side of the Swift, Passaconaway Road (which changes into Dugway Road) parallels the lower section of the river. This road offers additional access to the water.

Best Assets The Swift River is a wonderful mountain stream in the heart of the White Mountain National Forest. White Ledge, Blue Mountain, Potash Mountain, Haystack, Bear Mountain, and Scaur Peak are just a few of the mountains forming the backdrop to this splendid brook trout stream.

There is a lot of access to the Swift. Best of all, it has a fly-fishing-only section.

Biggest Drawback Like all free-flowing mountain streams, the Swift is subject to rapid changes in water level. If the Swift River Valley gets several days of heavy rain, you might want to delay your trip to the area until the stream has a chance to clear and drop back to more fishable levels.

Regulations The fishing season is from January 1 to October 15. The daily bag limit is a total of five trout, not to exceed 5 pounds. There is no length limit.

From the NH 113A bridge downstream to the NH 113 bridge: Fly-fishing only; the daily creel limit for brook trout is two fish.

Favorite Flies Olive Woolly Bugger (#10), Black Woolly Bugger (#10), Brown Woolly Bugger (#10), Woolly Worm (#10–12), Royal Coachman (#6–10), Hare's Ear Nymph (#8–14), Pheasant Tail Nymph (#8–14), Bead Head Nymph (#8–14), Olive Sparkle Caddis Pupa (#8–14), Brown Sparkle Caddis Pupa (#8–14), Cream Sparkle Caddis Pupa (#8–14), Olive Caddis Larva (#8–14), Brown Caddis Larva (#8–14), Elk Hair Caddis (#10–14), Adams (#10–14), Light Cahill (#12–16), March Brown (#8–12), Royal Wulff (#12), Adams Wulff (#12).

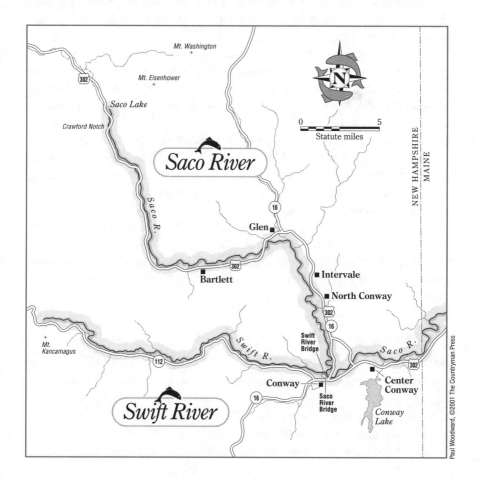

The Swift is one of the best-known rivers in New Hampshire. This reputation is well deserved, because the stream contains a good population of
nice-sized brown, rainbow, and brook trout. The river is also easily accessed,
providing a tourist with many opportunities to get on the water quickly.

The Swift begins near Mount Kancamagus in Livermore in the White
Mountain National Forest. This section of the river is a typical freestone
mountain stream, tumbling and cascading, forming plunge pools broken by
pocket water and riffles. The water is clear and cool, and the forest scenery
is wonderful. The native brook trout are strong and bright, but as in most
mountain streams, are on the small side, averaging 6 to 8 inches in length.
However, if you use lightweight tackle (perhaps a 2- or 3-weight rod) and
dry flies, you won't be disappointed.

Working your way downstream, you'll encounter more rainbow and
brown trout. The Swift River gets annual stockings of trout and, in addition
to the native brookies, has a good population of rainbows.

There is a lot of access to the Swift River from NH 112, which parallels
the stream for its entire length. Many pullouts, picnic areas, and campgrounds let you park and fish.

The best fishing on the Swift is from the last half of May through the
first week or two of July. Remember that the Swift is a mountain freestone
stream and subject to high water in spring from melting snow. If the area
experiences heavy spring rains, the river may not be in fishable condition
until the end of May.

Favorite flies for the Swift are high-floating attractor dry flies such as
the Royal Wulff, Humpys, and Elk Hair Caddis. I tie these flies on hook sizes
10 and 12. Weighted nymphs work well in the lower sections for catching
larger brown and rainbow trout. Small streamers, Woolly Buggers, and
Woolly Worms will round out your Swift River fly box.

When the main stem of the Swift heats up by the last half of July, try
fishing one of the many tributaries. These flow in the shade of the surrounding forest and stay cool throughout summer; the fishing for native
brook trout will remain good. Douglas Brook is a favorite, accessed along
Bear Notch Road out of Passaconaway.

THE SACO RIVER

Maps *The New Hampshire Atlas and Gazetteer*, pages 44 and 45.

Description The Saco River in New Hampshire starts in Crawford Notch State
Park at the outflow of Saco Lake. At this point the Saco is a freestone mountain stream. You can wade this part of the stream "wet" (without waders), a
particularly nice practice in the heat of summer.

The Saco gains size and strength by the time it reaches North Conway, but the entire river, all the way to the Maine border, is wadable. The lower stretch of the Saco in New Hampshire is also a good river to fish from a canoe.

Best Assets In addition to brook trout, the lower reach of the Saco contains some very large brown trout. The river is liberally stocked with brook, rainbow, and brown trout. Also be sure to check out the fly-fishing-only section in North Conway.

Biggest Drawback North Conway is a busy town, and the fly-fishing-only section can see a lot of anglers, especially during June. Midweek is the best time to fish this stretch.

Regulations The fishing season is from January 1 to October 15. The daily creel limit is a total of five trout, not to exceed 5 pounds. There is no length limit.

Note the special fly-fishing-only section: From a point at Lucy Brook marked by a sign downstream to the confluence of the river with Artists Falls Brook. The daily creel limit in this section is two brook trout.

Favorite Flies Olive Woolly Bugger (#10), Black Woolly Bugger (#10), Brown Woolly Bugger (#10), Woolly Worm (#10–12), Royal Coachman (#6–10), Hare's Ear Nymph (#8–14), Pheasant Tail Nymph (#8–14), Bead Head Nymph (#8–14), Olive Sparkle Caddis Pupa (#8–14), Brown Sparkle Caddis Pupa (#8–14), Cream Sparkle Caddis Pupa (#8–14), Olive Caddis Larva (#8–14), Brown Caddis Larva (#8–14), Elk Hair Caddis (#10–14), Hendrickson (#14), Adams (#10–14), Light Cahill (#12–16), March Brown (#8–12), Royal Wulff (#12), Adams Wulff (#12).

The Saco River is one of the many streams that begin in New Hampshire and flow east into Maine; the streams flowing west toward Vermont can get no farther than the Connecticut River. While the Maine portion of the Saco has brown trout averaging 10 inches in length, the river has a much better reputation for the quality of its striped bass fishery: The mouth of the Saco is one of the best places to catch stripers on the East Coast.

I'm also more interested in the stretch of the Saco lying on the New Hampshire side of the border because this part is more remote. Southern Maine is becoming heavily populated, and with the increasing numbers of people I'm also seeing an increase in the number of NO TRESPASSING signs.

In New Hampshire the Saco flows through the White Mountain National Forest and Grafton Notch State Park. Access to the river is excellent, and the scenery is wonderful. I may live in Maine, but when I think of trout fishing on the Saco, I think of New Hampshire.

The Saco River begins at Saco Lake, a small stillwater north of Grafton Notch State Park. The river quickly tumbles over Flume Cascade and Silver

Cascade. This section is remote and beautiful. US 302 closely parallels the upper Saco, providing access at many pullouts, picnic areas, and campgrounds.

By the time you reach Conway, New Hampshire, the banks of the Saco are getting crowded with houses and other development. This section of the river, however, still offers good fishing. In addition to stocked brook trout, you will also catch rainbow and brown trout. Some of the brown trout, especially as you approach and enter Maine, weigh several pounds. There are pullouts along the many main and side roads that follow the river, and this is a favorite section of canoeists. I suppose it depends upon what you want from your fly-fishing; if it's only large fish, head to the lower section of the Saco; if it's solitude, beautiful scenery, and the chance to catch wild trout, explore the upper reaches.

Your choice of tackle also depends upon where you fish. The lower section of the Saco is wider and the fish are larger; I would choose a standard 9-foot-long rod matched with a 6-weight line. For flies, Muddler Minnows, Black Ghosts, Woolly Buggers, and other streamers seem to work best. For the upper stretch, scale back to a 7-foot-long, 3- or 4-weight rod and high-floating attractor dry flies.

Other Stocked Trout Water Worth Exploring

Airport Pond (Jefferson), Armington Lake (Piermont), Atwood Pond (Thornton), Baker River (Campton), Baskin Pond (Chatham), Bean Pond (Ossipee), Bearcamp River (Sandwich), Beebe River (Campton), Beech River (Ossipee), Blue Pond (Madison), Bog Pond (Campton), Brackett Pond (Wentworth), Carroll Stream (Carroll), Carr Pond (Clarksville), Carter Pond (Beans Purchase), Cedar Pond (Milan), Chandler Brook (Landaff), Clay Brook (Bridgewater), Conway Lake (Eaton), Crawford Brook (Carroll), Big Dan Hole Pond (Ossipee), Dells Pond (Littleton), Duncan Lake (Ossipee), Durand Lake (Randolph), Echo Lake (Franconia), Ellis River (Bartlett), Ellis Stream (Jackson), Falls Pond (Albany), Flat Mountain Pond (Waterville), Fox Pond (Plymouth), French Pond (Haverhill), Garland Brook (Moultonborough), Upper Greeley Pond (Livermore), Guinea Pond (Sandwich), Hall Brook (Sandwich), Hamm Branch River (Franconia), Hancock Brook (Lincoln), Hatch Pond (Eaton), Higher Ground Pond (Wentworth), Hildreth Pond (Warren), Hutchins Pond (Effingham), Israel River (Jefferson), Jackman Brook (Woodstock), Jericho Pond (Landaff), Johns River (Dalton), Kiah Pond (Sandwich), Ledge Pond (Madison), Lonesome Lake (Lincoln), Loon Lake (Freedom), Lost River (Woodstock), Mountain Pond (Chatham), Mystery Pond (Ossipee), Oliverian Stream (Haverhill), Owl Brook (Ashland), Peabody River (Gorham), Pettyboro Brook (Bath), Phillips Brook (Stark), Pollard Brook (Ossipee), Salmon Hole River (Lisbon), Stearns Brook (Milan), Trout Brook (Lyme), Tunis Brook (Hanover).

Where to Stay in Central New Hampshire

Christmas Farm Inn Route 16B, Jackson Village, NH 03846 603-383-4313.

The Buttonwood Inn P.O. Box 1817, North Conway, NH 03860 603-356-2625.

Inn at Jackson P.O. Box 807, Jackson, NH 03846 603-383-4321.

Maple Haven Camping & Cottages Box 54, Route 112, North Woodstock, NH 03262 603-745-3350.

Knoll Motel 446 Main Street, Plymouth, NH 03264 603-536-1245.

The Silver Fox Inn 10 Snows Brook Road, Waterville Valley, NH 03215 1-888-236-3699.

Local Guide Services

William Bernhardt III P.O. Box 1401, North Conway, NH 03860 603-356-8366.

Akela Fishing Tours 113 Lehner Street, Wolfeboro, NH 03894 603-569-6035.

Richard Estes Jr. P.O. Box 506, Ossipee, NH 03864 603-539-7354.

Peter Grasso 95 Roller Coaster Road, Laconia, NH 03246 603-366-4115.

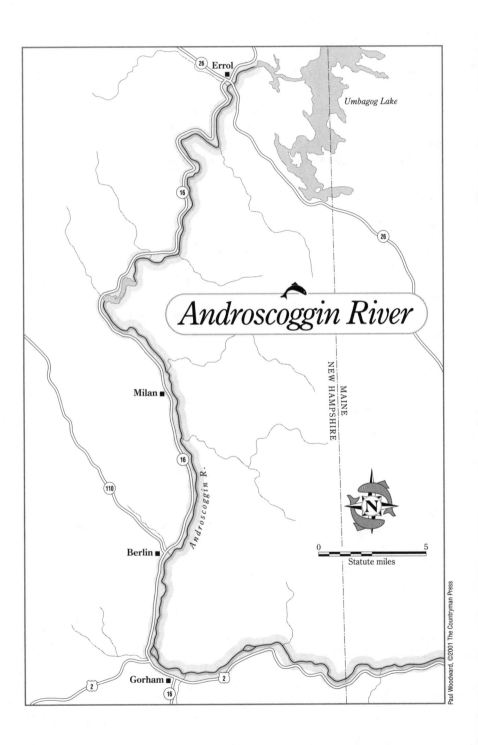

Errol

26

Umbagog Lake

16

Androscoggin River

26

MAINE
NEW HAMPSHIRE

Milan

16

110

Androscoggin R.

Berlin

N

0   5
Statute miles

Gorham

2

2

16

6 | Northern New Hampshire

As you drive toward the Canadian boarder, the population and development thin and you find increasing wilderness. Unfortunately, many people across the United States think of the entire Northeast as an overpopulated industrial wasteland; clearly, they've never visited northern New Hampshire.

This is a great place to come for a fishing vacation. The scenery is first-rate, the fishing is excellent, and there are many lodges catering to anglers.

THE ANDROSCOGGIN RIVER

Maps *The New Hampshire Atlas and Gazetteer,* pages 49, 50, and 51.

Description The Androscoggin is a medium- to large-sized river, especially when compared with other eastern rivers.

The Androscoggin River begins at the outflow of Lake Umbagog at the border between New Hampshire and Maine. The scenery along the river between Lake Umbagog and Berlin is particularly beautiful.

The river flows west for several miles to Errol, New Hampshire. It then heads almost directly south, gaining strength with the inflow of its many tributaries, most of which offer good to excellent fishing for brook trout. At Gorham the Androscoggin turns east and crosses the border into Maine. The river flows for a total of 53 miles in New Hampshire, all of it containing trout and landlocked salmon. You can either wade or fish the river from a canoe.

Access NH 16 closely parallels the upper Androscoggin River from Errol to Gorham. There are many pulloffs and campgrounds offering access to this wadable section of the river.

US 2 parallels the south side of the Androscoggin from Gorham to the Maine border, but the Canadian National Railway line runs between the road and the river, making access a little more difficult. North Road parallels the north side of the river in Shelburne near the Maine border. Here your best bet is to park near the two bridges over the river to gain access to the water.

Best Assets The Androscoggin is well stocked and gives you the opportunity to fish larger water. It's wide, offering ample casting room. There is also a lot of access to the river from Errol to Gorham, so the Androscoggin can comfortably accommodate a large number of anglers. If you choose to float the Androscoggin, you'll be able to fish many more miles of stream.

Biggest Drawback The section of the river below Pontook Dam contains several sets of rapids and can be very dangerous.

Regulations The fishing season is from January 1 to October 15.

From Errol Dam to the markers at the Bragg Bay deadwater: Fly-fishing only; the daily limit for brook trout is two fish; the minimum length for trout is 12 inches.

From the Dummer-Cambridge town line to Pontook Dam in south-central Dummer: The daily limit for trout is five, not to exceed a total weight of 5 pounds, and two landlocked salmon with a minimum length of 15 inches.

From Wheeler Bay in Dummer to the 12th Street bridge in Berlin: Taking trout and salmon between two hours after sunset and one hour before sunset is illegal—except brown trout, which may be taken any time of the day or night during the open season.

From the 12th Street bridge in Berlin to the Maine border: The daily limit for trout is five fish, not to exceed a total weight of 5 pounds, and two landlocked salmon with a minimum length of 15 inches.

Favorite Flies Hornberg (#6–10), Gray Ghost (#4–8), Black Ghost (#4–8), Mickey Finn (#6–8), Olive Woolly Bugger (#6–8), Black Woolly Bugger (#6–8), Brown Woolly Bugger (#6–8), Muddler Minnow (#4–8), Woolly Worm (#6–8), Royal Coachman (#6–10), Ballou Special (#4–8), Hare's Ear Nymph (#8–14), Pheasant Tail Nymph (#8–14), Bead Head Nymph (#8–14), Olive Sparkle Caddis Pupa (#8–14), Brown Sparkle Caddis Pupa (#8–14), Cream Sparkle Caddis Pupa (#8–14), Olive Caddis Larva (#8–14), Brown Caddis Larva (#8–14), Elk Hair Caddis (#10–14), Adams (#10–14), Hendrickson (#14), Royal Wulff (#12), Adams Wulff (#12), Light Cahill (#12–16), March Brown (#8–12).

The Androscoggin begins at Lake Umbagog on the border of New Hampshire and Maine. This is wild country, full of moose, beavers, and loons. The river flows northeast for only a mile or two before taking a sharp turn to the south.

It would be worth a long weekend to take a fishing trip to the upper Androscoggin. This section of the river flows between Errol and Milan, and is very easily accessed along NH 16. There are numerous pullovers and picnic sites along the river, and anglers remain spread apart; visit during the week and you'll have many nice pools to yourself. The river is stocked with brook, rainbow, and brown trout as well as landlocked salmon, so you'll have a nice chance at catching a variety of fish.

There are two dams on the upper Androscoggin that will impact your decisions about where to fish. The first is Errol Dam, which is above the town of Errol; the second, in southern Dummer, is called Pontook Dam. The river below Pontook Dam holds some very large fish, with some brown trout weighing up to 4 pounds. However, this section of the river is also dangerous to wade at times, so be mindful of the water levels coming from the dam, and always pay attention to changes in the water level.

The Androscoggin is wider than the typical New England trout stream. While I recommend lightweight tackle for fishing many streams throughout the region, a standard 9-foot-long rod fitted with a 5- or 6-weight line is perfect for the Androscoggin. You'll also want to come prepared with a selection of flies that includes Hendricksons, Blue Winged Olives, March Browns, Alder Flies, Elk Hair Caddises, weighted nymphs, and a variety of streamers.

The upper section of the Androscoggin is a combination of riffles, chutes, and pools. Concentrate on fishing in the faster water; the trout and salmon are rarely found in the long, slow sections of the river.

THE UPPER CONNECTICUT RIVER

Maps *The New Hampshire Atlas and Gazetteer,* pages 52 and 53.

Description The upper Connecticut River flows through mountainous Pittsburg, New Hampshire. This section of the river connects a series of dammed lakes and has good flows throughout the summer. The river is mostly gravel bottomed and easy to wade. There are excellent mayfly and caddisfly hatches, and a variety of streamers will catch very large trout.

There are many cabins and sporting lodges in the area, and Pittsburg remains a favorite destination among anglers.

Access US 3 is your key to fishing the upper Connecticut River. There are places to park and walk to the river below First Connecticut Lake and Second Lake. River Road, a well-maintained road south of US 3 below First Connecticut Lake, leads to additional places to fish.

Best Assets The upper Connecticut has excellent hatches beginning in spring and lasting into late summer. The river contains brook trout and landlocked

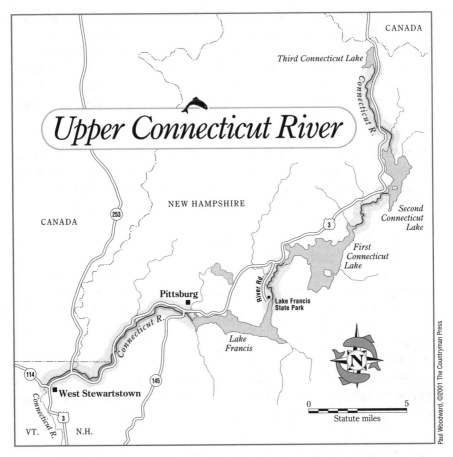

Paul Woodward, ©2001 The Countryman Press

salmon, as well as some very large brown trout. In addition to the river, the area contains several small streams and ponds with excellent trout fishing. This is the sort of place where you could fish for a couple of weeks and not get to all the water.

Be sure to check out the fly-fishing-only sections.

Biggest Drawback When the dams are generating a lot of water, forget it; the water will rise and make wading and fishing very difficult. Fortunately, this doesn't happen often.

Regulations The fishing season is from January 1 to October 15.

From the dam at Second Lake to the upstream side of the logging bridge on Magalloway Road: Fly-fishing only; all fish must be immediately released unharmed.

From the Magalloway Road bridge to the inlet at Green Point on First Connecticut Lake: Fly-fishing only; the daily creel limit for brook trout is two fish.

From First Connecticut Lake Dam to the signs on Lake Francis: Fly-fishing only; the daily creel limit for brook trout is two fish, with a minimum length of 12 inches.

Favorite Flies Hornberg (#6–10), Gray Ghost (#4–8), Black Ghost (#4–8), Mickey Finn (#6–8), Olive Woolly Bugger (#6–8), Black Woolly Bugger (#6–8), Brown Woolly Bugger (#6–8), Muddler Minnow (#4–8), Woolly Worm (#6–8), Royal Coachman (#6–10), Ballou Special (#4–8), Hare's Ear Nymph (#8–14), Pheasant Tail Nymph (#8–14), Bead Head Nymph (#8–14), Olive Sparkle Caddis Pupa (#8–14), Brown Sparkle Caddis Pupa (#8–14), Cream Sparkle Caddis Pupa (#8–14), Olive Caddis Larva (#8–14), Brown Caddis Larva (#8–10), Royal Wulff (#12), Adams Wulff (#12), Elk Hair Caddis (#10–14), Hendrickson (#14), Adams (#10–14), Light Cahill (#12–16), Green Drake (#4–6), March Brown (#8–12).

The upper section of the Connecticut River is one of the crown jewels in all of New England's fly-fishing. It really surprises me how few anglers living in the Northeast have fished this section. I once wrote that in some ways, visiting the upper Connecticut is a lot like going back in time: The lodges still have a rustic ambience, and the fishing is still good. The Connecticut River above the town of Pittsburg, New Hampshire, should definitely be on your list of places to fish in New England.

The upper Connecticut flows through a series of lakes, and some parts of the river are easier to get to than others. The river starts by flowing out of Third Connecticut Lake. You can get to this part of the river by hiking through the woods from US 3, but there are a couple of logging roads that cross the river and provide easier access.

The next access point is below Second Connecticut Lake. You can fish right below the dam, where you'll occasionally see a landlocked salmon jump up into the flowing water. I prefer using streamers in this section. Cast them out and let them swing through the flow.

The section of the river below First Connecticut Lake offers the most access. This is a good, fly-fishing-only section with four access points. The first is right below the dam at the lake. There is ample parking, and a short path will lead you to the river. This is a surprisingly nice area to fish. Although I say it's at "right below the dam," you're actually several hundred yards down from the dam in a lovely wooded valley.

The second access point to the trophy section is along River Road leading to Lake Francis State Park. About a mile down, River Road crosses Perry Stream, a small tributary of the Connecticut. Park near the stream and fish Perry Stream, or take a path leading down to the Connecticut.

About 200 yards back up the river, there is a dirt road to the right. This road also leads to a gated bridge and the river. There is parking near the bridge, and easy access to the water.

You can also gain access to the trophy section through Lake Francis State Park. A footpath leads up the river through a heavily forested area. Although the fishing is very good, you'll see far fewer people in this section than you will in the other stretches.

You can also gain access to the Connecticut River along US 3 below the town of Pittsburg. Here the river gradient smoothes out and the freestone gives way to gravel, but the entire river is fairly easy to wade. Remember: The Connecticut River is a tailwater, and you should always be aware of changes in the water level.

The Connecticut is fairly easy to fish. Much of the river is open and free of overhanging foliage. Your favorite 8- to 9-foot, 5- or 6-weight rod will work just fine.

The Connecticut is the home of some really impressive landlocked salmon and brown trout. To catch these fish, you'll want to use streamers: Gray Ghosts, Governor Aikens, and Nine-Threes.

The Connecticut is also a good dry-fly river. You won't want to be here without an assortment of Hendricksons, Cahills, Sulphurs, and Blue Winged Olives. The Elk Hair Caddis is also a good, all-around imitation for matching the river's many species of caddisflies.

The upper Connecticut River is a series of tailwaters. The river contains rainbow and brown trout, and landlocked salmon.

Nymphs also take their share of trout on the upper Connecticut. Weighted nymphs such as Bead Heads and Pheasant Tail Nymphs are among the favorites.

Tim Savard of Lopstick Lodge, one of the premier guiding services and places to stay in the area, gave me the lowdown on fishing the upper sections of the Connecticut.

"We use a drift boat in three different sections of the river: from West Stewartson to Colebrook, from Colebrook to Columbia, and from Columbia to North Stratford. It's fairly pastoral. The river widens and slows a bit, but because the water entering this section of the river comes from the bottom of the dam at Lake Francis, it remains cool throughout the summer. Even in August, the water temperatures remain in the 60s.

"It's all trout habitat: browns, rainbows, and a smattering of brook trout," continued Savard. "It's primarily dry-fly fishing. Our bread-and-butter fly is a *Baetis*. We see them from the beginning of June right until the end of the season when the autumn leaves choke the river and we can't fish."

What about the hatches in the sections of the river above Pittsburg?

"We have the usual group of Northeast flies in the early part of the season through June. We have some early caddis, and from July 1 on, it's pretty much all caddis, with some evening stonefly activity."

When do you like to start fishing?

"Right after ice-out, which averages around the first week of May. That's a totally different season. It's usually very short—seven days to three weeks long. It's when the salmon chase the smelt up the river.

"As that little mini season progresses, we begin to fish weighted nymphs," Savard went on. "In the 2000 season, we had some tremendous dry-fly fishing because many of the fish that entered to chase the smelt stayed. This was between First Lake and Second Lake.

"Next, we begin to concentrate on that section of the river between First Lake and Lake Francis. That's the trophy section. That season starts slow and begins to accelerate during the second, third, and fourth weeks of June. The beauty of this section is that the cold-water discharges from the dam keeps the river fishing well into the last week of July."

Do the dams ever generate so much water that it's impossible to fish?

"Not too often. In that second section, the normal water flow is around 100 to 150 cfs [cubic feet per second]. At times that can be fairly thin in terms of being able to hold decent fish in the river. What people don't understand about this river is that southern New Hampshire might be experiencing a terrible drought, but the upper Connecticut River will be in great shape. This is because the dams in the southern section of the state will be calling for more water, and they'll increase the flows coming out of our

Landlocked salmon are found in most of the major fly-fishing rivers throughout New England. These fish are strong fighters, and are caught with streamers, nymphs, and dry flies.

lakes . . . Because of the nature of the dam control, it's very rare that we'll have unfishable water."

How big are the fish in the upper Connecticut River?

"The average size of the brook trout is 11 to 12 inches long. The state also dumps in a ton of big spawners [brood stock from the hatchery], which go up to 3, 4, 5 pounds. The salmon average 20 to 21 inches in the spring. The salmon that stay in the river over the summer average 12 to 17 inches long. In the fall our salmon measure up to 24 inches."

What about the rainbow and brown trout?

"The rainbow trout come up out of the lakes. The rainbows coming up out of Lake Francis average 11 to 12 inches long. The brown trout, some of which weigh several pounds, also come out of the lakes."

Other Stocked Trout Waters Worth Exploring

Akers Pond (Errol), Back Lake (Pittsburg), Big Bear Brook Pond (Errol), Big Bear Brook (Errol), Big Brook Bog (Pittsburg), Bishop Brook (Stewartstown), Little Bog Pond (Odell), Boundary Pond (Pittsburg), Bragg Pond (Millsfield),

Carr Pond (Clarksville), Cedar Brook (Stewartstown), Cheesefactory Pond (Pittsburg), Clarksville Pond (Clarksville), Clear Stream (Dixville), Coon Brook Bog (Pittsburg), Corser Pond (Errol), Cranberry Bog Pond (Columbia), Big Diamond Pond (Stewartstown), Four Mile Pond (Dixs Grant), Harris Pond (Pittsburg), Indian Stream (Pittsburg), Little Peoples Pond (Berlin), Little Bog Pond (Odell), Lyman Brook (Columbia), Munn Pond (Errol), Simms Stream (Columbia).

Where to Stay in Northern New Hampshire

Colebrook House 132 Main Street, Colebrook, NH 03576 1-800-626-7331.

The Olde Morse Lodge 39 Portland Street, Lancaster, NH 03584 603-788-4600.

The Glenn First Connecticut Lake, Pittsburg, NH 03592 603-538-6500.

Lopstick Lodge & Cabins First Connecticut Lake, Pittsburg, NH 03592 1-800-538-6659.

Tall Timber Lodge Back Lake, Pittsburg, NH 03592 1-800-835-6343.

Guide Services of Northern New Hampshire

Lisa and Tim Savard RR 1, Box 49, Pittsburg, NH 03592 603-538-9955.

Thomas Remick Box 57B, Route 3, Pittsburg, NH 03592 603-538-7123.

Cindy Sullivan 231 Beach Street, Pittsburg, NH 03592 603-538-6651.

III | MAINE

I think most fly-fishers want to visit Maine at least once in their lives. It's a wonderful place to fish for several reasons.

First, the state hosts such a wide variety of fish species. If you like a mixed bag, you can fish for brook, brown, rainbow, and blueback trout, landlocked salmon, and a range of warm-water species—smallmouth bass, largemouth bass, northern pike, pickerel, and several varieties of panfish. There are days when I fish for sea-run striped bass in the morning and visit a local pond full of brook trout in the evening. In fall I'll be in a blind on a duck marsh at the crack of dawn and wet a line on the way home. Maine really is a sportsperson's paradise.

The other great thing about Maine is that so much of the good fishing—and hunting—is so readily available. Maine tradition holds that the land belongs to all residents. While southern Maine is becoming heavily developed, and much of the land is becoming posted against trespassing, huge areas throughout the state remain open to the public. This isn't public land; Maine has very little public land. About 90 percent of the state is owned by private individuals and large companies. The logging and paper industry is one of Maine's largest, and several corporations own hundreds of thousands of acres of forestland. Fortunately, the state of Maine, various sporting and conservation organizations, and the landowners work together to keep this land open to anglers, hunters, sightseers, and nature lovers. This is a unique situation, and all who enter and use these private lands should obey the rules set down by the landowners and show respect for their property.

Anglers are also drawn to Maine because of the state's rich sporting heritage—the lore of the Maine sporting camp and the big North Woods. And the state has been the home of some of the country's leading rod makers, fly-tiers, and canoe makers. I'll relate some of the more interesting historical highlights as I examine fly-fishing in Maine.

I travel and fish throughout much of the United States and Canada. There's great fishing all over North America, but I'm always happy to call Maine my home waters.

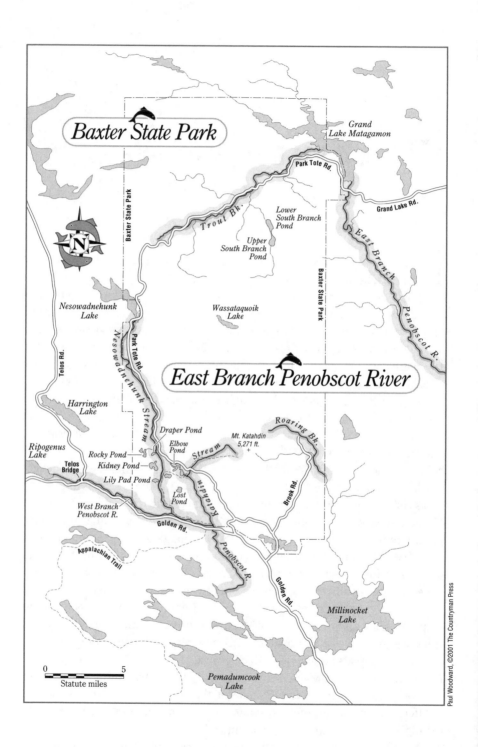

7 | Central Maine

Baxter State Park and the surrounding area of central Maine is one of my favorite areas to fish. I suspect you could spend most of your life fishing central Maine and never sample all the area has to offer. Whether you enjoy fishing ponds, streams, or large rivers, you'll find good fishing in central Maine. Because of the variety and quality of the landlocked salmon and trout, I think the Baxter State Park region is the crown jewel of Maine fly-fishing.

BAXTER STATE PARK

Maps *The Maine Atlas and Gazetteer,* Maps 50, 51, 56, and 57. The Baxter State Park Authority also supplies a variety of maps of the park. Some are free; there is a charge for others. For maps and additional information, contact the Baxter State Park Authority.

Description Baxter State Park is a wilderness area located in the central section of Maine in Piscataquis and Penobscot Counties. The park contains the highest mountains in Maine, including Mount Katahdin. The highest point on Mount Katahdin is Baxter Peak, elevation 5,271 feet.

Baxter State Park is a heavily forested region famous for its hiking trails, moose, and fine fishing. There are several streams of particular interest to the fly-fisher, as well several ponds containing large brook trout.

Baxter State Park offers camping and cabins, but accommodations are primitive. No potable water is available within the park (including the cabins), and there is no store or commissary; you must bring everything you'll need for your stay. Despite the lack of modern conveniences, the park attracts thousands of visitors every year, and the cabins and camping sites are booked months in advance.

Access There are two access points to Baxter State Park. First, you can take

Looking at Mount Katahdin across Daicey Pond in Baxter State Park. During the last half of June, the ponds of Baxter State Park feature a good hatch of *Hexagenia* mayflies.

Golden Road out of Millinocket, Maine (Millinocket is also a good place to fill your gas tank and pick up any last-minute supplies for your trip). Head west on Golden Road toward the park and the West Branch of the Penobscot (look for the signs along the road). After Golden Road crosses the confluence of Millinocket Lake and Ambajejus Lake, the road splits; the fork to the west continues along the West Branch of the Penobscot River, and the fork to the north leads to Baxter State Park (once again, signs point the way). Head north into the southern end of the park. The southern section contains the better fishing.

The second access point leads to the northeast corner of Baxter State Park. Take ME 159 west out of Patten, Maine. At Shin Pond, ME 159 turns into Grand Lake Road. Continue along Grand Lake Road until you reach the park entrance.

There are gates at both entrances. The park personnel will request your name, where you plan to visit in the park, and what you plan to do; they'll record your license plate number. Please don't be offended by these questions; this isn't a case of "big brother" watching over us. The Baxter State Park Authority works very hard to manage the thousands of people who visit the park every year, and this information proves helpful when someone becomes hurt or lost. Baxter State Park is largely a wilderness area, and many people come very unprepared for the primitive conditions.

There are no paved roads within Baxter State Park, and the dirt and gravel roads never seem to get graded. You'll be happier if you visit in a sturdy vehicle.

Best Assets The trout ponds. The ponds in the southern end of the park contain some very large brook trout. The streams also contain native brookies. The scenery is superb.

Biggest Drawbacks The road system is very primitive; some of the potholes will really cause your teeth to chatter (no matter how slow you drive). Renting a cabin (the Baxter State Park Authority charges premium prices compared with many commercial sporting camps) that doesn't have running water and in which you're not allowed to cook doesn't make a lot of sense to me; at the end of the day I like to wash off the insect repellent and cook away from the mosquitoes. On the other hand, if the roads were paved and the cabins were rated four-star, the park would be overrun with tourists and lose the sense of "wildness" so many visitors come to enjoy.

The fishing regulations are another disappointment. While it's unlawful to possess natural bait within the park, and you're permitted to keep only two trout per day, I wish at least a couple of the ponds would be managed under strict catch-and-release regulations. Today most fly-fishers are interested in catching large trophy fish, and many are willing to travel and pay a tidy sum for the privilege. Every year anglers travel to Labrador and other northern regions to catch really large brook trout. Historic records show that the waters of Maine once contained trout rivaling those caught today in Canada. Even if strict catch-and-release were instituted, the rivers, lakes, and ponds of Maine might not be able to produce the numbers of exceptionally large brook trout found in Canada because there might be other limiting factors. It would be wonderful if some of Baxter's ponds could be set aside, however, to see just how large the fish could grow. Anglers would travel from far and wide to hook, play, and then release big native trout.

Regulations A patchwork of regulations governs the ponds and streams of Baxter State Park, but these are the highlights.

The legal fishing season is from April 1 to September 30.

It is unlawful to possess natural bait—worms, minnows, natural salmon eggs, and so on—within the boundaries of Baxter State Park. At a minimum, all fishing requires at least the use of artificial lures.

Nesowadnehunk Stream, which runs north to south near the western border of the park, as well as Daicey, Kidney, Lost, Rocky, and Draper Ponds are fly-fishing only.

Favorite Flies Hornberg (#6–10), Gray Ghost (#4–8), Black Ghost (#4–8), Mickey Finn (#6–8), Olive Woolly Bugger (#6–8), Black Woolly Bugger (#6–8), Brown Woolly Bugger (#6–8), Muddler Minnow (#4–8), Woolly Worm (#6–8), Royal Coachman (#6–10), Ballou Special (#4–8), Hare's Ear Nymph (#8–14), Pheasant Tail Nymph (#8–14), Olive Wiggle Nymph (#6), Bead Head Nymph (#8–14), Olive Sparkle Caddis Pupa (#8–14), Brown Sparkle Caddis Pupa (#8–14), Cream Sparkle Caddis Pupa (#8–14), Olive Caddis Larva (#8–14), Brown Caddis Larva (#8–14), Elk Hair Caddis (#10–14), Adams (#10–14), Light Cahill (#12–16), Green Drake (#4–6), March Brown (#8–12), Royal Wulff (#10–12).

Baxter State Park is the product of visionary Governor Percival Baxter. He purchased large tracts of land, including some of the state's most outstanding mountains, and in 1931 deeded these to the state of Maine under the stipulation that the land remain "forever wild." This clause in the agreement between Governor Baxter and the state is taken almost literally. Although there are several campgrounds within the park, these are fairly primitive; you'll even have to carry in your own water. At many times of year, the gravel Park Loop Road is better described as a series of potholes. There are also cabins for rent—they were built as commercial sporting camps before the park was founded—but these, too, have no running water; cooking must be done outdoors. Despite these inconveniences, Baxter State Park is held dear to the hearts of many anglers, hikers, and nature lovers.

Baxter State Park is a fly-fisher's dream. The ponds and streams in the park are governed by strict fly-fishing-only regulations.

Baxter State Park boasts some of the best fishing for brook trout in Maine. The ponds here are especially good. If you visit Baxter State Park for a few days, then you must spend a couple of evenings fishing Daicey and Kidney Ponds, both in the park's southwest corner. If I had my choice, I would fish these ponds during the last week of June or maybe the first week of July (although the July 4 weekend is a very busy time in the park). This is when the *Hexagenia* mayfly hatches, and you'll have an excellent chance at catching very large brook trout. I envy the folks who live near Baxter State Park and can monitor the hatches every year; they have the best chance of fishing these ponds when the hatch is at its peak. Even if you don't hit the peak, though, big *Hexagenia* will be emerging at the end of June.

Living about three hours from Baxter State Park, I've had mixed results catching the peak of the hatch. Some years the *Hexagenia* have come off sporadically, but the trout are almost always willing to hit a *Hexagenia* nymph imitation. A tan-and-olive Woolly Bugger tied on a 3X- or 4X-long, size 6 hook is a good, simple imitation of this large mayfly nymph. A variety of large Wiggle Nymphs has been devised to imitate *Hexagenia* and green drake nymphs. I prefer using a sinking line and 6-foot-long leader when fishing Hex nymphs.

Earlier in the season, before the *Hexagenia* mayflies become the talk of the area, a variety of mayfly imitations will take fish on the local trout ponds in the evening. My favorite, however, is the Elk Hair Caddis. I cast an Elk Hair Caddis several feet in front of a cruising fish and give it a very light twitch. This enticing action often triggers a fast strike.

Draper and Tracy Ponds, also in the southwest corner of Baxter State Park, are other good bets for catching brook trout. These ponds are easily accessible from the road and are perfect for fishing from a canoe or float tube. If you'd like to take a hike, walk to Rocky Pond; the path starts at the parking lot for Kidney Pond. You can put a float tube on a pack frame and take the half-mile hike to the pond, or you can rent a canoe at the Kidney Pond ranger station. One of the nice things about Baxter State Park is that canoes are stationed at almost all of the ponds. These rent for about a dollar an hour, or a few dollars a day.

The northeast corner of Baxter State Park contains several other ponds you might want to try. Lower South Branch Pond is the easiest to reach from the road; Upper South Branch Pond requires a short hike. Once again, the prominent species is brook trout.

In addition to these stillwaters, Baxter contains several streams that offer good fly-fishing. These streams run through beautiful country and contain native brook trout.

Nesowadnehunk Stream is the most popular. This stream, which averages about 30 feet wide, begins at Nesowadnehunk Lake on the western boundary of the park. The main Park Loop Road follows the stream along much of its course, allowing for ample access. Nesowadnehunk Stream is loaded with caddisflies, and I've done best fishing small Olive, Tan, and White Caddis Pupae. June is the favorite time to fish Nesowadnehunk Stream.

If you enjoy fishing for native brook trout with a dry fly and dainty rod, you'll want to try Roaring Brook, which flows through the campground servicing the trails leading to Mount Katahdin and surrounding peaks. This is a busy area with all of the hikers passing through, but you'll probably have the fishing to yourself. The path to Mount Katahdin—the tallest point in Maine and the end of the Appalachian Trail—follows the stream for a short distance, and you can wade the rest of the way to fish pools that very few anglers ever visit. This is mountain-style fly-fishing: You'll need a short, lightweight rod; you'll be making tight casts in close quarters; and small, bushy dry flies catch the most fish. These small trout—they average 8 to 10 inches long—slash at the flies. Try fishing Roaring Brook in June and July, and again in September. And because you'll be doing a bit of hiking and scrambling over and around boulders, plan on wading "wet" (without waders).

If you're really up to the challenge, and measure the quality of the fishing by the solitude you find, you might want to try Katahdin Stream. This stream is accessed through the Katahdin Campground in the park's southwest corner. A part of the Appalachian Trail follows the stream, but you can be fairly certain that you'll have the fishing all to yourself. Katahdin Stream is a small mountain brook, requiring short, lightweight tackle and good casting ability.

Baxter State Park is a perfect fishing destination for a long weekend or even an entire week. I suggest fishing the streams during the day and visiting the ponds in the very early morning and early evening. This way you'll be able to fish a variety of water. You'll also have the bonus of being at the ponds when you're most likely to see moose. The cry of the loon, a moose wallowing in the shallows, and a brook trout on the end of the line: There's nothing quite as good.

THE PENOBSCOT RIVER

The Penobscot River, named for the tribe of Native Americans who made their home along this major waterway, is one of Maine's key angling features. It's a river of many faces, and whatever type of fishing you enjoy, you'll be able to do it on the Penobscot.

The mouth of the river boasts a wonderful striped-bass fishery. These oceangoing fish appear around Memorial Day and remain through September. As the numbers of fish increase, more local fly-fishers are pursuing this strong, sporty species.

The section of the Penobscot flowing through Bangor is famous for its Atlantic salmon fishing, although in recent years this fishery has fallen on hard times. Bangor was also the home of Hiram Leonard, the founder of the H. L. Leonard Rod Company. Leonard is generally credited as the first rod maker to offer large quantities of fine split-bamboo fly rods to the angling public. In 1881, he moved his company to New York State to be closer to the important New York City market. Bangor was also the home of the F. E. Thomas Rod Company. Fred Thomas was a disciple of Leonard who developed his own reputation for making fine rods.

It's curious, but few local anglers know about the full role Bangor played in the development of the fly-fishing trade. While many know about Fred Thomas, and some senior anglers still covet rods purchased directly from the F. E. Thomas Rod Company, very few are familiar with the Leonard connection. A couple of years ago, however, I received a flyer in the mail announcing a local sporting auction. Among the list of featured items for sale was a fly-rod listed as a "Bangor Leonard." I wondered: Could it really be a rod Hiram Leonard made while living in Bangor?

I attended the auction the following week and, sure enough, the rod was stamped H. L. LENOARD MAKER, BANGOR, ME. Being a maker and student of split-bamboo rods, I quickly noticed several things about the rod that led me to believe this was a transitional rod between Leonard's early work and the time when he was granted two patents by the U.S. Patent Office for improvements in the construction of split-bamboo fly rods. This rod was indeed an important find. The question was, of course, would I have any competition in the bidding?

A couple of hundred bidders attended the auction, but most were interested in the large assortment of shotguns and rifles; I was virtually alone in bidding for my prized rod, and I bought it for less than $100. What I like best about this rod, besides its historical significance, is the fact that it knocked around Bangor for more than 100 years before coming into my possession.

The section of the river above Bangor, especially the part flowing through Old Town—the home of the Old Town Canoe Company—contains excellent smallmouth bass fishing. These fish are plentiful, strong, and an excellent species to pursue with a fly-rod; all you need is a 6-weight and an assortment of poppers, Woolly Worms, and Muddler Minnows.

If you're interested in trout and landlocked salmon, however, head to the West and East Branches of the Penobscot River.

EAST BRANCH OF THE PENOBSCOT

Maps *The Maine Atlas and Gazetteer,* Map 51; also see map on page 120.

Description The East Branch of the Penobscot River starts as a small stream at East Branch Pond in Township 7, Range 11. It flows easterly into Third Matagamon Lake and Grand Lake Matagamon. This upper section of the East Branch, part of which flows through Baxter State Park, is remote and requires travel on a series of poorly maintained logging roads. The most easily accessed section of the East Branch lies below Grand Lake Matagamon.

The East Branch of the Penobscot is a big, wide river. However, when the dam at Grand Lake Matagamon is releasing only small amounts of water, the river is fairly easy to wade.

Access Access to the East Branch of the Penobscot is found by taking ME 159 west out of Patten, Maine. At Shin Pond ME 159 turns into Branch Lake Road. Continue until Branch Lake Road crosses the East Branch (this road also leads to the northeast entrance of Baxter State Park).

Dirt roads follow the west side of the river, providing access for fishing.

Best Assets The East Branch of the Penobscot doesn't get nearly as many visitors as the West Branch. The West Branch has more access along its length, so the rafting companies call that river home. Also, some anglers believe that the West branch offers better fishing (although I've done quite well on the East Branch). As a result, the East Branch offers more solitude.

During your visit to the East Branch, you can also quickly drive into Baxter State Park and fish the ponds and streams in the northeast corner of the park.

The East Branch is a very beautiful place to fish. The mountains of Baxter State Park provide an excellent backdrop.

Biggest Drawbacks Access is limited, and the river is subject to discharges from the dam at Grand Lake Matagamon.

Regulations Open to fishing from April 1 to September 30. Artificial lures only. Daily bag limit: two trout, minimum 10 inches in length; only one trout may exceed 12 inches. Minimum length on salmon: 10 inches.

Favorite Flies Hornberg (#6–10), Gray Ghost (#4–8), Black Ghost (#4–8), Mickey Finn (#6–8), Olive Woolly Bugger (#6–8), Black Woolly Bugger (#6–8), Brown Woolly Bugger (#6–8), Muddler Minnow (#4–8), Woolly Worm (#6–8), Royal Coachman (#6–10), Ballou Special (#4–8), Hare's Ear Nymph (#8–14), Pheasant Tail Nymph (#8–14), Bead Head Nymph (#8–14), Olive Sparkle Caddis Pupa (#8–14), Brown Sparkle Caddis Pupa (#8–14), Cream Sparkle Caddis Pupa (#8–14), Olive Caddis Larva (#8–14), Brown Caddis Larva (#8–14), Elk Hair Caddis (#10–14), Adams (#10–14), Light Cahill (#12–16), Green Drake (#4–6), March Brown (#8–12).

The East Branch is another fork of the Penobscot you might want to fish when visiting Baxter State Park. It's a tailwater, but it isn't as wide or turbulent as the West Branch. A dirt road travels down the west side of the river, providing access to easily fished water. There are also state campsites in the area, as well as commercial campsites. Because the East Branch is a tailwater, the river stays cool throughout much of the summer, and fishing remains good. Also be sure to keep your eye peeled for any beaver ponds in the area; I've enjoyed some excellent evening fishing for brook trout on the local beaver flowages.

I've had my best luck on the East Branch fishing streamers: Olive and Black Woolly Buggers, Mickey Finns, and Gray Ghosts. The East Branch contains primarily landlocked salmon averaging 14 inches, although it's possible to catch larger salmon in spring and fall.

THE WEST BRANCH OF THE PENOBSCOT RIVER

Maps *The Maine Atlas and Gazetteer,* Maps 49, 50, and 51.

Description The West Branch of the Penobscot is a big, wide river. While much of it is extremely difficult or even impossible to wade, there is enough wadable water that you could fish for several days and not visit the same pools twice.

The West Branch of the Penobscot flows out of the eastern arm of Seboomook Lake, in Seboomook Township, below Seboomook Dam. It flows in a northeasterly direction into Chesuncook and Ripogenous Lakes. It resumes at Ripogenus Dam, at the east end of Ripogenus Lake.

The West Branch of the Penobscot is famous for its large landlocked salmon, but it also contains brook trout.

Access The West Branch of the Penobscot is fairly easy to find, and there are many points at which you can enter the river.

The chief way to access the West Branch is by taking Golden Road west out of the town of Millinocket. After crossing the confluence of Millinocket and Ambajejus Lakes, look for signs pointing the way to the West Branch corridor. Golden Road will cross over and then follow the West Branch. This section of the river, almost 15 miles long, is the favorite among most fly-fishers; you could spend days just fishing this stretch.

If you want to see more of the West Branch, continue on Golden Road above Chesuncook and Caribou Lakes. Golden Road crosses the West Branch at a spot known as Hannibal's Crossing. You can continue on Golden Road to Seboomook Lake, and look for signs leading to Seboomook Dam. The dirt road to the south side of the West Branch leads along the headwaters, and follows the beginning of the river below the dam.

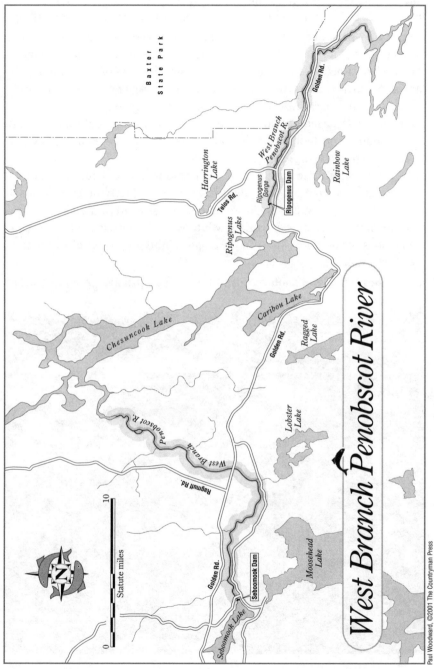

West Branch Penobscot River

Best Assets Big salmon. Lots of access. Plenty of water to fish. Many anglers consider the West Branch of the Penobscot the best landlocked salmon river in the United States. Many of the local ponds offer excellent trout fishing.

Biggest Drawback Because of its size and easy access, the West Branch is a very popular place among all sorts of river enthusiasts. As a percentage of the number of people who use the river, anglers are a very small group. The largest number of users are kayakers and rafters. Several large white-water companies offer party raft trips on the river. It's common to see a flotilla of these large rafts, each holding a dozen or so people, pass by. And although the whooping and hollering these folks carry on can be momentarily disturbing, keep two things in mind.

First, most of these rafters begin their trips within an hour or so of each other. Once they float by, you might have the river pretty much to yourself for the rest of the day. Second, it's going to take strength in numbers to protect our natural resources: Anglers, white-water enthusiasts, and everyone who enjoys the outdoors share in the responsibility to protect places such as the West Branch.

Regulations While you should consult the *Maine Open Water Fishing Regu-*

While much of the West Branch of the Penobscot is difficult to wade, there are sections where you can wade safely. This angler is releasing a nice landlocked salmon.

lations handbook for specifics, here is an outline of the regulations governing the West Branch of the Penobscot.

From Seboomook Dam to Chesuncook Lake: From April 1 to August 15, artificial lures only. Daily limit on salmon: one fish. Daily limit on trout: two fish. From August 16 to September 30, fly-fishing only. Daily limit: one trout or salmon.

From Ripogenus Dam downstream to the Telos Road bridge: From April 1 to September 30, fly-fishing only. Daily limit on salmon: one fish (minimum length 26 inches).

From the Telos Road bridge downstream to Debsconeag Falls: From April 1 to August 15, artificial lures only. Daily limit on salmon: one fish. From August 16 to September 30, fly-fishing only. Daily limit on salmon: one fish (minimum length 18 inches).

Favorite Flies Hornberg (#6–10), Gray Ghost (#4–8), Black Ghost (#4–8), Mickey Finn (#6–8), Olive Woolly Bugger (#6–8), Black Woolly Bugger (#6–8), Brown Woolly Bugger (#6–8), Muddler Minnow (#4–8), Woolly Worm (#6–8), Royal Coachman (#6–10), Ballou Special (#4–8), Hare's Ear Nymph (#8–14), Pheasant Tail Nymph (#8–14), Bead Head Nymph (#8–14), Olive Sparkle Caddis Pupa (#8–14), Brown Sparkle Caddis Pupa (#8–14), Cream Sparkle Caddis Pupa (#8–14), Olive Caddis Larva (#8–14), Brown Caddis Larva (#8–14), Elk Hair Caddis (#10–14), Hendrickson (#14), Adams (#10–14), Light Cahill (#12–16), Green Drake (#4–6), March Brown (#8–12), Royal Wulff (#10), West Branch Dry Fly (#4–6).

Many consider the West Branch of the Penobscot the best landlocked salmon fishery in the United States. While it certainly contains plenty of large salmon, I'm not going to hide the fact that it's also a tough river to fish. The West Branch is a big, brawny river, and some areas can be very dangerous to wade. In several sections, however, the riverbed is made of gravel and small stones, and wading is safe and comfortable.

The first section of the river worth considering is below Seboomook Lake. This part of the river contains salmon averaging 2 pounds, but fish weighing as much as 5 pounds are occasionally caught. The river flows out of Seboomook Dam, and you can enjoy good fishing in the stretch below the dam. The next easily reached section, is at Hannibal's Crossing, where a well-maintained bridge crosses the river. There is parking next to the bridge, and you can access to the river. The last time I crossed the bridge here, I saw a moose crossing the river downstream. Between Seboomook Dam and Hannibal's Crossing, the West Branch is largely inaccessible accept by canoe or raft.

The next section of the West Branch is below Ripogenus Dam. This is by far the most popular area, with both fly-fishers and white-water enthusiasts. It contains landlocked salmon as well as brook trout. There are many places to access this part of the West Branch from Golden Road leading out of Millinocket. The first access point is right below Ripogenus Dam. There is a landing high above the water at the hydropower plant from which you can fish; you can also climb down the rocks downstream from the power plant. I occasionally fish here because it yields good fish, but I don't linger for long; this area gets a lot of sightseers, and it's also the put-in spot for kayakers and rafters.

Ripogenus Gorge, which extends for about a mile below the hydro plant dam, is off-limits to the vast majority of anglers. The sheer granite walls prohibit access, and the angling potential of the gorge remains a secret from all but a very few fly-fishers. I know of only one guide, Ian Cameron of Penobscot Drift Boats, who offers fishing trips through Ripogenous Gorge. Cameron, probably the most knowledgeable guide on the river, got his start as a kayaker. Years ago he started stowing a fly-rod in his kayak and began exploring "Rip" Gorge. A few years back, he founded his guiding service by offering drift-boat trips on the lower sections of the West Branch, but he soon purchased a special raft and began taking passengers through the gorge. I was privileged to be the first client he took into Ripogenous Gorge, and it's a trip I'll never forget. The scenery is spectacular, and really big fish lurk in the deep, black holes in this part of the river.

Ian Cameron is probably the most expert guide on the West Branch of the Penobscot, and his advice is sound.

"Even though it opens April 1 for fishing," Cameron told me recently, "the best fishing is from the middle of May through the first two weeks of July. It picks up again from Labor Day to the close of the season on September 30."

I commented that it's too bad that the season on the West Branch isn't extended until the end of October, but he disagreed.

"Even though the landlocks spawn in November and December, the West Branch has a natural reproducing population of salmon. The biologists feel that these wild salmon don't need the trauma of being fished right before they spawn. If you want to fish in the late fall, there are other places to go, such as the East Outlet of the Kennebec."

What are Cameron's favorite West Branch flies?

"Gray Ghost, and the Black Ghost with a marabou wing. The Ripogenus Smelt and the Montreal Whore are also good patterns.

"The West Branch has good caddis- and stonefly hatches," he added. "Tan caddis and claret caddis. A size 16 stonefly dry fly tied with a Day-Glo green body and white wings does a nice job of imitating a bright green stonefly you'll find on the river. There's the usual grouping of early-summer

The West Branch of the Penobscot is considered the best landlocked salmon river in the country.

mayflies, as well as a hatch of sulphur mayflies. The sulphurs are sporadic, but they're there.

"I like a full-sinking line when fishing streamers on the West Branch, but a sinking tip will also work. Some of the pools are very deep. A 7- or 8-weight outfit works best for chuckin' streamers, but you can scale back to a 5- or 6-weight for the dry flies."

For most of us (I have fished through Ripogenous Gorge only twice myself), the next available spot to fish is a pool called Little Eddy. Most of the local anglers launch canoes or small boats at Little Eddy, paddle to the middle of the pool, and drop anchor. Although I do a lot of fishing and hunting from a canoe, I've never felt confident enough to canoe the swirling waters here; I'm too nervous about getting swept into the fast, dangerous water downriver. I suggest not fishing Little Eddy from a boat unless you are an expert paddler; there are simply too many more fishing trips to enjoy to risk an accident. But don't despair; I once visited Little Eddy in the evening at the height of the hatch, and there were several fish rising right along the bank. I don't think there's really any reason to get out in the middle of the pool.

The next logical place to fish the West Branch is upstream of the Telos

Road bridge. This is a popular area among fly-fishers, but the wading can be very tricky; one false step and you're up to your neck (or higher) in the river. Your best bet might be to leave the waders in the car and rock-hop along the edge of the river. There is plenty of good holding water containing salmon and book trout along the side.

Another popular area of the West Branch is accessed by crossing the river on the Telos Road bridge, turning right, and driving through the campground down to the water. The river in this stretch is fast, but the wading is fairly easy. This area contains some very large salmon.

Going downriver from the Telos Road bridge, Golden Road follows the West Branch, providing many access points to the river. From here on out, most of the accessible areas of the river are fairly easy to wade. Just remember that the West Branch of the Penobscot is a tailwater and subject to rapid rises in water level. Still, because it's a tailwater, the water remains cool and the fishing is good throughout most of the summer.

Some folks are a little dismayed by the number of rafters using the West Branch. Yes, the river gets crowded on summer weekends. However, this is a wide river that can accommodate a lot of traffic, and so is managed as a multiple-use waterway. Look at it this way: Because the white-water enthusiasts enjoy clean and clear rivers as much as we do, they are our natural allies in protecting this important natural resource. Try to keep that thought in mind the next time your solitude is broken by a group of boaters.

One of the best dry flies is a pattern called the West Branch Dry Fly. This unusual fly imitates a wounded smelt floating on the surface of the water. It can be cast upstream and fished with a dead drift, but it works better if given an occasional twitch. The West Branch Dry Fly triggers fierce rises from the salmon living in the West Branch.

The West Branch Dry Fly has a closed-cell foam core covered with pearl E-Z Body tubing. Its overall length is 3 to 4 inches. Similar floating bait fish imitations are being used today for all types of fishing, and you'll probably be able to find something very similar in your favorite fly shop.

THE KENNEBEC RIVER

Maps *The Maine Atlas and Gazetteer,* Maps 20, 21, 30, 40, and 41.

Description The Kennebec is one of the longest rivers in the state of Maine. It begins at Moosehead Lake, where the West and East Outlets flow out of the lake. The outlets converge at Indian Pond, about 3 miles from Moosehead. The Kennebec flows south out of Indian Pond, and converges with the Dead River at a place called The Forks. Much of the Kennebec from Indian Pond to The Forks is remote and inaccessible except by canoe. The river quickly widens from The Forks to Moscow, where it flows into Wyman Lake.

The Kennebec continues southward until it reaches the head of tide in Augusta. Much of the river below Wyman Lake is wide and provides many opportunities for float trips.

Access There are four favorite places to fish the Kennebec. The first is the East Outlet. Take ME 15 north out of Greenville for about 8 miles. The highway passes over the river, and there is ample parking and room to wade. The Forks, where the Kennebec and Dead Rivers meet, is the next popular fishing destination. Take US 201 north out of Moscow into the township of West Forks. The highway follows the east side of the Kennebec, offering access. Third, the section of the river below Wyman Dam in Moscow is accessed from the west side from ME 16. The final likely place to fish, and one of the best, is the section of the river below Shawmut Dam in Fairfield.

Best Assets Depending on where you fish, the Kennebec features brook trout, landlocked salmon, rainbow trout, and brown trout. The fish will rise to prolific hatches, offering fine opportunities to cast dry flies to large fish. The section of the river from the East and West Outlets to The Forks is big woods full of moose, bears, deer, and ruffed grouse. The sections of the river below Wyman and Shawmut Dams offers excellent wading.

Biggest Drawbacks Because of the distances involved, it's difficult to make the East Outlet a day trip; it's best to spend a couple of days to fish. This section of the river also sees a lot of anglers. The sections below Wyman and Shawmut Dams can also be quite busy. But that's the way it is with good water.

Regulations The Kennebec is a long river, and passes through several lakes and dams. As a result, different sections of the river are governed by different regulations. Although this can lead to some confusion and frustration on the part of anglers trying to obey the law, these regulations are designed to protect and enhance the fisheries in the various parts of the Kennebec.

You should consult the latest edition of the *Maine Open Water Fishing Regulations* booklet for specifics, but here is an outline of the regulations governing the Kennebec.

From the East Outlet to Indian Pond: Fly-fishing only. Open to fishing from May 1 to October 31. From May 1 to September 30, the total daily creel limit for trout and salmon is one fish (the minimum length on brook trout is 12 inches; on salmon, 14 inches). From October 1 to October 31, fly-fishing only, catch-and-release only.

From the West Outlet to Indian Pond: Open to fishing from May 1 to October 31. From May 1 to September 30, the daily creel limit for trout is two fish. From October 1 to October 31, artificial lures only, and all fish must be immediately released.

From Indian Pond to Central Maine Power Dam in Skowhegan: Open to

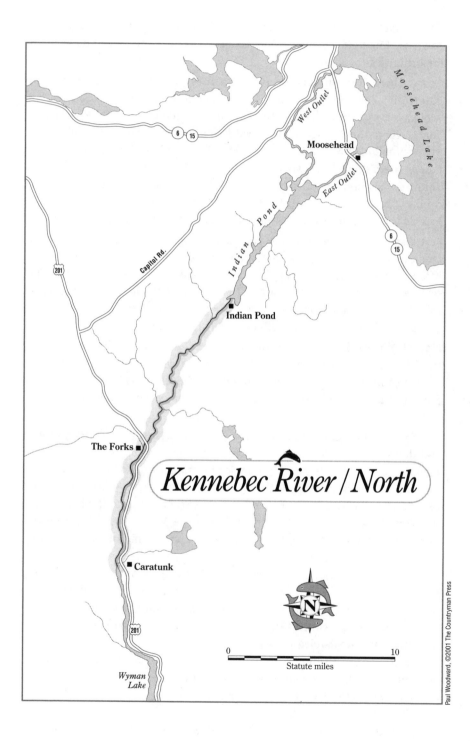

Kennebec *River* / *North*

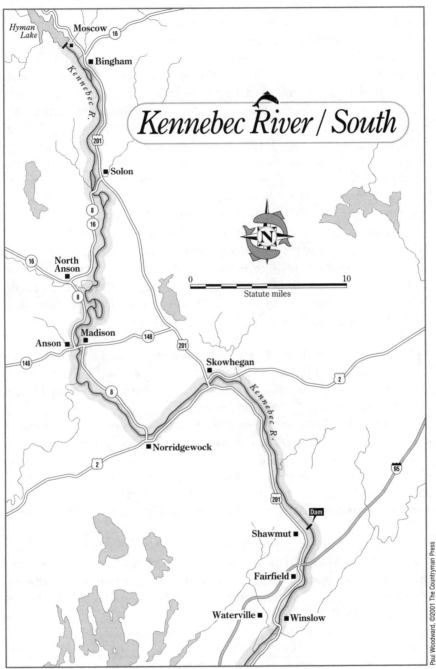

Kennebec River / South

Hyman Lake

Moscow 16

Bingham

Kennebec R.

201

Solon

8
16

16

North Anson

8

Madison 148

Anson 201

148

Skowhegan 2

8

Norridgewock

2

95

201

Dam

Shawmut

Fairfield

Waterville Winslow

N

0   10
Statute miles

fishing from April 1 to October 31. The daily creel limit on trout and salmon is two fish (the minimum length for brook trout is 10 inches; the minimum length for salmon, brown, and rainbow trout is 12 inches). From August 16 to October 31, artificial lures only.

From Central Maine Power Dam in Skowhegan to the head of tide in Augusta: Open to year-round fishing. The total daily creel limit on trout and salmon is two fish (the minimum length for trout and salmon is 12 inches).

Important exceptions to these regulations are the laws pertaining to the popular section of the river below Shawmut Dam. This water is fly-fishing only. The daily creel limit for trout and salmon is one fish (the minimum length is 16 inches). These strict regulations are helping to produce a fine trophy fishery in the Shawmut section of the Kennebec. I know quite a few serious fly-fishers who would be happy if the Shawmut section of the river was governed under catch-and-release regulations.

Favorite Flies Black Ghost (#2–8), Gray Ghost (#4–8), Muddler Minnow (#4–6), Colonel Bates (#4–8), Mickey Finn (#4–8), Royal Wulff (#12–14), Green Comparadun (#12), Brown Comparadun (#12), Hare's Ear Nymph (#12–16), Elk Hair Caddis (#12–18), Royal Coachman (#10–14), Hendrickson (#14–16), Olive Sparkle Caddis Pupa (#12–16), Brown Sparkle Caddis Pupa (#12–16), Humpy (#12–14).

The Kennebec River is an extremely important river in the history of Maine. It opened the state's interior to trappers and missionaries. Hard-scrabble loggers soon followed, and the lumbering and shipbuilding industries flourished along the banks of the Kennebec.

Much of the Kennebec River flows through forested, tough-to-access areas. You can take a canoe trip down the river, and a growing number of guide services are offering western-style drift-boat trips for anglers. These guides are in tune with the local hatches and can get you into sections of the river that receive the least amount of fishing pressure. On the other hand, there are several easily accessed parts of the river that offer excellent fishing.

Let's begin with the West Outlet of the Kennebec. It's 8 miles long, flowing from Moosehead Lake to Indian Pond. The West Outlet is accessed by driving 16 miles north on ME 15 out of Greenville, Maine. ME 15 crosses over the East Outlet. Look for a campground where you can launch a canoe and fish the quiet pool below the bridge.

The East Outlet is one of the Kennebec's most popular fishing spots. It flows from a dam on Moosehead Lake, and is easily found by driving 11 miles on ME 15 north out of Greenville. ME 15 crosses the East Outlet, and there is ample parking on both sides of the river.

Many anglers fish from the top of the dam, but it's almost impossible to lift a fish up the side of this 20-foot-high structure. There is plenty of wadable water downriver from the dam. The East Outlet below the dam is big, fast water requiring careful wading: Felt-soled waders and a wading staff are musts.

A gravel road follows the west side of the East Outlet, but travel is limited for low-slung vehicles. A good bet is to fish a huge, gravel-bottomed pool about half a mile south of ME 15. This section of the river contains good landlocked salmon and is fairly easy to fish. The East Outlet also contains brook trout averaging more than 12 inches in length.

Ian Cameron, owner of Penobscot Drift Boats, is one of the most knowledgeable guides on the East Outlet. He has plenty of good insights for visiting and fishing the East Outlet.

What's the best time of the year to fish the East Outlet?

"From Memorial Day to the end of June," said Cameron. "And then, starting after Labor Day until the end of October. It's one of the few rivers that's open to catch-and-release fishing until the end of October.

"It's not that you can't score on some beautiful fish at other times," he

The East Outlet of the Kennebec is wide and fast. It is also an excellent place to catch large landlocked salmon.

added. "For example, my wife caught a 22-inch salmon during the heat of the day in August."

And you're mostly fishing for landlocked salmon?

"Primarily salmon," said Cameron, "but there are also brook trout. It seems that the brook trout fishery has been improving over the past few years. These are stocked trout, but the Department of Inland Fisheries and Wildlife has created spawning beds for these fish. The spawning beds are marked with signs, and it is considered unsporting—at the least—to fish over them. If you do fish over the spawning beds, it's likely that someone will chuck a rock in your direction."

What's Cameron's choice in flies?

"In the spring it's the Gray Ghost, Winnipesaukie Smelt, and the Black Ghost. In the spring it seems that the salmon also prefer flies with a little bit of purple. As the season progresses, the East Outlet has some wonderful hatches and the fish do rise. Caddis- and stoneflies are very important. In the spring big Black and Golden Stonefly Nymphs work very well."

Cameron noted that the salmon rise to the adult stoneflies flittering over the water. "Stimulators work very well when the fish are turned on to the adult stoneflies—Olive and Royal Stimulators. When adult caddis are on the water, try light green, olive, brown, tan, and gray caddisflies tied all the way down to size 20. Also, in the summer try Olive and Black Woolly Buggers, and don't forget a selection of caddis pupae: olive, tan, and brown.

"In the fall one of the best streamers is the Montreal Whore. The body is fluorescent orange wool wrapped on the hook with a silver tinsel rib. The bucktail underwing is sparse blue, over sparse white, with sparse red on top. I add a few strands of pearl Krystal Flash to the underwing. The wing is a bunch of white marabou tied on top.

"Also in the fall, the fish seem to enjoy a Gray Ghost tied with a Day-Glo orange body.

"There's also very good mayfly hatches on the East Outlet," Cameron continued. "This past year there were excellent hatches of Hendricksons."

What about tackle selection?

"For hurling big streamers, a 7-weight works about the best. At other times, a 9-foot-long 6-weight is fine."

The East Outlet is only 3 miles long. Both the East and West Outlets flow into Indian Pond and form the main stem of the Kennebec River. It should be noted that Indian Pond is home to a good population of strong smallmouth bass.

Whether you're fishing for trout, salmon, or bass, favorite patterns include Mickey Finns, Matukas, Muddler Minnows, and Woolly Buggers.

As an added bonus, this section of the Kennebec River is open to fishing until October 30. You'll see few NO TRESPASSING signs in this part of

Maine, so you can also bring along your grouse gun and enjoy a bit of bird hunting. If you want to hunt really big game, you can enter the lottery to win a moose-hunting permit, but these coveted licenses are extremely hard to come by. Still, if you visit during the second full week in October, you'll see hunters returning to Greenville to have their moose tagged by game wardens and then turned over to the local butchers. This is a great time to be in Greenville; the entire town takes on a type of party atmosphere you can find only where fishing, hunting, and other traditional outdoors sports are still held in high regard.

The next most likely section for fly-fishers to try is below the confluence of the Dead and Kennebec Rivers. The flow in this part of the river is controlled by the dam at Indian Pond, and water levels fluctuate greatly. When the water is low, you'll find wading easy; when the water is high, wading is almost impossible. Still, this section of the Kennebec, near an area called The Forks, remains a productive and popular place to fish. When the water is down, you can find many nice pools and runs by hiking up the north side of the river. The Forks are reached by driving US 201 north out of Caratunk, Maine.

The section of the river below Wyman Dam is one of the best areas in the state to enjoy good opening-day fishing. While snow might still linger in the shadows beneath the pines, and most ponds and lakes are still locked in ice, the fast water below the dam is clear and offers fast fishing for land-locked salmon and rainbow trout, some weighing more than 6 pounds. Favorite patterns in spring are Gray Ghosts, Black Ghosts, Nine-Threes, and any of the other popular New England streamers.

The Kennebec River below Wyman Dam remains an excellent fishing destination throughout the summer. The water flows from the bottom of the dam and remains cool until August. Good flies in summer are weighted nymphs and attractor dry flies such as Humpies and Wulffs.

It's easy to find this middle part of the Kennebec. Some of the very best fishing is found right below Wyman Dam. Follow US 201 south out of Moscow and look for a road clearly marked as leading to the dam. There is a rough boat launch on the west side of the Kennebec on ME 16 opposite the town of Bingham, and you can also launch a canoe on the east side where US 201A crosses the river in Solon. This particular area has good hatches of mayflies and caddisflies in June.

The final section of the river worthy of serious consideration is below Shawmut Dam. Mike Holt, the owner of Fly-fishing Only, considers this area of the river above I-95 his home waters. Fly-fishing Only is a first-class fly shop situated only 37 feet from the river.

"The best times to fish the Shawmut area of the Kennebec are May and June, and then again in September and October," Holt told me. "The dominant fish is brown trout; the secondary species is rainbow trout. And it's not unusual to hook a 20-inch trout. The state stocks approximately 5,000 to 6,000 brown trout every year, and the Kennebec Valley Chapter of Trout Unlimited stocks an additional 2,000 rainbows. We have a good rainbow fishery, as well as a good brown trout fishery.

"However, there's very little natural reproduction. I've talked to the biologists about it, and they say that while there is a little reproduction taking place, the young-of-the-year trout are sensitive to high water temperatures. We do get higher water temperatures during the end of July and August, and the juveniles just don't make it."

Although this section of the Kennebec is a tailwater, Holt said that the water is rarely so deep as to prevent wading.

"The river drops during the first couple of weeks of May, and remains wadable throughout the summer and fall. The only time it rises again is when there is what they call a 'significant rain event.'"

"What's unique about the Shawmut fishery," Holt continued, "is that below the dam, for approximately 600 yards, you have all wadable water. I don't know of so much wadable water on any other part of the Kennebec. And this is pretty mild-mannered wading; it's not a steep gradient, there aren't strong flows, and there aren't many large boulders."

What about fly selection? Holt started with spring.

"Starting in May, our hatches run the gamut. When the temperature of the water reaches the mid-40s, sometime in May, we start seeing the blue-winged olives. Then, during the end of May and June, we'll see the quill Gordons, the blue quills, and the Hendricksons."

"Toward the end of May and the first of June, we're blessed with having *cornuta*, a larger type of blue-winged olive. They're around size 14."

What about fall?

"We get a lot of white mayflies in September," said Holt. "They hatch and lay their eggs almost simultaneously; they don't go to the streamside vegetation and return to mate. A size 14 White Wulff is a very popular pattern for matching the white mayfly. The white mayfly is a blessing in September, because all of the other insects are so small that time of the year."

In autumn the big trout also feed on small alewives, sea-run bait fish that ascend Maine rivers in spring and early summer.

"We refer to it as the alewife hatch," continued Holt. "The IF&W [Maine Inland Fisheries and Wildlife] traps and trucks alewives to ponds they normally can't reach. It's been a great success. They take some of the alewives to a pond that empties into the Kennebec above the Shawmut Dam. The alewives eventually migrate back into the river and school up above the dam. If we get a good rain and flush of water, or the dam operator opens the gates to allow the alewives to pass downstream, it becomes hog heaven. All of the big fish come up into the wading area below the dam to feed on the alewives. You'll see the big brown trout herding the alewives, just like striped bass herding and cornering bait fish. You'll see the alewives jumping out of the water trying to get away from the brown trout, and the seagulls will dive into the alewives from the air. You'll see big V-wakes, which are the trout chasing the alewives. It's really something to see."

What fly would you use when the big trout are turned on to the alewives?

"I like a Ballou Special. I tie this pattern on a size 6 or 4, 6X-long streamer hook. I tie on a lot of peacock herl on the top to imitate the dark back of an alewife."

Holt suggested using standard tackle for fishing the Kennebec River. "It's hard to go wrong with a 5- or 6-weight outfit. I do the majority of my fishing with a 9-foot-long, 5-weight rod. This is a good, all-purpose rod."

Beyond the first 600 yards of wadable water below the Shawmut Dam, Holt suggested taking a float trip. He offers guided float trips, but you can also float the river from your own canoe.

"It's not the most popular thing to do, but if you want to enjoy some really great fishing, you can float the river. This trip starts at the end of the wadable water below the dam and lasts for about 3 miles into the takeout in Fairfield. This is all good water, and no one fishes it. It's also very safe, Class I water. There are only three riffles in this section; there are no rapids that go across the entire river."

A special mention should be made of the Kennebec Valley Chapter of Trout Unlimited. This group of local anglers won Trout Unlimited's Golden Trout Award for 1999, the highest honor TU gives to a local chapter. The Kennebec Valley Chapter received the prestigious award for its work in the removal of Edwards Dam in downtown Augusta, Maine. On the Kennebec below Shawmut Dam, the chapter conducts river cleanups and buys rainbow trout for stocking. It also fights to maintain strict trophy regulations, a laudable goal in a state where so many anglers continue to gauge the quality of the fishing by how many fish rather than how many memories they take home.

There are many more miles of the Kennebec to fish before it reaches the Atlantic Ocean, but they contain mostly smallmouth bass, striped bass, and other nontrout species. There is also a very small run of Atlantic salmon. Because of the Kennebec's wide variety of fish, many local anglers spend their entire lives fishing this river to the exclusion of almost any other. You could fish for the Kennebec for a couple of weeks and just scratch the surface of what this magnificent waterway has to offer.

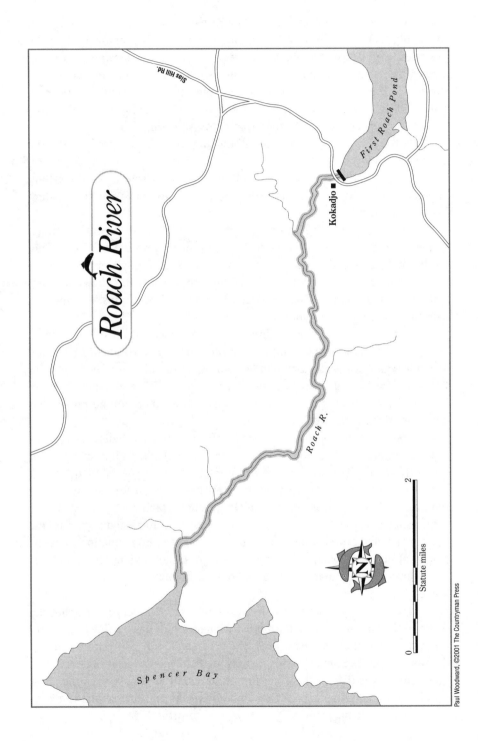

Roach River

Sias Hill Rd.

First Roach Pond

Kokadjo

Roach R.

Spencer Bay

N

0   2

Statute miles

Paul Woodward, ©2001 The Countryman Press

THE ROACH RIVER

Map *The Maine Atlas and Gazetteer,* Map 41.

Description The Roach is a small but important river in central Maine. It begins at First Roach Pond and flows for about 7 miles before entering Spencer Bay in Moosehead Lake. The Roach is a moderately wide, wadable river offering excellent fishing for landlocked salmon and brook trout.

Access Take Lily Bay Road north out of Greenville, Maine. Drive approximately 15 miles to the town of Kokadjo. The Roach River flows from below a dam on First Roach Pond. Look for paths leading down the sides of the river and to the pools.

Best Asset In spring and fall the Roach river offers excellent fishing for salmon and brook trout. Fall is an especially good time for salmon.

Biggest Drawback It's tough to easily access much of the river. As a result, those pools that are accessible get quite crowded. In fall I've met anglers on other rivers who said they tried fishing the Roach, but left because of all the crowds.

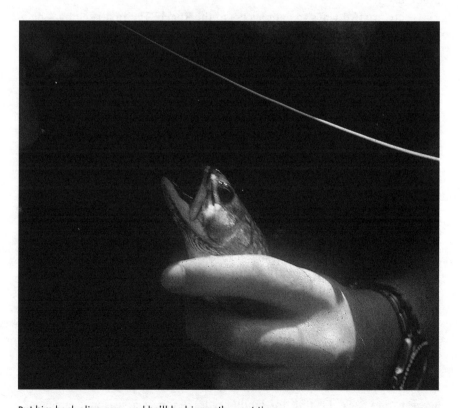

Put him back alive now, and he'll be bigger the next time.

Regulations From the dam at First Roach Pond downstream to the red markers on the shore at Moosehead Lake, the river is open to fishing from May 1 to September 30. Fly-fishing only. All fish must be released alive at once.

Flies Hornberg (#6–10), Gray Ghost (#4–8), Black Ghost (#4–8), Mickey Finn (#6–8), Olive Woolly Bugger (#6–8), Black Woolly Bugger (#6–8), Brown Woolly Bugger (#6–8), Muddler Minnow (#4–8), Woolly Worm (#6–8), Royal Coachman (#6–10), Ballou Special (#4–8), Hare's Ear Nymph (#8–14), Pheasant Tail Nymph (#8–14), Bead Head Nymph (#8–14), Olive Sparkle Caddis Pupa (#8–14), Brown Sparkle Caddis Pupa (#8–14), Cream Sparkle Caddis Pupa (#8–14), Olive Caddis Larva (#8–14), Brown Caddis Larva (#8–14), Elk Hair Caddis (#10–14), Adams (#10–14), Light Cahill (#12–16), Green Drake (#4–6), March Brown (#8–12).

The Roach River is one of the streams on the must-fish lists of anglers making the swing through central Maine near Baxter State Park. It's easily accessed and offers good landlocked salmon fishing, with some fish weighing up to 4 pounds. The Roach River also contains some excellent brook trout.

There are two ways to gain access to the Roach. The first is along a path starting in the tiny town of Kokadjo. This path leads to a series of good pools that are easy to wade. The second alternative is to launch a boat at Jewett Cove on Moosehead Lake and motor to the mouth of the river. Here you will find several good pools that hold fish.

GRAND LAKE STREAM

Map *The Maine Atlas and Gazetteer,* Map 35.

Description Grand Lake Stream is a short, medium-wide river flowing out of West Grand Lake and into Big Lake in eastern Maine. The river contains brook trout and smallmouth bass, but the main attraction—bringing anglers from all over the country—is landlocked salmon. The streambanks are mostly wooded, wading isn't difficult, and you'll have a chance at catching a trophy salmon.

Access Take US 1 north out of Princeton, Maine. A paved road on the left leads to Grand Lake Stream (look for the signs). This road leads into the village of Grand Lake Stream Plantation. The stream runs through the center of this small village; you won't miss it.

Best Asset Grand Lake Stream is geared toward serving sportsmen and -women. There are lodges and cabins to fit every pocketbook, guides, and a general store that carries all the basics (flies, tackle, food, et cetera).

Biggest Drawbacks Fishing for landlocked salmon is a seasonal endeavor;

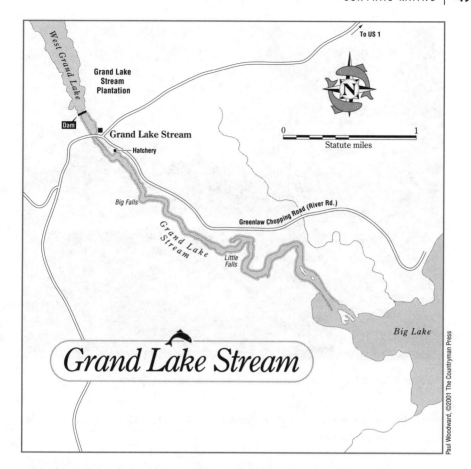

once the water gets too warm, from about the middle of July until the middle of autumn, forget it. Grand Lake Stream can also get very crowded, but most of the anglers are friendly.

Regulations Fly-fishing only. Legal fishing season is April 1 to October 20. From April 1 to August 16, the daily limit on trout is two fish, and the limit on salmon is one fish. From August 16 to September 30, the total bag limit is one fish. From October 1 to October 20, all fish must be immediately released.

Favorite Flies Barnes Special (#6–8), Gray Ghost (#4–8), Black Ghost (#4–8), Mickey Finn (#6–8), Olive Woolly Bugger (#6–8), Black Woolly Bugger (#6–8), Brown Woolly Bugger (#6–8), Muddler Minnow (#4–8), Woolly Worm (#6–8), Royal Coachman (#6–10), Ballou Special (#4–8), Hare's Ear Nymph (#8–14), Pheasant Tail Nymph (#8–14), Bead Head Nymph (#8–14), Olive Sparkle Caddis Pupa (#8–14), Brown Sparkle Caddis Pupa (#8–14), Cream Sparkle Caddis Pupa (#8–14), Olive Caddis Larva (#8–14), Brown Caddis Larva (#8–14), Elk Hair Caddis (#10–14), Hendrickson (#14), Royal

The dam at Grand Lake Stream. Both sides of the river offer good fishing.

Wulff (#12), Adams (#10–14), Light Cahill (#12–16), Green Drake (#4–6), March Brown (#8–12).

Few of northern New England's rivers rival Grand Lake Stream for importance in the history of fly-fishing. While Maine is famous for its contributions to the development of streamers, the first of these flies may have been used—in Maine, at least—at Grand Lake Stream.

Col. Joseph Bates Jr., the noted fly-fishing historian, told a delightful story about the first of these flies. In his book *Streamer Fly Tying and Fishing*, Bates quoted a story from the April 1910 edition of *National Sportsman* magazine. According to the author of that article:

> There was a time when the chanticleers of Grand Lake Stream used to rule the yards with uplifted white tails; but their pride was crushed when a guide named Alonzo Stickney Bacon demonstrated that a hen's long feathers made attractive lures for ouananiche (landlocked salmon). This is how it came about.
>
> Alonzo was in his canoe, fishing with artificial flies. He could not get a rise. He was seated on a cushion filled with hen's feathers. There was a hole in the cushion and a long white feather protruded. Alon-

zo plucked the feather from the cushion, tied it to a hook, and used it as a lure. The ouananiche took it with avidity. Other fishermen copied the lure. Soon in all the barnyards of the plantations all of the hens were rifled of their caudel appendages, and the stream was flecked with anglers using a long straggly fly, misnamed by Boston flymakers the Morning Glory. All things great are wound up in some things little, but I am convinced that this recital is true.

No one knows if Alonzo Stickney Bacon really was the first Mainer to tie a streamer. What's important is that a simple fly, known locally as Rooster's Regret, became the model for numerous other long-feathered streamers. These flies were little more than a few feathers, almost always in the natural colors as they came from the chickens, tied to the hooks; an extravagant Rooster's Regret would have a tinsel body. These flies were designed to imitate smelt, a favorite bait fish of the region's large landlocked salmon and trout.

Grand Lake Stream is famous for another important contribution: the Grand Lake canoe. Before the development of gasoline-powered outboard motors, anglers fished the surrounding lakes using traditional canoes, and a visiting sport could hire a guide and canoe for $2 per day. When outboard motors were introduced, someone got the idea of sawing the pointed end off the stern of a canoe and filling the hole with a flat board for mounting a motor. With a motorized square-stern canoe, an angler could cover far more territory and spend more time fishing rather than paddling. This craft was also safer because the passengers could get off a lake quickly when the weather turned foul. More important, a guide using a motorized canoe could charge $5 per day. That's all most guides had to hear before they demanded that local boatbuilders develop a craft suited to their needs.

A Grand Lake canoe, known locally as a Grand Laker, is usually about 20 feet long, beamy, and has a high, rounded bow. A 10-horsepower motor mounted on the square stern can whisk the canoe and its occupants up and down the tree-lined shores of Maine's lakes. Grand Lakers are still handcrafted in the village of Grand Lake Stream, and they adorn the yards and poke out of the barns and garages of many local homes. As one craftsman said, "If it's not made in Grand Lake Stream, it's not a Grand Laker."

Grand Lake Stream flows through the heart of Grand Lake Stream Plantation, a small village that caters mostly to anglers and hunters. Some year-round inhabitants work in the logging industry, and a couple trap during the winter, but the most important activities are still fishing and hunting. Grand Lake Stream isn't a long piece of water, so it's the perfect destination for anyone interested in a weekend fishing trip.

Grand Lake Stream flows out of West Grand Lake, an immense body of water containing lake trout, brook trout, landlocked salmon, and smallmouth bass. The stream flows for about 2½ miles through a mixed-hard-wood and fir forest before flowing into Big Lake. Although it's relatively short, Grand Lake Stream contains fast pocket water, long glides, big salmon, and the occasional brook trout.

Grand Lake Stream, which is governed by fly-fishing-only regulations, begins at West Grand Lake by pouring over a small timber-and-rock dam. Below the dam is the Dam Pool (what else?), the first major fishing area of the stream. There is ample parking near the dam, and you can look out over the Dam Pool from your automobile.

The Dam Pool is a big, swirling hole of cold water; while there are other major pools on the stream, nothing matches the width and depth of this one. There is easy access to both sides of the Dam Pool—you can walk over the top of the dam to get to the other side of the stream—and fishing from either bank is productive. You'll see two options when you look down Grand Lake Stream from the top of the dam. On your right a small embankment leads down to the stream. At the base of the embankment is a sandbar providing safe, comfortable wading. Since you must wade out onto this sandbar to get to the fishable water, you'll have plenty of room for your backcast. The left bank of the Dam Pool is lined with rocks and small boulders, and the water is too deep to wade. The trees lining this bank limit your casting room, but the water at your feet holds fish; a roll cast will get your fly over any salmon holding in this side of the pool.

The overflow from the Dam Pool glides out of the back end of the pool, flows through a fairly narrow channel—about 50 feet wide—and passes by a landlocked salmon hatchery operated by the Maine Department of Inland Fisheries and Wildlife. There is parking available at the hatchery, and you can walk along the bank and fish. The current here is fast and strong, and wading is best done near shore with the aid of a wading staff. This is a chal-lenging area to fish, and a nymph cast upstream and allowed to drift with the current can be productive. Casting a streamer across the current will also raise fish.

At the end of the hatchery is the popular Hatchery Pool. A lot of anglers fish this area, but I don't think it contains any more fish than other spots on the river; it's just close to the sporting lodges. This is also an easy area to wade and can accommodate several fishermen. When I go to Grand Lake Stream, I occasionally fish the Dam and Hatchery Pools. They contain fish, but seem to hold just as many anglers. I usually concentrate my efforts down-stream; sometimes I don't even stop to look at the Dam and Hatchery Pools.

Greenlaw Chopping Road, also known as River Road, parallels Grand Lake Stream and takes you to other, more forested spots on the river. I've never seen a sign for Greenlaw Chopping Road—I discovered its name on a map—but it's easy to find. The road begins in the center of town and heads

Netting a fall salmon on Grand Lake Stream.

south toward Big Lake. As you drive, you'll pass several footpaths leading through the woods to the right. These paths head to the river and are worth exploring. Some lead to fast pocket water requiring nimble wading; others take you to sedate pools that are more comfortable to fish. Except for the occasional rustic cabin, these sections of the stream are wooded and beautiful.

Continuing along Greenlaw Chopping Road, you'll pass a dirt road and a wooden sign maintained by the Grand Lake Stream Guides Association. At one time you could pull off of the paved road here and drive up to the river. Today the association gates the dirt road and maintains a small parking area near the road. From the parking area it's a very short walk to the river, and this change is helping to preserve the beauty of Grand Lake Stream.

This part of the river, which is the end of the easily accessible water, offers several fishing opportunities. When you walk down from the parking area, you'll see a large pool flowing from a remote section of the stream. The pool flows from the right, makes a fast curve away from you, and dumps over a small waterfall called Little Falls. This pool contains small boulders and several deep cuts, but it's easy to wade. I've caught many nice salmon here, and both streamers and nymphs produce fish. There are two productive ways to fish this pool. First, you can walk along the bank and enter the stream at the head of the pool. Here the stream is lined with medium-sized gravel and is easy to wade. Start by casting a streamer to the far bank, then let the fly swing across the current. Make a cast, step downstream, and make another cast. Repeat this procedure until you cover the entire pool.

The second approach is to begin fishing at the back end of the pool and cast a nymph or dry fly upstream. Allow the fly to drift with the current; in the case of the nymph, pay attention for the slightest twitch or hesitation of the line indicating a strike. I have used this method to catch many large fish here.

Below this big pool are several other areas you should consider fishing. An abandoned dirt road follows the river for a distance of about 100 yards and takes you to a mix of riffle and pocket water, all containing fish.

The dirt road eventually peters out into a path. Most visiting anglers don't explore this path and miss out on one of the most beautiful and productive pools on the river: the Meadows, a long, slow pool flowing through a marshy area of the stream. The Meadows itself is a little too slow to attract many salmon, but fish lie at the tail of the pool where the current speeds up. During the early evening at the end of May and the first half of June, this area can come alive as big salmon rise to a host of hatching mayflies and caddisflies.

It's important to remember that the water flowing out of West Grand Lake passes through a very small dam. As a result, the temperature of the water in the stream is strongly influenced by the surface temperature of the lake. During summer, as the temperature of the lake increases, the temperature of the stream rises, too. Fishing action slows by the middle of July and remains tough throughout August; by the first of August, many fish simply flee the stream for the deeper, cooler water in the lakes.

There are three times of the year to visit Grand Lake Stream and know you'll at have a chance at catching a big (3- to 5-pound) landlocked salmon. This stream is one of New England's traditional opening-day fishing destinations. Salmon enter the river in fall to spawn and remain in the stream throughout winter. In spring these fish provide fast action for anglers willing to brave the cold. Streamers are the best choice for this early-season fishing; be sure to dress warmly and bring a thermos of hot chocolate. The season begins April 1, and there's a good chance that snow will be lingering in the shadows of the trees.

If you're not interested in fishing with ice on your rod guides, visit Grand Lake Stream at the end of May. This is when the hatches begin, and you can enjoy some of the best dry-fly-fishing of the year. The most important insect is locally known as the brown caddis. This hatch begins near the end of May and continues for about two weeks. The hatch starts as the sun drops over the horizon and lasts until dark. During this period the surface of the water is covered with swirling masses of caddisflies, and salmon eagerly strike a size 12 Elk Hair Caddis. Although Grand Lake Stream can be crowded with anglers throughout the day, I usually have the main pools to myself during the height of the brown caddis hatch; most visitors return to the lodges for supper and miss the best fishing!

While the brown caddis hatch is *the* dry-fly fishing event of the year on Grand Lake Stream, several mayflies also get the attention of the fish. March browns and dark Hendricksons are fairly common. A size 14 Dark Hendrickson is an excellent all-around imitation for matching the mayfly hatches. Sometimes, even at the height of the brown caddis hatch, a Dark Hendrickson catches more fish than any other fly.

September brings frosty nights and cooler water temperatures. The salmon start reentering the stream by the middle of September. Now we're getting into my favorite time of the year on Grand Lake Stream: the fall spawning run.

For years the fishing season closed on the last day of September. This was unfortunate, because often the salmon run was just beginning to heat up. In recent years the closing of the season on Grand Lake Stream, and a few other choice waters in Maine, has been pushed back to October 15. Now you can visit Grand Lake Stream in fall and be assured that the salmon are back in the river. You can do a little duck or grouse hunting, too.

The salmon run varies from year to year; much of it depends on the temperature of the water. If your calendar is open, try scheduling your trip as close to end of the fishing season as possible. This is when the water will be its coolest, the autumn foliage will be its brightest, and the greatest number of salmon will be in the river. Most biologists agree that landlocked salmon are genetically identical to wild sea-run Atlantic salmon. When it comes to the behavior of Grand Lake Stream salmon during the spawning run, I agree: Though a pool may be full of salmon (sometimes you'll see two or three fish around every large rock), they're usually lockjawed. Streamers are the favorite flies during the fall, but I have better success using size 8 and 10 Hare's Ear Nymphs. My technique is simple: I pick out a fish (or an area where I've seen fish) and cast the fly upstream. I allow the nymph to sink and drift through the area, and I stay alert for a strike. If nothing happens, I try again. These salmon don't seem interested in eating at this time of year, and I've found it best to get the fly as close as possible to them, almost sticking it in their mouths. This technique sounds tedious, but it works. I can't tell you the number of times I've seen other anglers march into the stream, cast a streamer for half an hour without success, and leave; I, on the other hand, continue to drift a nymph past the fish until I find a taker. On most October days I catch five or six salmon; not a lot, but each weighs 2 to 3 pounds.

It's easy to plan a fishing trip to Grand Lake Stream. There are lodges in the village as well as cabins for rent. If you'd like more personalized service on the water, guides are also available. On the other hand, if you like going it alone, stop by the Pine Tree Store, the hub of activity in the village. Here you can get the latest information on stream conditions and more specific directions about where to fish.

Today much of Grand Lake Stream is protected from development. Conservation easements and lands purchased for inclusion in the Maine Coast Heritage Trust, a nonprofit organization dedicated to preserving wilderness and waterways for public use, guarantee that future generations of fly-fishers enjoy this historic landlocked-salmon fishery.

Although there are many of square miles of forests and water around Grand Lake Stream Plantation, Grand Lake Stream is a kind of angler's oasis; salmon and trout fishing is marginal in the rest of the area. While you might want to sample the fine fishing in nearby West and East Grand Lakes, Big Lake, and the other lakes and ponds in the area, you will probably want to make one of the lodges in Grand Lake Stream your base of operations.

I've devoted more space to this one stream than to any other piece of water, but I've always wanted to write this little essay. And besides, Grand Lake Stream stands apart from just about any other river in New England. Only the Batten Kill and Upper Dam, Maine, compare in their historical significance in the annals of fly-fishing.

Other Stocked Trout Waters Worth Exploring

Allen Pond (Greene), Bartlett Pond (Livermore), Brettun's Pond (Livermore), Crystal Pond (Turner), Little River (Lisbon), Meadow Brook (Durham), Moose Brook (Auburn), Newell Brook (Durham), Nezinscot River (Turner), Lower Range Pond (Poland), Middle Range Pond (Poland), Upper Range Pond (Poland), Royal River (Auburn), Tripp Pond (Poland), Bernard Pond (Eustis), Beal Pond (Madrid), Blanchard Pond (Alder Stream Township), Bug Eye Pond (Chain of Ponds Township), Clearwater Pond (Industry), Didge Pond (Rangeley), Eddy Pond (Sandy River Plantation), Little Greely Pond (Dallas), Grindstone Pond (Kingfield), Haley Pond (Rangeley), Hills Pond (Perkins Township), Hurricane Pond (Kibby Township), Little Jim Pond (Jim Pond Township), Loon Lake (Dallas), Lufkin Pond (Phillips), McIntire Pond (New Sharon), Midway Pond (Sandy River Plantation), Moxie Pond (Township D), Otter Pond (Chain of Ponds Township), Saddleback Pond (Sandy River Plantation), Schoolhouse Pond (Avon), Staples Pond (Temple), Webb River (Carthage), Flanders Pond (Sullivan), Georges Pond (Franklin), Echo Lake (Fayette), Flying Pond (Vienna), Messalonskee Stream (Waterville), Upper Narrows Pond (Winthrop), Lower Narrows Pond (Winthrop), Sebasticook River (Clinton), Cold River (Stow), Concord River (Albany Township), Saco River (Fryeburg), Spears Stream (Peru), Twitchell Brook (Greenwood), Webb River (Dixfield), Wild River (Batchelders Grant), Cold Stream Pond (Enfield), Fitts Pond (Clifton), Hermon Pond (Hermon), Jerry Pond (Millinocket), Wassataquoik Stream (Township 3, Range 8), Weir Pond (Lee), Abol Pond (Township 2, Range 9), Alder Stream (Atkinson), Upper Bean Pond (Rainbow Township), Bennett Pond (Parkman), Doe Pond (Monson), Fowler Pond (Township 3, Range 11), Frost Pond (Township 3, Range 11), Horseshoe Pond (Willimantic), Lily Pond (Monson), Piper Pond (Abbot), Prong Pond (Greenville), Sebec River (Milo).

Where to Stay in Central Maine

White House Landing Wilderness Camps P.O. Box 749, Millinocket, ME 04462 207-745-5116.

Allagash Gateway Campsite P.O. Box 396, Millinocket, ME 04462 207-723-9215.

Camp Wapiti P.O. Box 340, Patten, ME 04765 207-528-2485.

Frost Pond Camps Box 620E, HCR 76, Greenville, ME 04441 207-695-2821.

Pleasant Point Camps P.O. Box 929, Millinocket, ME 04462 207-746-7464.

Driftwood Lodge P.O. Box 239, Shin Pond, ME 04765 207-528-2936.

Pray's Big Eddy Campground P.O. Box 548, Millinocket, ME 04462 207-723-9581.

Leen's Lodge Grand Lake Stream Plantation, ME 04367 1-800-995-3367.
Indian Rock Camps P.O. Box 117, Grand Lake Stream Plantation, ME 04637
207-796-2822.
Rideout's Lodge Danforth, ME 04424 1-800-594-5391.

Local Guide Services

Penobscot Drift Boats RFD 1, Box 926, Stonington, ME 04681 207-843-
6292.
Matagamon Wilderness Box 220, Patten, ME 04765 207-446-4635.
Mountain Man Guide Service 119 Knox Street, Millinocket, ME 04462
207-723-8500.
Alvah Harriman P.O. Box 156, Grand Lake Stream, ME 04637 207-796-
5494
Gilpatrick's Guide Service P.O. Box 461, Skowhegan, ME 04976
207-453-6959.
Northern Forest Guide Service 403 Aroostook Avenue, Millinocket, ME
04462 207-723-5872.

8 | Maine's Western Mountains

The western mountains of Maine are rich in history and good fishing. You can return many times and almost always fish a new piece of water. Streams and ponds abound, and there are also points of historical interest for visiting anglers.

Plan to try at least a couple of pieces of water when you visit. If you'd like to save a few bucks and don't mind roughing it, the region is peppered with primitive campsites. If you like to camp but still want to take a shower in the evening, or if you vacation in an RV, numerous commercial campgrounds will fill the bill.

Another option is to stay at a full-service sporting camp. Maine's western mountains boast some of the most famous—and oldest—lodges in North America. These are the places that dream trips are made of: rustic cabins, homey lodges, terrific food, and excellent service. Some of these lodges control large acreages that contain many ponds and streams, guaranteeing that the fish receive little pressure from other anglers. Guides are usually available at the lodge (inquire about availability and rates), but your host will be on top of the best fishing and can point you in the right direction.

This region is also known for its wildlife; be sure to bring your camera and plenty of film. Loons, moose, deer, and beavers are common sights, but don't be surprised if you see a black bear.

UPPER DAM

Maps *The Maine Atlas and Gazetteer,* Map 18 and 28.

Description Upper Dam is an old wooden and stone-block dam on the Rapid River between Mooselookmeguntic and Upper Richardson Lakes in Richardson Township. Traveling east on ME 16 in Adamstown Township, look for the dirt road marked UPPER DAM ROAD. The gates near the head of the road are

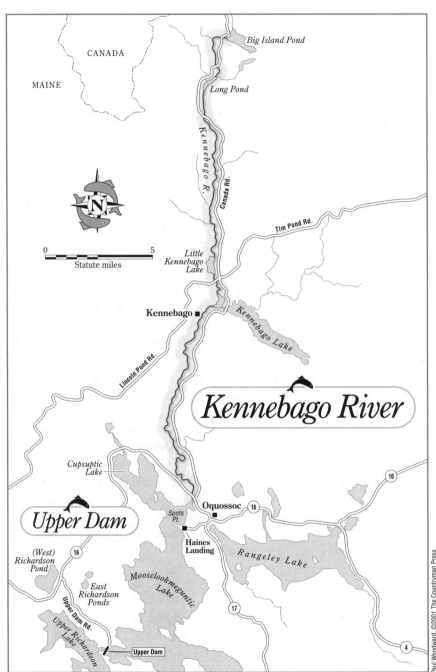

CANADA

MAINE

Big Island Pond

Long Pond

Kennebago R.

Canada Rd.

Tim Pond Rd.

0   5
Statute miles

*Little
Kennebago
Lake*

Kennebago ■

Kennebago Lake

Lincoln Pond Rd.

Kennebago River

*Cupsuptic
Lake*

Upper Dam

*Spots
Pt.*

Oquossoc (16)

(16)

**Haines
Landing**

(West)
*Richardson
Pond*

(16)

Rangeley Lake

*East
Richardson
Ponds*

*Mooselookmeguntic
Lake*

(17)

Upper Dam Rd.

*Upper Richardson
Lake*

Upper Dam

(4)

closed during certain times of year, but there is ample parking. At short walk down Upper Dam Road will take you to the dam.

Access Fish Upper Dam from the platforms at the base of the dam or from the banks. If you don't mind carrying a canoe, you can launch near the base of the dam and fish the middle of the stream (be sure to take an anchor).

Best Assets There are three major assets to visiting Upper Dam. First, you can say you've been there. That sounds silly, but it's true: You'll be visiting one of the most important locations in the history of fly-fishing and fly-tying. Second, there is ample access at the base of the dam and the sides of the river. Finally, there are almost always fish in the pool below Upper Dam. Even in August, when most fish leave the warm rivers for the cooler lakes, you'll see trout and salmon resting along the edges of the casting platforms.

Biggest Drawbacks Upper Dam, after all, is a dam. Its saving grace is that it retains its old look, and the nearby cabins fit the scene perfectly. Still, if you're looking for solitude, Upper Dam is not the place to go; people are always strolling by, and you'll probably have to share the casting platform with at least a couple of other anglers. Also, if the gate on Upper Dam Road is closed, you'll have to hike down to the river.

Regulations Upper Dam is fly-fishing only. It opens to fishing on April 1 and closes October 31. There is a total one-fish-per-day limit on trout and salmon. The trout must be at least 12 inches long, and the salmon must be at least 18 inches. From October 1 to October 31, all fish caught must be immediately released.

Favorite Flies Any Carrie Stevens–style streamer: The Grayhound, Shang's Favorite, Tomahawk, and Lady Miller are just a few examples (#2–8). And how could you visit Upper Dam without fishing Carrie Stevens's most famous fly, the Gray Ghost (#2–8)? After you've paid your respects to the memory of Mrs. Stevens, try these other flies: Edson Dark Tiger (#4–8), Edson Light Tiger (#4–8), Mickey Finn (#4–8), Dr. Burke (#4–8), Ballou Special (#4–8), Hare's Ear Nymph (#4–8), Bead Head Nymph (#4–8).

It may seem strange to include a dam as a destination in a book about trout fishing, but Upper Dam, near Rangeley, Maine, is no ordinary dam. This is one of the most historic locations in fly-fishing. It was here that Carrie Gertrude Stevens tied her famous series of feather-wing streamers, including the legendary Gray Ghost.

I remember the first time I visited Upper Dam. I wanted to see the dam, as well as the house in which Carrie Stevens lived. The gate blocking the road to the dam was closed, so I took the quarter-mile hike down to the water.

The dam is still standing, and a small flotilla of aluminum skiffs—plus two or three genuine wooden Rangeley guide boats—lined the bank of the

Famed Upper Dam, the place where Carrie Stevens first tried her most famous fly, the Gray Ghost.

pool below the dam. In his book *Streamers and Bucktails,* Col. Joseph Bates described how the guides launched their boats onto the big swirling pool below the dam. The boats would bob around on the churning water, and the guides would drop their anchors when they were in the best positions for their sports to catch fish. No one was on the water that hot August day, but the boats lay at the ready and the big whirlpool was still spinning below the dam.

Upper Dam lies at the mouth of Lake Mooselookmeguntic. After a very short journey, the rushing water enters Lake Richardson. Upper Dam has been modified over the years—you can see where fresh railroad ties and concrete have been added—but the short dam retains much of the outline seen in early photographs.

There is a network of rigid scaffolding on the back side of the dam, giving anglers access to the water. While these walkways are perfectly safe for adults, small children should not be allowed onto the dam; there are no railings on the fishing platforms, and one misstep could end up with a child falling into the rushing water. Casting can also be a bit tight on these platforms if other anglers are fishing, but you really don't have to cast far to reach the fish.

I didn't have a Gray Ghost on my first visit to Upper Dam, but I rummaged through my fly boxes and found a Golden Witch, another of Carrie's famous patterns. On the second cast a large landlocked salmon came from the deep water near the side of the dam and swirled under the fly. While I didn't catch that fish, it was still a thrill to use one of Carrie's patterns on the spot where she fished.

Your trip to Upper Dam won't be complete until you visit Carrie Stevens's house. Walk over the rock-and-wooden dam, and continue on the dirt road leading along the top of the earthen portion of Upper Dam. Carrie Stevens's house lies on the right side of the road. Today the house has new out-of-state summer residents, but it can be viewed from the road. On the left side of the road is a plaque commemorating Carrie Stevens and her contributions to fly-fishing.

Once upon a time, the journey to Upper Dam was a romantic adventure. The trip began with a train ride to Bemis, Maine, a prosperous logging town on the shores of Mooselookmeguntic Lake. From Bemis, a steamer ferried eager anglers across the lake to Upper Dam. Today you can reach Upper Dam by auto. Take ME 16 west out of Rangeley, Maine, approximately 15 miles. Look for signs that say MAINE PUBLIC RESERVE LAND (land owned by the state of Maine for public use). Turn left on the first maintained gravel road; this is Upper Dam Road, and will take you to the dam. A gate is locked across the road during certain times of year, and you must walk the last quarter mile.

There are three options for fishing Upper Dam. First, you can fish from the back side of the dam. At the turn of the 20th century brook trout were the only game fish to come from these waters. Trout, some weighing several pounds, stacked below the raceways in the dam. Later, as landlocked salmon were stocked throughout the state, these fish began to appear at Upper Dam. It's very simple to walk out onto the ramps and scaffolding on the dam and cast a streamer into swirling water below. Favorite spots are in the swirling eddies on each end of the dam, as well as the clear water between each raceway.

A second option is to walk downstream from the dam and fish the moving water between the lakes. There is a large walkway leading out over the water, or you can fish from shore or wade.

A third possibility is to launch a canoe onto Upper Dam Pool. Drop anchor so that you can cast along the edges of the water flowing from the dam. Now you're fishing in the style of the sports who visited Upper Dam so many years ago.

There are two schools of thought as to how to fish below Upper Dam. The traditionalists favor streamers: Gray Ghosts, Black Ghosts, Edson Tigers, and marabou-wing patterns. Today growing numbers of anglers are using

You may fish off the platforms below Upper Dam. While I don't spend all day fishing off these platforms—I prefer more secluded waters—this is some of the most important water in the history of fly-fishing. It has changed very little over the decades.

Bead Head Nymphs. These flies sink quickly and are effective in the slower eddies at the ends of the dam. I confess that while I make split-bamboo rods and tie the traditional New England feather-wing streamers, I get a little tired of the misty-eyed romanticizing I hear about these things; I also think the average angler just wants to catch a fish. Still, when I visit Upper Dam, I also use streamers, especially Carrie Stevens's patterns. Sure, I might catch more fish with Bead Heads, but on this particular piece of water it just doesn't seem right.

Keep in mind that the water below Upper Dam is designated fly-fishing only. That means different things in different parts of the country. Maine takes a pretty restrictive view of fly-fishing only. Specifically, no pieces of shot may be added to your leader in order to get the fly to sink. Be forewarned of this law or the local game warden will give you a ticket.

Favorite times to fish Upper Dam are the end of May through the end of June, and throughout September. While the brook trout average 10 to 12 inches in length, and the salmon weigh about 1½ to 2 pounds, larger fish gather below Upper Dam in spring and late September.

After exploring and fishing Upper Dam, cap off the day with a bit of pond fishing. The two East Richardson Ponds are near the intersection of Upper Dam Road and ME 16 (if you're traveling back toward ME 16 on Upper Dam Road, the ponds will be on the right), and West Richardson Pond is across ME 16 where you turned onto Upper Dam Road. All of these ponds require a canoe or float tube.

KENNEBAGO RIVER

Map *The Maine Atlas and Gazetteer,* Map 28.

Description The Kennebago River starts at Big Island Pond in Seven Ponds Township, a remote, hard-to-access forested part of Maine near its border with Quebec. The river flows roughly south through Little Kennebago Lake, and gains strength with the outflow of Kennebago Lake. The Kennebago ends where it flows into Cupsuptic Lake near Haines Landing.

Access Access to the Kennebago is found where ME 16 crosses over the river. Look for the dirt road on the east side of the river (travel north) to reach the Steep Bank Pool and other pools along the lower stretch of the river. The best access along the main stem of the river is through private sporting camps. Access to the upper Kennebago is along Canada Road heading north; this is a rough logging road requiring a sturdy vehicle.

Best Asset Once the water drops, which is usually by the first two weeks of June, the Kennebago River offers good dry-fly fishing throughout much of the season. Go prepared with a selection of Wulff patterns and a spool of light tippet material. Fishing with a 4-weight dry-fly rod is especially fun.

The Kennebago River contains trout and landlocked salmon. In the fall, some of the salmon weigh several pounds.

Biggest Drawback Unless you elect to stay at one of the sporting camps along the Kennebago, access can be a problem. However, fishing a short section of this river should be on your itinerary when you visit the mountains of western Maine.

Regulations The Kennebago officially opens on the first of April, but this isn't the best time to visit. The real fishing doesn't begin until ice-out comes to the lakes and the fish begin entering the river, usually around the middle of May. The river closes to fishing on September 30. At the time of this writing, there is a proposal before the state government to extend the season until October 15. If this takes effect, the first two weeks of October will be an excellent time to visit the Kennebago.

The entire river is fly-fishing only. All of the tributaries are closed to fishing. The daily limit on brook trout is two fish per day, a minimum of 10 inches in length, and only one fish may measure more than 12 inches. You may keep one landlocked salmon per day. Note that strict catch-and-release regulations take effect from August 15 to the close of the season.

Favorite Flies Black Ghost (#2-8), Gray Ghost (#4-8), Muddler Minnow (#4 and 6), Colonel Bates (#4-8), Mickey Finn (#4-8), Royal Wulff (#14-12), Green Comparadun (#12), Brown Comparadun (#12), Hare's Ear Nymph (#12-16), Elk Hair Caddis (#12-18), Royal Coachman (#10-14), Hendrickson (#14-16), Olive Sparkle Caddis Pupa (#12-16), Brown Sparkle Caddis Pupa (#12-16), Humpy (#12-14).

The Kennebago is one of Maine's more noteworthy rivers. It's a tough river to fish because so much of it is beyond easy access. Your best bet is to take ME 16 west out of Rangeley. Drive 8 miles and look for a wide gravel road on the right (if you cross over the river on a concrete bridge, you've gone too far). This gravel road, which lacks a regular maintenance program (low-slung vehicles beware), leads along the lower portion of the river. The most famous area in this stretch of the Kennebago is called the Steep Bank Pool. You can take that name quite literally: A steep bank leads down to a wide, deep pool in the river. Although the Steep Bank Pool attracts a lot of anglers, it can contain some nice brook trout and landlocked salmon.

Above the Steep Bank Pool you'll find several sets of riffles worthy of attention. Besides the fish, this is a nice area to wet a line, because the surrounding woods are undeveloped.

You can also try your luck where ME 16 crosses the Kennebago. A convenient landmark is a sign for the OQUOSSOC ANGLING ASSOCIATION (according to the sign, this club was established in 1868). Oquossoc is a nearby hamlet populated mostly by summer residents. There is parking near the bridge, and you can walk down the embankment to the river. This is a rocky portion of the river offering riffles and some pocket water.

Much of the Kennebago River is controlled by commercial camps. For about the price of a motel room in the city, you can enjoy a nice cabin, delicious meals, and plenty of great trout and salmon fishing. Grant's Kennebago Camps is one of Maine's legendary sporting destinations. Grant's controls a private section of the river containing more than 20 named pools. Although this part of the river is open only to those who stay at Grant's, manager Jim Collins told me that the entire river contains good fishing.

"June is the very best time to visit the Kennebago," said Collins. "A lot of it depends upon when the ice goes out in the lakes. The fish usually begin entering the river during the last two weeks of May. Fishing peaks in June, and can remain good into July if the weather remains cool and we get rain. August is a tough month because the water level drops and the

Steep Bank Pool on the Kennebago River.

temperature rises, but things pick up again during the last three weeks of September when the fish begin to spawn.

"The eastern brook trout is our main fish" he continued. "It's not uncommon to catch a 2- to 3-pound brookie. That's a nice brook trout. Next, we have landlocked salmon. These fish don't grow as large as in some other areas. The biologists say the Kennebago salmon don't get real big because the river doesn't get a heavy run of smelt.

"In addition to the brook trout and salmon, anglers catch a few brown trout every year. We don't have many, but they are very large—between 4 and 6 pounds."

What about fly selection?

"The favorite streamers are Nine-Threes, Mickey Finns, Black Ghosts, Gray Ghosts, Colonel Bateses, and Muddler Minnows," said Collins. "We use these throughout the season.

"The Kennebago is also a very good dry-fly river. The Royal Wulff is the most popular dry fly. During the first half of June, we have hatches of green drakes and brown drakes. Be sure to bring a selection of flies to match these insects."

Once again, basic tackle works best: "A 9-foot-long rod is the favorite. Most anglers use a 5- or 6-weight outfit. You could get by with hip waders, but there are some deep pools and you'll manage better with chest waders. And don't forget the insect repellent."

While the Kennebago River is known as a fly-fishing destination, everyone in your group can also enjoy the river. "A lot of nonfishing visitors like to float the river with a canoe. We're also providing kayaks for our guests. These are becoming very popular."

Although the hatches of mayflies and caddisflies are not as dependable as on some other rivers, the Kennebago offers excellent chances at trophy fish. In addition to the flies that Collins mentioned, a selection of Elk Hair Caddises is valuable when there is a caddis hatch, and they do a fine job of imitating the few stoneflies that emerge on the Kennebago. Favorite nymphs include Bead Head Nymphs and the Gold Ribbed Hare's Ear. When the salmon are running into the river in the fall, streamers are a good choice. You can bet that when Carrie Stevens was living at nearby Upper Dam, some of her flies got a workout on the Kennebago.

In addition to the lower portion of the river, you can drive a set of logging roads to the upper Kennebago. There are two ways to get to this portion of the river. The first is to take ME 16 west out of Rangeley approximately 15 miles. You'll pass a sign for GRANT'S KENNEBAGO CAMPS. Turn onto the first well-maintained gravel road on your right. Drive 3 miles until this road intersects with another large gravel road. This second road is the Lincoln Pond Road (don't bother looking for a sign—there isn't one). Turn right

The New England brook trout is a magnificent game fish.

and drive approximately 8 miles until the road crosses the river. Turn left onto a gravel road that follow the river. On some maps this road is called Kennebago River Road; the last time I fished the Kennebago, however, a sign nailed to a tree read CANADA ROAD.

You can get to this same part of the Kennebago by taking ME 27 north out of Stratton, Maine. Drive 6 miles and look on your left for the sign to Tim Pond Camps, another old-line sporting camp. Turn left onto the gravel road and drive 15 miles until the road crosses the river. This is the same road described above, except that east of the river it's called Tim Pond Road.

The upper portion of the Kennebago flows along the base of the Kennebago Divide. The banks in this area are lined with alders, but the river isn't large and wading is comfortable. If you visit during June or the first of July, launch a canoe onto Little Kennebago Lake in the evening. This small lake is near the intersection of Lincoln Pond (Tim Pond) and Kennebago River Roads. The river flows into the lake from the north, and exits at the south. Try fishing near the inlets and outlets, and look for trout rising to evening hatches of mayflies and caddisflies.

THE PARMACHENEE COUNTRY (MAGALLOWAY RIVER)

Maps *The Maine Atlas and Gazetteer,* Maps 27 and 28.

Description The Parmachenee Country is a series of streams and ponds running along the border between Maine and New Hampshire. The heart of the area is the Magalloway River, which contains trophy brook trout. The area also contains several good lakes and ponds worth fishing in the evening when the insects emerge and the trout begin rising. In the heat of summer, explore any of the tributaries leading into the Magalloway, especially where the cool mountain water enters the main stem of the river.

Access Travel west on ME 16 toward Errol, New Hampshire. Look for a well-maintained dirt road on the right in Wilsons Mills, Maine (you'll see a sign for BOSEBUCK MOUNTAIN CAMPS). This road leads into the heart of the Parmachenee area.

ME 16 west parallels the Magalloway starting in Wilsons Mills, and provides additional access to the river.

Best Assets This area sees few anglers. It's very possible to fish all day and see only two or three other fishers. This is also big woods, and it would be rare to visit a local pond in the evening and not see moose.

Biggest Drawbacks You must go prepared; bring plenty of food, fill your gas tank, and don't forget the insect repellent. It's a long way back to town if you forget something. Also, as I will discuss, much of the best and most historic water is behind a locked gate. Bosebuck Mountain Camps, which is very nice and affordable, has access to many miles of river.

Regulations The Magalloway River is fly-fishing only. It is open to fishing from April 1 to September 30 (but for all practical purposes, the real fishing doesn't begin until near the end of May). You may keep one trout or salmon per day. All trout less than 8 inches or longer than 12 inches must be released. From August 16 to September 30, all fish must be released.

Favorite Flies Gray Ghost (#4–8), Black Ghost (#4–8), Mickey Finn (#4–8), Muddler Minnow (#4–8), Woolly Bugger (#4–8), Ballou Special (#4–8), Hare's Ear Nymph (#8–14), Bead Head Nymph (#8–12), Pheasant Tail Nymph (#8–12), Royal Coachman (#10–12), Olive Sparkle Caddis Pupa (#10–14), Brown Sparkle Caddis Pupae (#10–14), Royal Wulff (#12–14), Hendrickson (#14–18), Elk Hair Caddis (#12–16), Quill Gordon (#12), March Brown (#12–16).

This part of Maine, on the border with New Hampshire, is one of the most historic in New England fly-fishing. President Dwight Eisenhower visited Parmachenee Camps, situated on one of the islands on Parmachenee Lake.

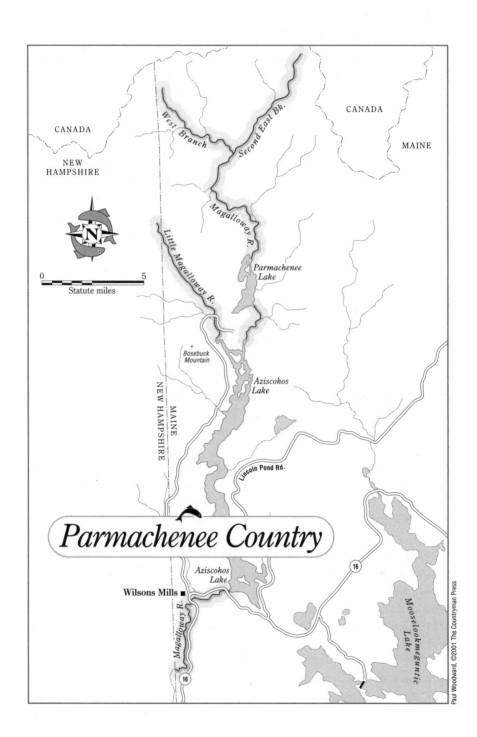

CANADA

NEW
HAMPSHIRE

CANADA

MAINE

West Branch

Second East Br.

Magalloway R.

Little Magalloway R.

N

0   5
Statute miles

*Parmachenee
Lake*

+
Bosebuck
Mountain

*Aziscohos
Lake*

MAINE
NEW HAMPSHIRE

Lincoln Pond Rd.

Parmachenee Country

*Aziscohos
Lake*

Wilsons Mills ■

Magalloway R.

16

16

*Mooselookmeguntic
Lake*

These are no longer commercial camps, but a plaque on the Magalloway River marks the spot where the president did a bit of trout fishing.

The road into the Parmachenee area is gated, but Carroll Ware, head guide at Bosebuck Mountain Camps, leads anglers into the area to fish and learn the rich history of the region.

"This area was home to an Indian named Chief Metalluck," said Ware. "He had a daughter named Parmachenee. The lake was named for the daughter, and of course the fly called the Parmachenee Belle was also named for her.

"President Eisenhower fished an area of the Magalloway called Little Boy Falls," he continued. "According to legend, Chief Metalluck came across two trappers and a kidnapped boy near the falls. The chief rescued the boy and returned him to his parents in Canada. Ever since then, the pool in that part of the river has been called Little Boy Falls."

And what about Bosebuck Mountain, for which Bosebuck Camps are named?

"According to one story, a group of geologists climbed the mountain and became trapped in a snowstorm in the 19th century. They didn't have enough food, and so were in a bit of a predicament. One of the men had a

An old bridge on the Magalloway River.

Little Boy Falls on the Magalloway River was fished by President Dwight Eisenhower.

dog named Bo. It's said that Bo killed a buck deer and saved the group from starvation. And there you have it: 'Bo's buck.'"

If you're not interested in venturing beyond the gated road, you can still go into the Parmachenee area to enjoy excellent brook trout fishing on the Magalloway River. Take ME 16 west out of Rangeley for nearly 20 miles. Look for the sign to Bosebuck camps on the right. Turn onto this gravel road and drive 3 miles. Turn right onto a second gravel road (there will be a second sign to Bosebuck camps) and continue driving another 10 miles, until the road crosses the river. There is a pulloff and place to park on the side of the road, and a path leads you down to the river. This is a beautiful place to fish; sweeping vistas of the mountains provide the backdrop, and large brook trout, some measuring almost 20 inches, inhabit the pools. Late September is especially good, because the larger trout run into the river out of Aziscohos Lake. Remain quiet as you fish and a moose might wander out of the woods and join you on the river.

Standard nymphs—Gold Ribbed Hare's Ears and Bead Heads—work well on the Magalloway River and the other waters of the Parmachenee Country. Streamers also work well, and guide Carroll Ware is especially fond of leech patterns.

THE DEAD RIVER

Maps *The Maine Atlas and Gazetteer*, Maps 28, 30, and 40.

Description Despite its great length as well as fishing and canoeing opportunities, the Dead River gets little attention. The South Branch of the Dead River starts at Saddleback Lake and flows north to Flagstaff Lake. The North Branch starts at Lower Pond in the Chain of Ponds in Chain of Ponds Township; it then travels southeast into Flagstaff Lake. The single main stem of the Dead River then flows out of the northeast corner of Flagstaff Lake until it joins the Kennebec River at The Forks in West Forks.

Access There are three major places to wet a line along the Dead River.

South Branch of the Dead River: Access to the South Branch is largely accomplished along ME 16, which follows the river along much of its course. There is ample parking along the banks. The lower section of the South Branch is accessible by canoe.

North Branch of the Dead River: Access to the North Branch is largely accomplished along ME 27. There is ample parking along the road and plenty of opportunities to fish. Floating the river by canoe is an excellent way to access many lightly fished areas of the river.

The Dead River from Flagstaff Lake to The Forks: It's tough to gain access to much of the river above The Forks. A series of logging roads lead to different areas in this section. Gain access to the river below the dam at Flagstaff Lake from Long Falls Dam Road north out of North New Portland. This is a typical logging road requiring a sturdy vehicle. The next access to the main stem of the Dead River is along US 201 in The Forks. A short dirt road, called Two Mile Road, follows the north shore of the river briefly, offering additional access.

Best Assets If you're adventuresome, the Dead River offers excellent opportunities to take a float trip and get away from the crowds. There is ample access to the upper branches of the river. This is another big-woods area, full of moose and other wild game.

Biggest Drawbacks The upper sections of the river run very low as summer wears on. Look elsewhere to fish from the middle of July until the fall rains replenish the river. Although these sections are easily accessed, the low, warm water forces the fish to retreat to the cooler depths of Flagstaff Lake.

The lack of ready access is the biggest drawback to the lower main stem of the Dead River. However, you can enjoy what fishing there is on the lower section, and fish the Kennebec River and nearby ponds.

Regulations South Branch: Open to fishing from April 1 to October 31. The daily bag limit is five trout, minimum 6 inches in length. From October 1 to October 31, artificial lures only, and all fish must be released.

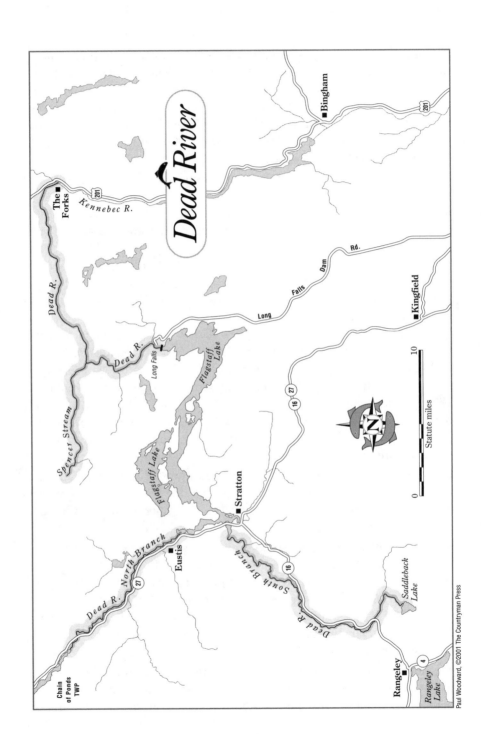

Dead River

North Branch: Open to fishing from April 1 to September 30. Fly-fishing only. The daily bag limit is five trout, minimum 6 inches in length.

Main stem below Flagstaff Lake: Open to fishing from April 1 to September 30. The minimum length for salmon and rainbow trout is 12 inches; for brook trout, 10 inches. Daily bag limit: two fish. From Flagstaff Lake to the confluence with Spencer Stream, you may fish from October 1 to October 31, artificial lures only, and all fish must be released.

Favorite Flies Black Ghost (#2–8), Gray Ghost (#4–8), Muddler Minnow (#4 and 6), Colonel Bates (#4–8), Mickey Finn (#4–8), Royal Wulff (#12–14), Green Comparadun (#12), Brown Comparadun (#12), Hare's Ear Nymph (#12–16), Elk Hair Caddis (#12–18), Royal Coachman (#10–14), Hendrickson (#14–16), Olive Sparkle Caddis Pupa (#12–16), Brown Sparkle Caddis Pupa (#12–16), Humpy (#12–14).

I admit that the Dead River doesn't have the most appealing of names. But what's in a name? The river has been a favorite among local anglers, and has also become a popular destination among white-water canoeists.

The North Branch of the Dead River is easily accessible by traveling north on ME 27 out of Eustis, Maine. The paved road follows the river, providing many access areas. The North Branch is fast water, and is a favorite among canoeists. However, there are plenty of fishable pools, and even the pocket water in the faster sections holds brook trout and landlocked salmon.

The best fishing on the North Branch begins below the dam at Lower Pond. This part of the river is rocky, so it's best to wade with a wading staff. Another excellent spot is where Alder Stream flows into the North Branch. Here's a hint for when fishing in the North Country: When the water in a river warms, seek out an area where a small stream flows into the river. The fish tend to congregate in the cooler water here.

ME 27 goes all the way to the province of Quebec (approximately 20 miles from Eustis) through the Chain of Ponds region. The Chain of Ponds is a stillwater angler's delight. There are numerous ponds, from little spits of water perfect for float tubing to slightly larger pieces where you'll appreciate the speed of a canoe. Most of these ponds contain brook trout averaging 10 to 12 inches, but larger fish are always possible. The end of May through the first half of July is the perfect time to be in the Chain of Ponds. This is also when the North Branch of the Dead River is best. Try fishing the river during the day, and then heading to a pond in the late afternoon for the evening hatch.

The South Branch is easily accessed by traveling west on ME 16 out of Stratton, Maine. The road travels along much of the river, and there are ample places to park and begin wading. Ten-inch brook trout are the most common fish, and you'll rarely see another angler.

The Dead River is alive with good trout fishing.

The Dead River below Flagstaff Lake contains excellent brook trout, some weighing as much as 2 pounds. Maine guide Hal Blood, of Cedar Ridge Outfitters, was kind enough to share some of his insights about fishing this area.

"Fly-fishing the Dead River near The Forks is good anytime. We fish from the outlet of Spencer Stream down to The Forks. This is primarily brook trout water, but there are also salmon. There are some very nice trout in the river. These aren't just the little trout you'd normally find in a brook. There's some really good water—deep pools—that holds fish. And there's good fly hatches."

What kinds of flies does Blood recommend?

"The most common insects are caddis. The river has a lot of smaller mayflies. The nearby ponds contain good numbers of green drakes. They start hatching around July 4 and go until the first of August. If the weather stays cool and we get rain, the hatches and fishing will hold up pretty well.

"For the river, a Hornberg is a good pattern. It works just about anywhere. You can fish it dry, or you can fish it wet. Muddlers are also very good. Well, I guess a Muddler is supposed to look like a little minnow, but I think a small Muddler—say size 8 or 10—also looks like a caddis case drifting along.

"As for as tackle, I recommend using a 5- to 8-weight rod. It depends upon the skill of the fisherman. We sometimes get into big trout, and new fly-fishers might not know how to play a large fish. They'd be better off with a heavier rod."

Harley Hunkler, of Northern Outdoors, agreed with Blood's observations.

"We fish from the end of May until the first of October. Some of the best fishing is where the Dead and Kennebec Rivers come together in The Forks," said Hunkler. "Some anglers try to wade the river, but it can be tough. There are a lot of boulders and deep pools. You need chest waders and heavy-duty footwear. Right now we're looking at floating and fishing the Dead River with rafts."

Hunkler also warned about the difficulty of accessing much of the lower Dead River. "The roads leading into the area are in pretty tough shape—it's four-wheel-drive territory."

And Hunkler's choice of flies?

"Caddis are the big hatches. We get a few stoneflies. Bring dry flies as well as a variety of nymphs. But I also like to use streamers: Gray Ghosts, Black Ghosts, Mickey Finns, and Muddler Minnows. And a 7-weight outfit is adequate."

And what do the nonfishing folks do?

"Hiking, moose-watching, mountain biking—there's plenty to do," said Hunkler.

Other Stocked Rivers, Streams, and Ponds in Maine's Western Mountains

Attean Pond (Attean Township), Little Austin Pond (Bald Mountain Township), Basin Pond (Pierce Pond Township), Black Hill Pond (Embden), Carrabassett River (Anson), Chase Pond (Moscow), Clearwater Pond (Prentiss Township), Crocker Pond (Dennistown Plantation), Big Dimmick Pond (Caratunk), Dodge Pond (Rangeley), East Pond (Smithfield), Fish Pond (Moxie Gore), Haley Pond (Rangeley), Heald Stream (Jackman), Kilgore Pond (Pierce Pond Township), Knights Pond (Squaretown Township), Long Pond (The Forks Plantation), Lost Pond (Pleasant Ridge Plantation), Moose Pond (Hartland), Mosquito Pond (The Forks Plantation), Otter Pond (Bowtown Plantation), Sandy Stream (Jackman), Smith Pond (Forsyth Township), Spruce Pond (Lexington Township), Sugar Berth Pond (Dennistown Plantation), Supply Pond (Moose River), Wyman Pond (Caratunk).

Where to Stay in Maine's Western Mountains

Bosebuck Mountain Camps P.O. Box 1213, Rangeley, ME 04970 207-474-5460.

Nugent's Chamberlain Lake Camps HCR 76, Box 632, Greenville, ME 207-944-5991.

Cedar Ridge Outfitters P.O. Box 744, Jackman, ME 04945 207-668-4169.

Tim Pond Wilderness Camps Box 22, Eustis, ME 04936 207-243-2947.

Grant's Kennebago Camps P.O. 786, Rangeley, ME 04970 207-864-3608

Local Guide Services

Blair Barrows P.O. Box 266, Oquossoc, ME 04964 207-864-2615.

Tim Casey P.O. Box 777, Jackman, ME 04945 207-668-5091.

Clayton Eastlack Box 284, Route 17, Oquossoc, ME 04964 207-864-3416.

Northern Outdoors P.O. Box 100, The Forks, ME 04985 207-663-4466.

Fly-fishing Only 230 Main Street, Fairfield, ME 04937 207-453-6242.

9 | Maine's North Woods

Northern Maine was once a remote, almost inaccessible destination for the average sportsperson. There were few roads, and many ponds and streams were rarely fished. About the only way to travel through the North Woods was by canoe. Hardy sports packed their provisions into canoes, hired a guide, and set off for adventure that could be called a fishing safari.

Today a well-developed network of logging roads has opened much of northern Maine to truck and automobile travel. While this has been a boon to anglers wishing to wet a line, it's generally believed that these roads have worked to the detriment of the fishery. Brook trout weighing 3 or more pounds were once common throughout northern Maine. Today, in part due to the increase in fishing pressure, the average trout measures about 10 to 12 inches. Large fish are still caught, however, and the odds are that you'll still be able to find a piece of water and have it all to yourself.

THE ALLAGASH RIVER

Maps *The Maine Atlas and Gazetteer,* Maps 55, 56, 61, 62, and 66.

Description The Allagash River is the heart of the Allagash Wilderness Waterway, one of the most famous destinations for anglers, hunters, canoeists, and other outdoors enthusiasts in the northeastern United States.

The Allagash River begins in Chamberlain and Eagle Lakes in north-central Maine. The Allagash Wilderness Waterway is heavily forested, and features many rivers, streams, lakes and ponds. You could spend many years fishing the Allagash and surrounding waters and not sample everything the region has to offer.

The headwaters and much of the Allagash are deep in the Maine woods. Be sure to bring all of the supplies you'll need for your stay, including plenty of gasoline. It's many miles to the nearest store and service station.

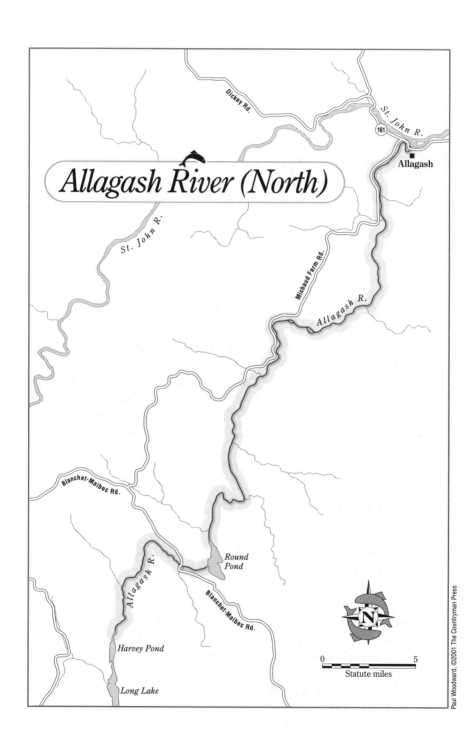

Allagash River (North)

Dickey Rd.

St. John R.

161

Allagash

St. John R.

Michaud Farm Rd.

Allagash R.

Blanchet-Malbec Rd.

Allagash R.

Round Pond

Blanchet-Malbec Rd.

Harvey Pond

Long Lake

N

0 5
Statute miles

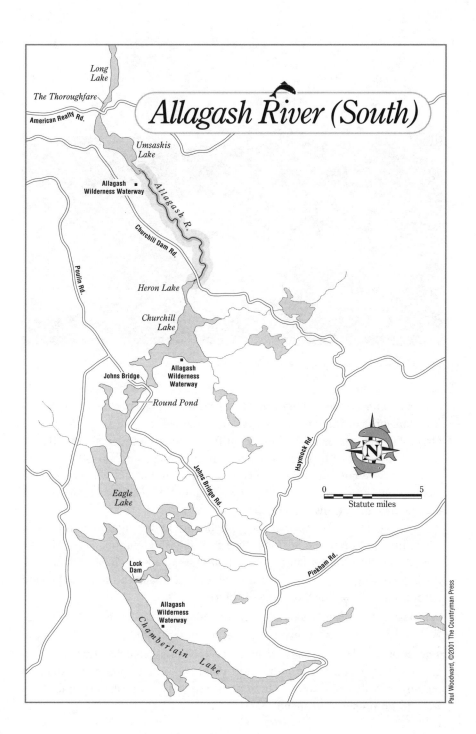

Long
Lake

The Thoroughfare

American Realty Rd.

Umsaskis
Lake

Allagash
Wilderness Waterway

Allagash R.

Churchill Dam Rd.

Poulin Rd.

Heron Lake

Churchill
Lake

Johns Bridge

Allagash
Wilderness
Waterway

Round Pond

Haymock Rd.

Eagle
Lake

Johns Bridge Rd.

Lock
Dam

Pinkham Rd.

Allagash
Wilderness
Waterway

Chamberlain Lake

Allagash River (South)

N

0   5
Statute miles

Paul Woodward, ©2001 The Countryman Press

The Allagash is northern Maine's most important river.

Access I could describe many ways to get to the Allagash Wilderness Waterway, but most of them require travel on unnamed logging roads. Most logging roads are numbered, and are identified by small wooden signs nailed to trees at intersections. Over the years, however, the signs fall off the trees, new roads are cut, and other roads wash out. The loggers who work these woods don't seem to mind a bit; they navigate this region as easily as you or I get around our own neighborhoods.

The easiest access to the Allagash begins at the mouth of the river, where it empties into the St. John River in Allagash Plantation. Take ME 161 west out of Fort Kent, Maine. After the highway crosses the Allagash, look for a gravel logging road, called Michaud Farm Road, on the left. Michaud Farm Road follows the west side of the river.

Best Assets The deep woods are full of wildlife. The Allagash Wilderness Waterway is also one of the premier canoeing destinations in the Northeast.

Biggest Drawbacks The roads are tough on low-slung vehicles. This is also an area that requires preparation to visit; you just don't drop into the Allagash region for a day of fishing. Much of the river is quite remote, and you'll want to go prepared to spend several days.

Regulations The Allagash River flows between a series of lakes and ponds, and has many tributaries. As a result, no uniform set of regulations governs the entire river. Consult the *Maine Open Water Fishing Regulations* booklet for the specific regulations governing the waters you fish. In general, the Allagash Wilderness Waterway is open to fishing April 1 to September 30.

Favorite Flies Hornberg (#6–10), Gray Ghost (#4–8), Black Ghost (#4–8), Mickey Finn (#6–8), Olive Woolly Bugger (#6–8), Black Woolly Bugger (#6–8), Brown Woolly Bugger (#6–8), Muddler Minnow (#4–8), Woolly Worm (#6–8), Royal Coachman (#6–10), Ballou Special (#4–8), Hare's Ear Nymph (#8–14), Pheasant Tail Nymph (#8–14), Bead Head Nymph (#8–14), Olive Sparkle Caddis Pupa (#8–14), Brown Sparkle Caddis Pupa (#8–14), Cream Sparkle Caddis Pupa (#8–14), Olive Caddis Larva (#8–14), Brown Caddis Larva (#8–14), Elk Hair Caddis (#10–14), Adams (#10–14), Light Cahill (#12–16), Green Drake (#4–6), March Brown (#8–12), Royal Wulff (#12), Adams Wulff (#12), Humpy (#12).

The Allagash is one of Maine's most legendary rivers. It was once a major artery for trappers and missionaries; eventually woodcutters used it to transport their logs downriver. The Allagash drains a vast region of the North Woods, flowing north 98 miles before emptying into the St. John River at Allagash. Today much of the river is protected as part of the Maine Public Reserve Lands and Allagash Wilderness Waterway.

The headwaters of the Allagash flow among a series of lakes: Chamberlain, Eagle, Churchill, Umsaskis, and several others. The moving water between the lakes offers a variety of white-water challenges, making the Allagash a popular destination for canoeists. Because the river is interspersed with lakes, there are a number of access points for canoeists, and trips ranging from four to seven days can be arranged through several outfitters. If you are an experienced outdoorsperson and would like to take a self-guided trip, just remember to take ample food and other supplies. Many adventurers strike out with the barest of provisions, planning to eat the trout they catch along the way. The folks in the town of Allagash tell too many tales of canoeists showing up very hungry.

Don't despair if you're not interested in taking a long canoe trip; you can easily reach the Allagash from the logging roads intersecting the river. Probably the easiest access is near the mouth of the Allagash. Take ME 161 east out of St. Francis. Travel through Allagash Village, cross over the river, and look for a large, well-maintained gravel road on the left. There is a gate operated by the North Woods Association near the beginning of this road, and a small fee is charged to gain access to this area. The person operating the gate can give you the local fishing conditions, as well as information

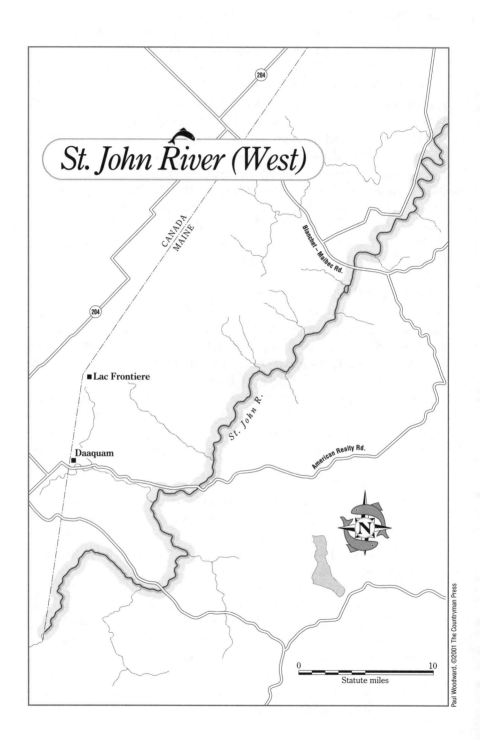

St. John River (West)

about where to camp and sightsee. This road travels along the lower reaches of the Allagash, providing a wealth of fishing opportunities. Some access points are quite obvious; others require a short walk through the woods to the water.

The lakes along the Allagash contain lake trout, whitefish, and landlocked salmon, but the river itself contains brook trout averaging 10 to 12 inches long. The month of June is the best time to fish the Allagash; the water is cool, and brook trout can be found in almost all of the deep runs. As the temperature increases in July and August, the trout migrate to below the spring holes and the mouths of cool feeder streams. While it might be difficult to find the springs, it's fairly easy to find the fish concentrated below the tributaries. The best tributaries are the small streams flowing through the woods. The foliage keeps the temperatures cool, and if the water is still flowing, especially during the dry, hot month of August, it's a good bet that the stream is spring fed. Hike down such a stream to where it flows into the main river. Cast small streamers and wet flies into the river below the mouth of the stream.

You can enjoy good dry-fly fishing throughout June and early July. Be sure to bring a supply of Blue Winged Olives, March Browns, and Light Cahills.

ST. JOHN RIVER

Maps *The Maine Atlas and Gazetteer,* Maps 54, 60, 66, 67, 68, 69, and 70.

Description The St. John is another river flowing through the deep woods of far northern Maine. The area is full of moose, ruffed grouse, deer, and black bears, as well as good fishing. This is a favorite river among canoe campers.

The St. John begins as a small stream near Maine's far eastern border with Quebec. It flows in a northerly direction, gaining strength and size as it goes.

The Allagash River empties into the St. John in Allagash Plantation. Gaining considerably in size, the St. John turns to the east and forms a part of the valley between Maine and New Brunswick, Canada. The forests give way to a variety of agricultural uses, primarily potato fields.

Access There are two ways to access the St. John. Both require travel on gravel logging roads. These roads are usually well maintained, but there are no guarantees; if the loggers are not working in an area, they have no reason to maintain the road. Fortunately, the roads leading to the St. John are main arteries in the working forest and are graded and maintained.

To reach the southern end of the St. John, follow Golden Road west out of Millinocket to Ragmuff Road (*The Maine Atlas and Gazetteer,* Map 49). In

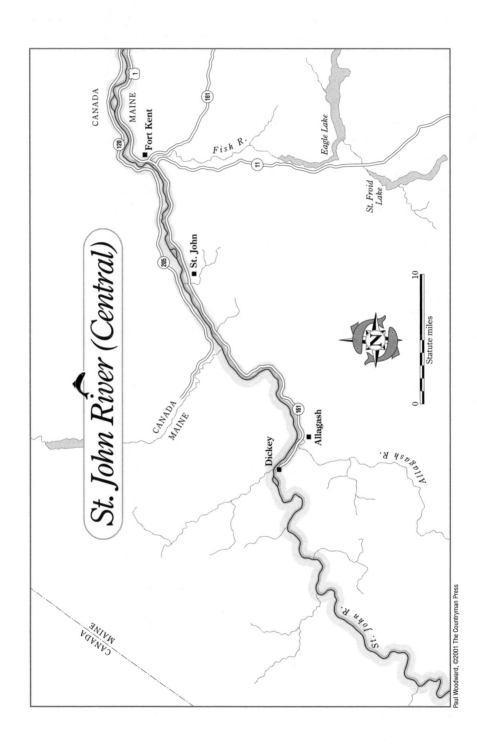

St. John River (Central)

CANADA
MAINE

Fort Kent

Fish R.

Eagle Lake

St. Froid Lake

St. John

CANADA
MAINE

Dickey

Allagash

Allagash R.

St. John R.

CANADA
MAINE

Statute miles

0   10

Paul Woodward, ©2001 The Countryman Press

The Maine Atlas and Gazetteer, you'll see that Ragmuff Road turns into Loon Lake Road, and then Caucombomoc Road. Caucombomoc Road intersects with St. Aurelie Road at St. Francis Lake in Township 8, Range 16 (*The Maine Atlas,* map 54). Take St. Aurelie Road west to Baker Lake. The Baker Branch of the St. John, which flows north out of Baker Lake, is the beginning of the St. John River canoe trip. A series of logging roads will take you to other sections of the upper St. John.

The second access point is from the northern section of the St. John. US 1 north out of Van Buren, Maine, follows the St. John, offering many places to park and fish. ME 161 continues following the south side of the St. John from Fort Kent to Dickey in Allagash Plantation. From Dickey, a well-maintained logging road called Dickey Road and a series of unnamed roads follow the river, offering additional access points to the water.

Best Assets Remoteness. Only diehard outdoorspeople visit the St. John. You'll be able to fish and enjoy the river without seeing a lot of other people.

Be sure to check out the many small streams and ponds in the area. They almost all contain brook trout.

Biggest Drawback Remoteness. Only experienced outdoorspeople enjoy visiting a place like this. If you travel to the upper St. John around Baker Lake, be sure to take everything you'll need for your stay, especially gasoline. It's many miles back to town, and there are no deep-woods convenience stores.

Regulations Note that the regulations governing the portion of the St. John forming the border between the Maine and New Brunswick are different from those pertaining to the river as it flows through Maine.

The portion of the St. John River forming the border between Maine and New Brunswick: Open to fishing April 15 to September 30. The daily bag limit on trout, salmon, and lake trout is five fish, not to include more than two salmon or two lake trout; all five may be trout. The total weight of these fish is not to exceed 7½ pounds. The minimum length for salmon is 14 inches; for lake trout, 18 inches.

The portion of the St. John River flowing in Maine: Open to fishing April 1 to September 30. The daily bag limit is five trout, minimum 6 inches in length.

Favorite Flies Hornberg (#6–10), Gray Ghost (#4–8), Black Ghost (#4–8), Mickey Finn (#6–8), Olive Woolly Bugger (#6–8), Black Woolly Bugger (#6–8), Brown Woolly Bugger (#6–8), Muddler Minnow (#4–8), Woolly Worm (#6–8), Royal Coachman (#6–10), Ballou Special (#4–8), Hare's Ear Nymph (#8–14), Pheasant Tail Nymph (#8–14), Bead Head Nymph (#8–14), Olive Sparkle Caddis Pupa (#8–14), Brown Sparkle Caddis Pupa (#8–14), Cream Sparkle Caddis Pupa (#8–14), Olive Caddis Larva (#8–14), Brown

A northern Maine brook trout.

Caddis Larva (#8–14), Elk Hair Caddis (#10–14), Adams (#10–14), Light Cahill (#12–16), Green Drake (#4–6), March Brown (#8–12).

The St. John River is another of those large Maine rivers that once supported trappers, adventurers, and log drives. It's a big, wide waterway; it's almost intimidating when you first encounter it. But it holds large numbers of brook trout, especially early in the season. While much of the St. John travels through Maine, a considerable portion forms the northern boundary between Maine and New Brunswick, Canada.

Like the Allagash, the St. John is popular among canoeists, and various float trips can be arranged through local outfitters. June is a favorite time to fish the St. John, and there are good hatches of mayflies and caddisflies. As the season progresses, concentrate your fishing below the mouths of feeder streams.

The water level of the St. John can fluctuate quickly depending on the amount of rain. By August the river is warm, and the trout actually enter the feeder streams.

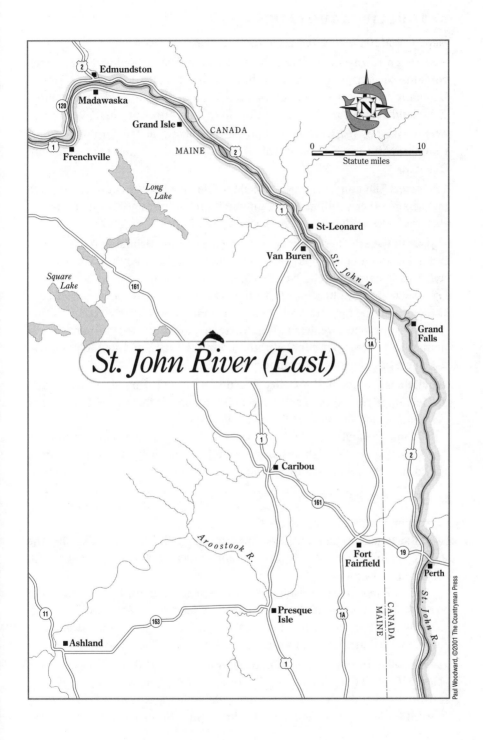

St. John River (East)

DEBOULLIE MOUNTAIN

Maps *The Maine Atlas and Gazetteer,* Maps 62 and 63.

Description Township 15, Range 9, locally known as Deboullie (De-boo-lee), contains several ponds that hold brook trout. Located in northern Maine, Deboullie features deep woods, an abundance of wildlife, and good fishing. You could spend a week in Deboullie and fish a different pond every day.

Access Take ME 161 west out of Fort Kent. Look on the left for the St. Francis Checkpoint in St. Francis. This well-maintained logging road leads into Deboullie.

Best Assets The pond fishing is excellent. This is also a great area to watch moose and other wildlife. Although you'll probably see a few other anglers, this area doesn't get a large number of visitors.

Biggest Drawback There are one or two lodges in the Deboullie region offering good accommodations and food; other than that, you'll have to camp out. This is normally fine, but the campsites I've seen in this area aren't the best—several are right adjacent to the gravel roads. After a couple of days without rain, the roads dry out, and your campsite will be covered in a cloud of dust every time a vehicle passes. There are, however, several campsites in more remote areas not situated right along the roads, and you'll be able to use one of these if they are unoccupied.

Regulations The regulations vary depending on which pond or stream you are fishing. Here are the general guidelines (consult the *Maine Open Water Fishing Regulations* booklet for more specifics).

Deboullie Pond, Gardner Pond: Open to fishing April 1 to September 30. The possession of live fish as bait is prohibited. The daily creel limit on trout is two fish, minimum length 8 inches; only one fish may exceed 12 inches.

Denny Pond, Upper Pond: Fly-fishing only. Open to fishing April 1 to September 30. The daily creel limit on trout is two fish, minimum length 8 inches; only one fish may exceed 12 inches.

Mud Pond, Togue Pond: Open to fishing April 1 to September 30. The daily creel limit on trout is two fish, minimum length 8 inches; only one fish may exceed 12 inches.

Perch Pond: Open to fishing April 1 to September 30. The possession of live fish as bait is prohibited. The daily creel limit on trout is two fish, minimum length 8 inches; only one fish may exceed 12 inches. From October 1 to October 31, artificial lures only, and all fish must be released.

Favorite Flies Hornberg (#6–10), Gray Ghost (#4–8), Black Ghost (#4–8), Mickey Finn (#6–8), Olive Woolly Bugger (#6–8), Black Woolly Bugger (#6–8), Brown Woolly Bugger (#6–8), Muddler Minnow (#4–8), Woolly Worm (#6–8), Royal Coachman (#6–10), Ballou Special (#4–8), Hare's Ear

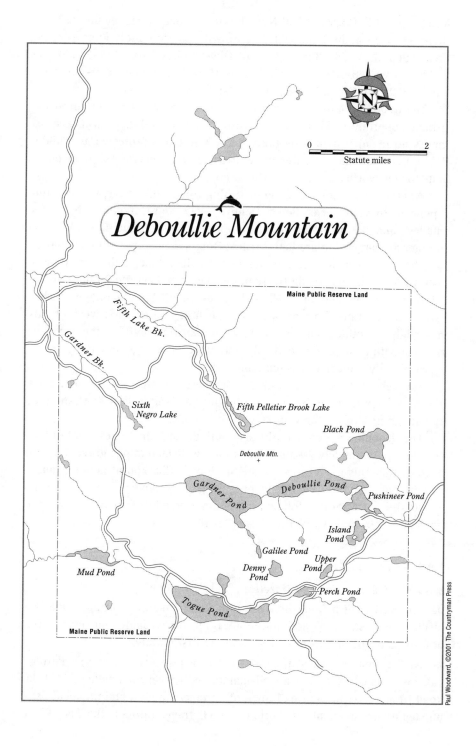

Deboullie Mountain

Statute miles

0   2

Maine Public Reserve Land

Fifth Lake Bk.

Gardner Bk.

Sixth
Negro Lake

Fifth Pelletier Brook Lake

Black Pond

Deboullie Mtn.
+

Gardner Pond

Deboullie Pond

Pushineer Pond

Island
Pond

Galilee Pond

Upper
Pond

Mud Pond

Denny
Pond

Perch Pond

Togue Pond

Maine Public Reserve Land

Paul Woodward, ©2001 The Countryman Press

Nymph (#8–14), Pheasant Tail Nymph (#8–14), Bead Head Nymph (#8–14), Olive Sparkle Caddis Pupa (#8–14), Brown Sparkle Caddis Pupa (#8–14), Cream Sparkle Caddis Pupa (#8–14), Olive Caddis Larva (#8–14), Brown Caddis Larva (#8–14), Elk Hair Caddis (#10–14), Adams (#10–14), Light Cahill (#12–16), Green Drake (#4–6), March Brown (#8–12).

The Deboullie Mountain area of northern Maine is an overlooked fly-fishing opportunity. This entire township (that's a relative term, because there's no town) is owned by the state of Maine and protected as a Maine Public Reserve Land. The Deboullie area contains several excellent ponds and streams worthy of serious fishing, however.

Whether you enjoy canoeing or fishing from a float tube, you can find a pond to fit your needs. Perch, Denny, Upper, and Galilee Ponds are the smallest, and can be easily fished from a float tube; Togue, Deboullie, and Gardner are larger and are better fished from a canoe or small powerboat.

There are several campgrounds in Deboullie. June is the best time to visit, with brook trout rising freely in the evenings. Favorite fly patterns are Elk Hair Caddises and Blue Winged Olives. Small Woolly Buggers fished with a sinking line also work well. In late June and the first week of July you might encounter hatches of large *Hexagenia* mayflies; these can be matched with an appropriate dry-fly imitation, but a large mayfly nymph or brown Woolly Bugger will catch more fish.

The Deboullie region is another area where you must go prepared; it's a long way back to town. Be sure to fill your gas tank in Fort Kent and pick up enough provisions for your stay in the woods.

The Deboullie region is fairly easy to find. Take ME 161 east out of Fort Kent for approximately 20 miles. Look for a well-maintained gravel road on the left. Take this gravel road to the St. Francis Checkpoint (about a quarter mile from ME 161). The attendant at the gate can give you the latest fishing conditions. Continue following this gravel road to Deboullie; there are signs along the way, so you won't get lost.

THE FISH RIVER

Maps *The Maine Atlas and Gazetteer,* Maps 63 and 67.

Description The Fish River between Fish River Lake and Portage Lake is a medium-wide stream containing brook trout. It's wadable and remote. The best times to fish are from mid-May to the first of July.

Access The first section of the river, between Fish River Lake and Portage Lake, is reached by taking a well-maintained gravel road called Fish Lake Road from ME 11 in the small town of Portage. Supplies and the local fishing report are available in Portage. You'll travel through the Fish River

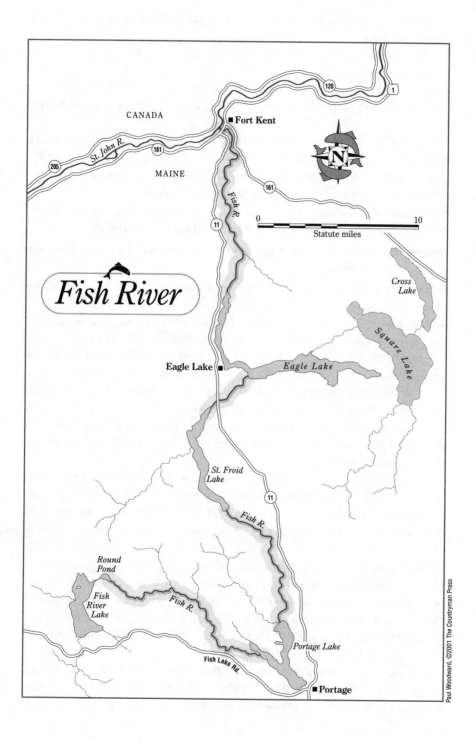

Checkpoint on your way to the river, where you can obtain maps and additional directions.

The second section of the Fish River, lying between Portage Lake and St. Froid Lake, can be fished in its entirety from a canoe. You can reach the middle of this section by taking a dirt road off ME 11 (the road will be on your left if you're heading north on ME 11). This road leads to a hand-carry boat launch.

The third section of the Fish, from Eagle Lake to Fort Kent, is easily accessed from ME 11 south out of Fort Kent. There is canoe access at the small town of Soldier Pond. Sly Brook Road, which intersects with ME 161 south of Fort Kent, offers access to much of the upper river.

Best Assets Few anglers visit the Fish River in the early part of the season. This is a favorite river among anglers who like to canoe and fish.

Biggest Drawback The river drops and warms by mid-July, knocking the wind out of the good fishing.

Regulations The Fish River connects several lakes, and the regulations differ somewhat depending on which piece of water you fish. The legal fishing season is from April 1 to September 30. The following regulations apply to the sections of the river that are of greatest interest to fly-anglers.

From Fish River Lake to Portage Lake: Open to fishing from April 1 to September 30. The daily bag limit is five trout, minimum 6 inches in length.

Fish River Thoroughfares (the stretches of the river connecting Long, Mud, Cross, Square, Eagle, and St. Froid Lakes): Open to fishing from April 1 to September 30. From August 16 to September 30: Fly-fishing only. The daily creel limit is two brook trout, minimum 12 inches in length; only one may exceed 14 inches.

From the US 1 bridge in Fort Kent upstream to Eagle Lake: Open to fishing from April 1 to September 30, artificial lures only. The daily creel limit for brook trout is two fish, minimum length 12 inches; only one fish may exceed 14 inches. From August 16 to September 30, the daily creel limit is one fish.

Favorite Flies Hornberg (#6–10), Gray Ghost (#4–8), Black Ghost (#4–8), Mickey Finn (#6–8), Olive Woolly Bugger (#6–8), Black Woolly Bugger (#6–8), Brown Woolly Bugger (#6–8), Muddler Minnow (#4–8), Woolly Worm (#6–8), Royal Coachman (#6–10), Ballou Special (#4–8), Hare's Ear Nymph (#8–14), Pheasant Tail Nymph (#8–14), Bead Head Nymph (#8–14), Olive Sparkle Caddis Pupa (#8–14), Brown Sparkle Caddis Pupa (#8–14), Cream Sparkle Caddis Pupa (#8–14), Olive Caddis Larva (#8–14), Brown Caddis Larva (#8–14), Elk Hair Caddis (#10–14), Adams (#10–14), Light Cahill (#12–16), Green Drake (#4–6), March Brown (#8–12).

The Fish is a remote river that you can enjoy in solitude.

The Fish River is one of those places visited mostly by locals. It's never been publicized, but it does contain some excellent fishing.

As with so many rivers in Maine, the moving water flows between a series of lakes. As a result, the Fish River can be broken into three sections. The first section of interest to fly-fishers flows between Fish River Lake and Portage Lake. There is an excellent campsite at the head of the river at Fish River Lake. This is a particularly good area to see moose, deer, and other wildlife. Much of the river in this section is remote, making for an excellent canoe trip. Begin at Round Pond, a small pond next to Fish River Lake, and take out at Portage Lake approximately 10 miles downstream. And don't overlook Round Pond; it can offer fast fishing in the early evening.

The next section, from Portage Lake to St. Froid Lake, is wider and more remote. It can be fished from a canoe, or you can gain access to the river from an unmaintained boat launch midway in this stretch. The fish here include brook trout, landlocked salmon, and, early in spring, lake trout weighing up to 5 pounds.

The final section of the Fish River that I'll discuss is from Eagle Lake to Fort Kent. I think the better fly-fishing is in the first section, but Soldier Pond—a wide, slow piece of water about 2 miles north of Eagle Lake—is a good place to try in the early evening.

The best fishing in the entire Fish River is from the last half of May through June. The first section of the river contains brook trout and the occasional landlocked salmon. As the water warms during summer, the salmon return to the lakes until the autumn rains cool the river, when the salmon return.

The Fish River is a nice destination if you'd rather not get too far back into the deep woods. Lodging, food, and gasoline are readily available along ME 11 and ME 161.

Other Stocked Waters Worth Exploring

Arnold Brook Lake (Presque Isle), Beau Lake (Township 19, Range 11), Beaver Tail Pond (Township 14, Range 10), Black Pond (St. John Plantation), Caribou Stream (Caribou), Carry Lake (Littleton), Cochrane Lake (New Limerick), Daigle Pond (New Canada Plantation), Deering Lake (Weston), Dickwood Lake (Eagle Lake), Hanson Brook Lake (Mapleton), Island Pond (Township 14, Range 8), Logan Pond (Houlton), East Mattawamkeag River (Oakfield), North Meduxnekeag River (Monticello), Monson Pond (Fort Fairfield), Mud Pond (Linneus), Nickerson Lake (New Limerick), Pleasant Lake (Island Falls), Portage Lake (Portage Lake), Rock Crusher Pond (Island Falls), Rockabema Lake (Moro Plantation), Round Mountain Pond (Township 11, Range 8), Rowe Lake (Township 11, Range 8), St. Froid Lake (Winterville Plantation), Spaulding Lake (Oakfield), Timoney Lake (Oakfield), Ugh Lake (Township 12, Range 14), Umsaskis Lake (Township 11, Range 13).

Where to Stay in Northern Maine

Libby Camps P.O. Box V, Ashland, ME 04732 207-435-8274.
Fish River Lodge P.O. Box 202, Eagle Lake, ME 04739 207-444-5207.
Red River Camps Box 320, Portage, ME 04768 207-435-6000.
Macannamac Camps P.O. Box B, Patten, ME 04765 207-528-2855.

Local Guide Services

Magnetic North Guide Service Box 306, 181 Main Street, Presque Isle, ME 04769 207-768-9421.
Dana Shaw 6 Winchester Street, Presque Isle, ME 04769 207-764-0494.
Wildwood Outfitters & Guide Service P.O. Box 538, Windham, ME 04062 207-892-9849.

Streamers

GRAY GHOST

Hook: 6X- to 8X-long streamer hook, sizes 2 to 8.
Thread: Black 6/0.
Tag: Flat silver tinsel.
Body: Orange floss.
Rib: Flat silver tinsel.
Throat: A bunch of white bucktail and strands of peacock herl.
Belly: A golden-pheasant crest feather, curving up.
Underwing: A long golden-crest feather, curving down.
Wings: Two gray hackles for each wing.
Shoulder: Silver-pheasant body feather.
Cheeks: Jungle cock.

BLACK GHOST

Hook: 6X-long streamer hook, sizes 4 to 8.
Thread: Black 6/0.
Tag: Flat silver tinsel.
Tail: Yellow hackle fibers.
Body: Black floss.
Rib: Flat silver tinsel.
Throat: Yellow hackle fibers.
Wings: Two white hackles for each wing.
Cheek: Jungle cock.

JOE'S SMELT

Hook: 6X-long streamer hook, sizes 2 to 8.
Thread: Black 6/0.
Tail: Red calf tail hair.
Body: Silver Mylar tubing.
Throat: Red paint.
Wing: Pintail flank feather tied flat on top of the body (mallard is a good substitute).
Painted eyes: Yellow with black pupils.

BALLOU SPECIAL

Hook: 6X-long streamer hook, sizes 4 to 8.
Thread: Black 6/0.
Tail: A golden-pheasant crest feather curving down.
Body: Flat silver tinsel.
Underwing: A bunch of red bucktail.
Wing: Two white marabou feathers tied on flat.
Topping: A dozen strands of peacock herl.
Cheeks: Jungle cock.

ALLAGASH AL

Hook: 4X-long streamer hook, sizes 2 to 8.
Thread: Black 6/0.
Body: Flat silver tinsel.

Rib: Oval silver tinsel.

Throat: A small bunch of red marabou.

Underwing: A small bunch of red bucktail.

Wings: Two furnace saddle hackles for each wing.

Cheeks: Jungle cock.

BARNES SPECIAL

Hook: 6X-long streamer hook, sizes 2 to 8.

Thread: Red 6/0.

Body: Flat silver tinsel.

Rib: Oval silver tinsel.

Underwing: Red bucktail, over which is a small bunch of white bucktail.

Wings: Each wing is made of two yellow saddle hackles and one grizzly saddle hackle on the outside.

BATTENKILL SHINER

Hook: 6X-long streamer hook, sizes 4 to 8.

Thread: Black 6/0.

Butt: Red floss.

Body: White floss.

Rib: Flat silver tinsel.

Throat: Gray hackle fibers.

Wing: Two blue saddle hackles with a badger saddle hackle on each side.

Cheeks: Jungle cock.

MICKEY FINN

Hook: 4X- or 6X-long streamer hook, sizes 4 to 8.

Thread: Black 6/0.

Body: Flat silver tinsel.

Rib: Oval silver tinsel.

Wing: A small bunch of yellow bucktail, over which is a small bunch of red bucktail, over which is a larger bunch of yellow bucktail (marabou is an excellent substitute for the bucktail).

BLACK NOSED DACE

Hook: 6X-long streamer hook, sizes 4 to 10.

Tail: A short piece of red yarn.

Body: Flat silver tinsel.

Rib: Oval silver tinsel.

Wing: A small bunch of white bucktail, over which is a small bunch of black bucktail, over which is a small bunch of brown bucktail.

LITTLE BROOK TROUT

Hook: 6X-long streamer hook, sizes 4 to 8.

Thread: Black.

Tail: A short section of red floss, over which is a small bunch of green bucktail.

Body: Cream fur dubbing.

Rib: Narrow flat silver tinsel.

Throat: A small bunch of green bucktail.

Wing: Four bunches of hair stacked: white bucktail, over which is orange bucktail, over which is green bucktail, over which is barred badger.

Cheeks: Jungle cock.

LITTLE BROWN TROUT

Hook: 6X-long streamer hook, sizes 4 to 8.

Thread: Black.

Tail: A small breast feather, with dark center removed, of a ring-necked pheasant.

Body: White wool.

Rib: Flat gold tinsel.

Wing: Four bunches of hair, stacked: yellow bucktail, over which is red bucktail, over which is gray squirrel tail, over which is brown squirrel tail.

Cheeks: Jungle cock.

EDSON LIGHT TIGER

Hook: 4X- or 6X-long streamer hook, sizes 4 to 10.

Thread: Black 6/0.

Tag: Flat gold tinsel.

Tail: A section of barred wood duck flank feather.

Body: Peacock herl.

Wing: Yellow bucktail.
Topping: The tips of two small red hackles.
Cheeks: Jungle cock.

EDSON DARK TIGER

Hook: 4X- or 6X-long streamer hook, sizes 4 to 10.
Thread: Yellow 6/0.
Tag: Flat gold tinsel.
Body: Narrow yellow chenille.
Throat: The tips of two small red hackles.
Wing: A bunch of brown bucktail dyed yellow.
Cheeks: Jungle cock.

GOLDEN SHINER

Hook: 6X-long streamer hook, sizes 6 to 10.
Thread: Black.
Tail: Orange hackle fibers.
Body: White floss.
Rib: Flat gold tinsel.
Throat: White bucktail, under which is a very small bunch of orange hackle fibers.
Shoulders: A blue dun saddle hackle.
Cheeks: Jungle cock.

GOVERNOR AIKEN

Hook: 6X-long streamer hook, sizes 4 to 8.
Thread: Black 6/0.
Tail: A section of barred wood duck flank feather.
Body: Flat silver tinsel.
Rib: Oval silver tinsel.
Throat: A bunch of white bucktail, under which is a section of red goose feather.
Wing: Lavender bucktail.
Topping: Six strands of peacock herl.
Cheeks: Jungle cock.

GRAND LAKE STREAMER

Hook: 6X-long streamer hook, sizes 2 to 8.

Thread: Black 6/0.
Body: Black floss.
Rib: Two pieces of narrow flat gold tinsel, tied in at the base of the tail and wound in opposite directions to form a diamond pattern.
Throat: Brown bucktail.
Wing: Four brown saddle hackles.
Cheeks: Jungle cock.

WINNIPESAUKIE SMELT

Hook: 6X-long streamer hook, sizes 2 to 8.
Thread: Black 6/0.
Tail: A bunch of golden-pheasant tippet fibers.
Body: Flat silver tinsel.
Rib: Oval silver tinsel.
Throat: Red hackle fibers.
Wing: A bunch of white marabou.
Topping: Six black ostrich herls.
Shoulders (optional): Jungle cock body feathers.

YORK'S KENNEBAGO STREAMER

Hook: 6X-long streamer hook, sizes 4 to 8.
Thread: Black 6/0.
Tag: Flat silver tinsel.
Tail: Golden-pheasant crest feather, curving up.
Butt: Scarlet floss.
Body: Flat silver tinsel.
Rib: Oval silver tinsel.
Throat: Red hackle fibers.
Wing: 4 golden badger saddle hackles.
Topping: Red hackle fibers.
Cheeks: Jungle cock.

MUDDLER MINNOW

Hook: 4X-long streamer hook, sizes 4 to 8.
Thread: Black 3/0.
Tail: Red hackle fibers.
Body: Flat gold tinsel.
Wing: Two strips of mottled turkey tail.
Head: Deer body hair, spun and clipped to form the head of a small bait fish.

WHITE MARABOU MUDDLER MINNOW

Hook: 4X-long streamer hook, sizes 4 to 8.
Thread: Black 3/0.
Tail: Red hackle fibers.
Body: Flat gold tinsel.
Wing: White marabou.
Head: Deer body hair, spun and clipped to form the head of a small bait fish.

WOOLLY BUGGER

Hook: 4X-long streamer hook, sizes 4 to 10.
Thread: Black 6/0.
Tail: Black or olive marabou.
Body: Black or olive wool yarn.
Hackle: Black or olive saddle hackle, tied on at the base of the tail and wound up the body.

MAGOG SMELT

Hook: 4X- or 6X-long bucktail, sizes 4 to 8.
Thread: Black 6/0.
Body: Flat silver tinsel.
Throat: Red hackle fibers.
Wing: A bunch of white bucktail, over which is bunch of yellow bucktail, over which is a bunch of violet bucktail.
Topping: Six strands of peacock herl.
Shoulders: Teal body feathers.

NINE-THREE

Hook: 6X-long streamer hook, sizes 2 to 8.
Thread: Black 6/0.
Body: Flat silver tinsel.
Wing: A small bunch of white bucktail, over which are three green saddle hackles tied on flat, over which are two black saddle hackles tied on upright.
Cheeks: Jungle cock.

GRAY SMELT

Hook: 6X-long streamer hook, sizes 2 to 10.

Thread: Gray 6/0.
Tail: One golden-pheasant crest feather tied curving up.
Body: White floss.
Rib: Flat silver tinsel.
Wing: Two green saddle hackles, with one blue dun saddle hackle on each side.
Cheeks: Jungle cock.

SILVER MINNOW

Hook: 6X-long streamer hook, sizes 4 to 8.
Thread: Red 6/0.
Body: Flat silver tinsel.
Rib: Oval silver tinsel.
Throat: Red hackle fibers.
Wing: A bunch of white bucktail, over which is a bunch of gray squirrel tail hair.
Topping: Five strands of peacock herl.

Dry Flies

BLUE QUILL

Hook: Regular dry-fly hook, sizes 14 to 18.
Thread: Gray 8/0.
Tail: Blue dun hackle fibers.
Body: Stripped peacock quill.
Wing: Sections of mallard wing feathers.
Hackle: Blue dun.

BLUE WINGED OLIVE PARACHUTE

Hook: Regular dry-fly hook, sizes 14 and 16.
Thread: Olive 8/0.
Tail: Blue dun hackle fibers.
Body: Olive dry-fly dubbing.
Wing post: Silver or white poly yarn.
Hackle: Blue dun hackle, wound around the base of the wing post.

BLUE WINGED OLIVE SPINNER

Hook: Regular dry-fly hook, sizes 14 to 18.
Thread: Olive 8/0.
Tail: Blue dun hackle fibers.

Body: Olive dry-fly dubbing.
Wings: Gray Antron yarn, tied in the spent position.

EASTERN GREEN DRAKE

Hook: 2X-long dry-fly hook, sizes 2 to 6.
Thread: Olive 8/0.
Tail: Mallard flank fibers dyed olive.
Body: Olive-brown dry-fly dubbing.
Wing: A bunch of mallard flank fibers dyed olive.
Hackle: Blue dun.

GREEN DRAKE PARACHUTE

Hook: 2X-long dry-fly hook, sizes 2 to 6.
Thread: Olive 8/0.
Tail: Blue dun hackle fibers.
Body: Olive dry-fly dubbing.
Wing post: White poly yarn.
Hackle: Grizzly dyed olive, wound around the base of the wing post.

HENDRICKSON COMPARADUN

Hook: 2X-long dry-fly hook, sizes 14 to 18.
Thread: Cream 8/0.
Tail: Tan Microfibbetts.
Body: Hendrickson pink dry-fly dubbing.
Wing: Natural elk hair.

HENDRICKSON PARACHUTE

Hook: Regular dry-fly hook, sizes 14 and 16.
Tail: Ginger hackle fibers.
Body: Hendrickson pink dry-fly dubbing.
Wing post: White poly yarn.
Hackle: Grizzly hackle wound around the base of the wing post.

HENDRICKSON SPARKLE DUN

Hook: 2X-long dry-fly hook, sizes 14 to 18.
Thread: Cream 8/0.
Tail: Tan Antron yarn.

Body: Hendrickson pink dry-fly dubbing.
Wing: Natural elk hair.

PALE MORNING DUN EMERGER

Hook: Regular dry-fly hook, sizes 16 and 18.
Thread: Tan 8/0.
Tail: Pheasant tail fibers.
Abdomen: Stripped ginger hackle quill.
Thorax: Tan dubbing.
Wing: White poly yarn.

PMD SPARKLE DUN

Hook: Regular dry-fly hook, sizes 16 and 18.
Thread: Olive 8/0.
Tail: Olive Antron yarn.
Body: Olive dry-fly dubbing.
Wing: Natural elk hair.

PMD PARACHUTE

Hook: Regular dry-fly hook, sizes 14 and 16.
Thread: Olive 8/0.
Tail: Grizzly hackle fibers.
Body: Olive dry-fly dubbing.
Wing post: Gray poly yarn.
Hackle: Grizzly hackle wound around the base of the wing post.

PMD SPINNER

Hook: Regular dry-fly hook, sizes 16 and 18.
Thread: Orange 8/0.
Tail: Clear Microfibbetts.
Body: Pinkish orange dry-fly dubbing.
Wings: White Antron yarn, tied in the spent position.

BLUE WINGED MAHOGANY PARACHUTE

Hook: 2X-long dry-fly hook, size 14.
Thread: Brown 8/0.
Tail: Blue dun hackle fibers.
Body: Brown dry-fly dubbing.
Wing post: Gray poly yarn.
Hackle: Blue dun wrapped around the base of the wing post.

HEXAGENIA COMPARADRAKE

Hook: 2X-long dry-fly hook, size 2.
Thread: Yellow 6/0.
Tail: Tan deer hair.
Body: Tan deer hair, tied on near the hook eye, pulled back, and spiral-wrapped with thread to form an extended body.
Wing post: Light elk hair.
Hackle: Ginger hackle wound around the base of the wing post.

ROYAL WULFF

Hook: 2X-long dry-fly hook, sizes 8 to 14.
Thread: Red 8/0.
Tail: Brown deer hair.
Body: Red floss with fore-and-aft butts of peacock herl.
Wings: White goat or calf body hair.
Hackle: Brown, wrapped very heavy.

TARANTULA

Hook: 4X-long dry-fly hook, sizes 8 to 12.
Thread: Brown 6/0.
Tail: Yellow poly yarn.
Body: Yellow poly yarn.
Wing: Gray squirrel tail.
Legs: Rubber legs.
Head: Deer hair, spun and clipped to the shape of a head on a Muddler Minnow.

ADAMS

Hook: Regular dry-fly hook, sizes 14 and 16.
Thread: Gray 8/0.
Tail: Mixed brown and grizzly hackle fibers.
Body: Gray dry-fly dubbing.
Wing: Grizzly hackle tips.
Hackle: Brown and gray hackles.

ADAMS PARACHUTE

Hook: 2X-long dry-fly hook, sizes 14 and 16.
Thread: Gray 8/0.
Tail: Mixed brown and grizzly hackle fibers.
Body: Gray dry-fly dubbing.
Wing post: Gray poly yarn.
Hackle: Brown and gray hackles, wrapped around the base of the wing post.

GRIFFITH'S GNAT

Hook: Regular dry-fly hook, sizes 18 to 22.
Thread: Black 8/0.
Body: Peacock herl.
Hackle: Grizzly, palmered up the body.

GINGER QUILL

Hook: Regular dry-fly hook, sizes 14 to 18.
Thread: Tan 8/0.
Tail: Ginger hackle fibers.
Body: Stripped peacock herl.
Wing: Strips of mallard wing feathers.
Hackle: Brown and ginger hackles.

TAN ELK HAIR CADDIS

Hook: Regular dry-fly hook, sizes 12 to 18.
Thread: Tan 8/0.
Body: Tan thread or dubbing.
Hackle: Ginger, palmered up the body.
Wing: Tan elk hair.

GRAY ELK HAIR CADDIS

Hook: Regular dry-fly hook, sizes 12 to 18.
Thread: Gray 8/0.
Body: Gray thread or dubbing.
Hackle: Grizzly, palmered up the body.
Wing: Elk hair dyed gray.

LIGHT CAHILL

Hook: Regular dry-fly hook, sizes 14 to 18.
Thread: Cream 8/0.
Tail: Cream hackle fibers.
Body: Cream dry-fly dubbing.

Wing: Wood duck flank feathers.
Hackle: Light ginger.

LIGHT CAHILL PARACHUTE

Hook: 2X-long dry-fly hook, sizes 14 to 18.
Thread: Cream 8/0.
Tail: Ginger hackle fibers.
Body: Cream dry-fly dubbing.
Wing post: White poly yarn.
Hackle: Light ginger, wrapped around the base of the wing post.

Nymphs and Emergers

ADAMS EMERGER

Hook: Bent-shank nymph hook, sizes 14 to 18.
Thread: Gray 8/0.
Tail: Gray poly yarn.
Body: Gray dry-fly dubbing.
Wing post: White poly yarn, clipped short after the fly is completed.
Hackle: Grizzly, wrapped around the base of the wing post.

GREEN DRAKE CDC EMERGER

Hook: Bent-shank nymph hook, sizes 8 to 12.
Thread: Olive 8/0.
Tail: Olive poly yarn.
Abdomen: Olive dry-fly dubbing.
Thorax: Olive dry-fly dubbing.
Hackle: Blue dun CDC feather.
Wing: Gray poly yarn, tied in between the abdomen and thorax and looped over the top of the thorax.

OLIVE DEEP SPARKLE PUPA

Hook: Regular wet-fly hook, sizes 12 to 18.
Thread: Olive 8/0.
Weight: Lead wire.
Body: Olive rabbit dubbing.
Outer body skin: Olive Antron yarn, tied in at the end of the hook shank and pulled up the top, bottom, and sides of the hook to loosely encase the body.
Legs: Dun hackle fibers.
Head: Gray peacock herl.

TAN DEEP SPARKLE PUPA

Hook: Regular wet-fly hook, sizes 12 to 18.
Thread: Tan 8/0.
Weight: Lead wire.
Body: Tan rabbit dubbing.
Outer body skin: Tan Antron yarn, tied in at the end of the hook shank and pulled up the top, bottom, and sides of the hook to loosely encase the body.
Legs: Ginger hackle fibers.
Head: Brown peacock herl.

BROWN DEEP SPARKLE PUPA

Hook: Regular wet-fly hook, sizes 12 to 18.
Thread: Brown 8/0.
Weight: Lead wire.
Body: Brown rabbit dubbing.
Outer body skin: Brown Antron yarn, tied in at the end of the hook shank and pulled up the top, bottom, and sides of the hook to loosely encase the body.
Legs: Brown hackle fibers.
Head: Brown peacock herl.

CREAM DEEP CADDIS PUPA

Hook: Regular wet-fly hook, sizes 12 to 18.
Thread: Cream 8/0.
Weight: Lead wire.
Body: Tan rabbit dubbing.
Outer body skin: Cream Antron yarn, tied in at the end of the hook shank and pulled up the top, bottom, and sides of the hook to loosely encase the body.
Legs: Light ginger hackle fibers.
Head: Brown peacock herl.

OLIVE EMERGING SPARKLE PUPA

Hook: Regular wet-fly hook, sizes 12 to 18.
Thread: Olive 8/0.
Tail: Olive Antron yarn.
Body: Olive rabbit dubbing.
Outer body skin: Olive Antron yarn, tied in at the end of the hook shank and pulled up the top, bottom, and sides of the hook to loosely encase the body.
Legs: Dun hackle fibers.
Head: Gray peacock herl.

TAN EMERGING SPARKLE PUPA

Hook: Regular wet-fly hook, sizes 12 to 18.
Thread: Tan 8/0.
Tail: Tan Antron yarn.
Body: Tan rabbit dubbing.
Outer body skin: Tan Antron yarn, tied in at the end of the hook shank and pulled up the top, bottom, and sides of the hook to loosely encase the body.
Legs: Ginger hackle fibers.
Head: Brown peacock herl.

BROWN EMERGING SPARKLE PUPA

Hook: Regular wet-fly hook, sizes 12 to 18.
Thread: Brown 8/0.
Tail: Brown Antron yarn.
Body: Brown rabbit dubbing.
Outer body skin: Brown Antron yarn, tied in at the end of the hook shank and pulled up the top, bottom, and sides of the hook to loosely encase the body.
Legs: Brown hackle fibers.
Head: Brown peacock herl.

CREAM EMERGING CADDIS PUPA

Hook: Regular wet-fly hook, sizes 12 to 18.
Thread: Cream 8/0.
Tail: Cream Antron yarn.
Body: Tan rabbit dubbing.

Outer body skin: Cream Antron yarn, tied in at the end of the hook shank and pulled up the top, bottom, and sides of the hook to loosely encase the body.
Legs: Light ginger hackle fibers.
Head: Brown peacock herl.

HARE'S EAR NYMPH

Hook: 2X-long nymph hook, sizes 10 to 18.
Thread: Brown 6/0.
Weight: Lead wire.
Tail: Pheasant tail fibers.
Body: Brown rabbit dubbing.
Rib: Gold wire.
Wingcase: Mottled turkey tail.

BEAD HEAD HARE'S EAR

Hook: 2X-long nymph hook, sizes 10 to 18.
Thread: Brown 6/0.
Head: Brass bead, sized to fit the hook.
Tail: Pheasant tail fibers.
Body: Brown rabbit dubbing.
Rib: Gold wire.
Wingcase: Mottled turkey tail.

PRINCE NYMPH

Hook: 2X-long nymph hook, sizes 12 to 16.
Thread: Black 6/0.
Weight: Lead wire.
Tail: Two brown goose biots.
Body: Peacock herl.
Rib: Oval gold tinsel.
Wing: Two white goose biots.

PHEASANT TAIL NYMPH

Hook: 2X-long nymph hook, sizes 12 to 16.
Thread: Brown 6/0.
Weight: Lead wire.
Tail: Pheasant tail fibers.
Abdomen: Pheasant tail fibers wrapped up the hook shank.
Rib: Gold wire.
Throax: Peacock herl.

Wingcase: Pheasant tail fibers.
Legs: Pheasant tail fibers cut to length.

BEAD HEAD PHEASANT TAIL NYMPH

Hook: 2X-long nymph hook, sizes 12 to 16.
Thread: Brown 6/0.
Head: Brass bead, sized to match the hook.
Tail: Pheasant tail fibers.
Abdomen: Pheasant tail fibers wrapped up the hook shank.
Rib: Gold wire.
Thorax: Peacock herl.
Wingcase: Pheasant tail fibers.
Legs: Pheasant tail fibers cut to length.

APPENDIX II: NORTHERN NEW ENGLAND HATCH CHART

Species	April	May	June	July	August	September
Early black stonefly (*Taeniopteryx nivalis*)	▮					
Hendrickson (*Ephemerella subvaria*)		▮				
Quill gordon (*Epeorus pleuralis*)		▮				
Blue-winged olive (*Ephemerella attenuata*)		▮	▮			▮
American march brown (*stenonema vicarium*)		▮	▮			
Grey fox (*stenonema fuscum*)		▮	▮			
Black quill (*Letophlebia cupida*)			▮			
Brown caddis (*cheumatopsyche campyla*)			▮	▮	▮	
Sulphur (*Ephemerella dorothea*)				▮		
Light cahill (*stenonema ithaca*)			▮	▮		
Yellow Sally stonefly (*Alloperla caudata*)			▮	▮		

Lime Sally stonefly
(*Alloperla inbecilla*)

Green drake
(*Ephemera guttulata*)

Hexagenia
(*Hexagenia limbata*)

White mayfly
(*Ephoron album*)

Trico
(*Tricorythodes stygiatus*)

Terrestrials
(grasshoppers, crickets, ants)

Books from The Countryman Press
and Backcountry Guides

We offer many more books on hiking, bicycling, canoeing and kayaking, travel, nature, and country living. Our books are available at bookstores and outdoor stores everywhere. For more information or a free catalog, please call 1-800-245-4151, or write to us at The Countryman Press, P.O. Box 748, Woodstock, Vermont 05091. You can find us on the Internet at www.countrymanpress.com